Collecting
Baseball Memorabilia

SECOND EDITION

Collecting Baseball Memorabilia

A Handbook

SECOND EDITION

DAN ZACHOFSKY

Foreword by BROOKS ROBINSON

McFarland & Company, Inc., Publishers
Jefferson, North Carolina, and London

LIBRARY OF CONGRESS CATALOGUING-IN-PUBLICATION DATA

Zachofsky, Dan, 1951–
Collecting baseball memorabilia : a handbook / Dan Zachofsky ;
foreword by Brooks Robinson. — 2nd ed.
p.   cm.
Includes bibliographical references and index.

ISBN 978-0-7864-4166-2
softcover : 50# alkaline paper ∞

1. Baseball — Collectibles — United States — Handbooks, manuals, etc.
I. Title.
GV875.2.Z35   2009   796.357'0973075 — dc22   2009000164

British Library cataloguing data are available

Cover image ©2009 Index Stock

Manufactured in the United States of America

*McFarland & Company, Inc., Publishers
Box 611, Jefferson, North Carolina 28640
www.mcfarlandpub.com*

To my wife, Gail, and my daughter, Amy,
and to the memory of my parents,
Adele and Morris Zachofsky,
and my father-in-law, David Rabinowitz.
You will be remembered forever.

Acknowledgments

I want to thank my wife, Gail who has provided support and endured my passion for baseball for more than 30 years. My beautiful daughter, Amy, accompanied me on many road trips to Dodgertown during her childhood, and we had fun together collecting baseball memorabilia. She is now a young professional pursuing her own dreams.

I am most appreciative to Joe Orlando, president of Professional Sports Authentication Services, who provided me a perspective about authentication and the process that his company employs. He sent me a great image of a Babe Ruth signed baseball that his company authenticated in a private sale. Joe Orlando provided excellent information on the importance of authentication.

I want to thank Chris Rodriguez from Bud's Sports Cards & Collectibles for allowing me to photograph Bob Gibson at his baseball show and include photographs of commemorative bats and a single-signed baseball collection with cube holders in the store. I am grateful to Edd Langdon for his input on framing techniques for fine works of art.

I want to thank the Brooklyn Dodgers and Hall of Fame players who signed different types of memorabilia for me over the years and put up with all of my autograph requests. You deserve a most heartfelt thank-you. I want to thank my spring training colleague and friend Cory Nightingale, a sports editor with the *Miami Herald,* who read the entire manuscript in rough draft and provided practical ideas from an editor's perspective. I'm looking forward to seeing you at spring training.

Above all, my parents, Adele and Morris Zachofsky, always inspired me to work hard and strive for excellence. I know you will enjoy this book, too.

Table of Contents

Foreword
by Brooks Robinson

Dan Zachofsky and I met at the 2006 Joe DiMaggio Memorial Classic, a silent auction to provide funds for the Joe DiMaggio Children's Hospital. Dan had me sign a copy of his first edition *Collecting Baseball Memorabilia: A Handbook*, a very informative book about collecting different types of baseball memorabilia and how to design and preserve a baseball collection with excellent ideas about starting a baseball collection.

In this book, Dan has provided a unique approach for collecting memorabilia and suggestions for collectors to initiate a baseball collection. You will learn how to acquire autographs, how to design a memorabilia room and display your collection, and above all, have fun participating in a great hobby.

Dan has presented ways to collect memorabilia in person and through the mail, as well as interacting with other collectors. He provides excellent suggestions on beginning a Hall of Fame collection, how to approach the players, and provides information about authenticity when purchasing items from reputable dealers and from auctions.

I have enjoyed participating in baseball shows for many years and have been impressed by the unique memorabilia that children and adults ask me to sign at these events. I am honored to have met Dan, and I know you will enjoy reading this interesting and informative book.

Preface

When I began teaching in Fort Lauderdale, Florida, in 1974, I was an ardent baseball fan who was suddenly able to attend spring training at the Yankees camp, located nearby, and the Dodgers camp, just down the road in Vero Beach. I would soon meet my heroes — the likes of Sandy Koufax, Don Drysdale, Maury Wills, Duke Snider, Johnny Podres, Steve Garvey, Ron Cey, Kirk Gibson and Orel Hershiser. In 1975 I started a single-signed Dodger baseball collection — with the aforementioned players and added the signatures of the new players each season. In the five years that followed, I accumulated signatures for a team-signed baseball, obtaining signatures from roughly 30 Dodger players.

At Fort Lauderdale Stadium, a short drive from my home, I initiated a single-signed baseball collection of Yankees greats, including Joe DiMaggio, Mickey Mantle, Yogi Berra, Phil Rizzuto, Whitey Ford, Jim "Catfish" Hunter, Tommy John, Bob Lemon, Reggie Jackson, Don Mattingly, Wade Boggs and many others. In 1996, after the Yankees moved to Tampa, the Orioles took up residence in Fort Lauderdale Stadium, and I had access to a new batch of players, including Cal Ripken, Jr., and Jim Palmer, whose autographs were easily obtained. My collection took shape, growing substantially from one spring training to the next. I was living where most fans traveled hundreds of miles to get to each February and March, and collecting signed memorabilia seemed a very obvious and enjoyable thing for me to do.

By 1988, when I first visited the Baseball Hall of Fame Museum in Cooperstown, New York, I had become hooked. I was entranced by all that I saw in the museum, spending hours poring over the plaques and exhibits. My next project would be a single-signed baseball collection of all of the living members (and future inductees). From the players I met — again, mostly in spring training — I requested that they not only sign their names on a ball but add "HOF" and the year they were inducted. Other related collections soon grew out of this one. Players noted the dates that they achieved certain milestones — e.g., "3,000 Hits" — on baseballs and photographs. The Hall of Fame Museum had transformed me into a historical collector. Eventually the interest in history led me to start a few unorthodox collections, including one of baseballs signed by U.S. presidents. In time, I had to give over part of my house to signed memorabilia. Today, as the collection continues to grow, it's a challenge to accommodate it all.

In 2000 the first edition of *Collecting Baseball Memorabilia: A Handbook* was published to provide collectors with six approaches to collecting baseball autographs. These approaches are meeting a player in person, mailing a written request to a player, trading with other collectors, networking online with others (email and the Internet), purchasing from reputable dealers and from online auctions. The hobbyist was provided a step-by-step approach to design a single-signed player and team collection, more specialized Hall of Fame baseball and photograph collections, handwritten responses to surveys and letters, as well as quirkier collections such as my batch of presidential autographs of signatures of actors who had baseball roles. Collectors were provided detailed instructions for designing a memorabilia room and displaying their collections, which are a source of great pride.

The second edition of *Collecting Baseball Memorabilia: A Handbook* updates material and provides new strategies for the collector. In addition to the six approaches to collecting baseball memorabilia, the book outlines strategies for coping with the fast-rising costs of collecting. The increasing popularity of online purchasing, collecting, and exhibiting is discussed, along with the consignments and sales that auction companies have encouraged.

Other topics include the role of authenticity in the hobby. Concerns about forgery and counterfeiting make third-party authentication imperative when people want to purchase signed memorabilia. The Professional Sports Authentication Services Company has designed a four-step authentication process that has changed the way signed memorabilia is being collected. That process is covered in this edition.

There have been changes in the items we hope to have signed, too. In 2000, Commissioner Bud Selig eliminated the American and National League presidents' positions, unifying the leagues. The new baseball available to the teams and hobby stores throughout the United States is the Rawlings Official Major League Baseball, with carries the "Allan H. Selig, Commissioner" inscription. Some hobby stores may have the Rawlings Official American and National League baseballs.

Over the past eight years there has been an increased interest in what I've referred to as simply "unorthodox collecting." Baseball items signed by presidents are especially popular. New information about presidential and other signings is included, as is a presidential listing with the price, auction company involved in the purchase and the date the baseball was sold.

The Hall of Fame Baseball Collection chapter includes 17 new (living) Hall of Fame inductees with information about the best approach to add these players to a collection. Members who have passed away have been referenced with the date of their death. The best approach to add these players to a collection is by purchasing items from reputable dealers and buying from online auctions. The use of performance-enhancing drugs by great players and possibly future Hall of Fame inductees may affect their election into the Hall. These players may have violated the rules for induction. These issues are presented in Chapter 4, The Hall of Fame Baseball Collection. In Chapter 5, "The Sleaze Factor," important tips on authentication and tips on avoiding forged memorabilia are shared.

In 2007 special event baseballs were produced when Barry Bonds hit the historic record-breaking 756th home run. The baseball was purchased online for $752,467 by fashion designer Marc Ecko. After asking fans to vote online whether the ball should carry an asterisk, he marked the ball with one, in accordance with the voting. The asterisk reflected that the accomplishment may be questionable as Bonds has been linked to using performance-enhancing drugs. In 2008 the Hall of Fame accepted Bond's record-breaking baseball, complete with asterisk.

The 2008 All-Star game was the final one at Yankee Stadium because after 85 years, the Yankees are moving into a new stadium. The New Era Cap Company produced three different All-Star Game hats for collectors to commemorate the 2008 All-Star game. Information is provided on these special event hats in Chapter 7, "The Hat Collection."

Game-used bats from the players are strongly preferred by collectors over batting-practice or store-bought bats. They are also more costly. No doubt because of the expense, alternatives such as the commemorative bats produced by the Cooperstown Bat Company, which are more moderately priced, have become popular. In 2007 the company produced a limited edition (1,000 bats) Cal Ripken, Jr., bat featuring a photo of Ripken, the Hall of Fame logo and colorful graphics. More information on these bats and the newest trends in bat collecting can be found in Chapter 8.

In Chapter 9, "The Photograph Collection," new themes, including a World Series team photograph collection and a photograph collection of World Series accomplishments noting game-winning hits, home runs and players scoring the winning runs are provided. Most collectors use digital cameras, which can record sound and video as well as take still photographs. Some cameras can record images in dim lighting and can take action shots, six frames per second. Discussion of these features, and the uses they're put to, is included in the chapter.

The written survey collection discussed in Chapter 10, "In Their Own Words," has been slightly modified. The surveys make good writing projects for children in the classroom, and students and other young collectors are encouraged to be creative and elicit their own responses to the survey items.

The greatest accomplishment for a collector is designing a memorabilia room and display. Discussions on designing five new storage displays have been added, along with new material on archival framing techniques for rare or vintage photos and fine art.

The last chapter, on spring training, includes a new section on etiquette for the autograph seeker. With spring-training attendance higher than ever, it can be an unpleasant experience to negotiate the crowds, but a little restraint and thoughtfulness can make a difference. So can knowing what to say and when.

1. Getting Started and Acquiring Autographs

Enter the quaint village of Cooperstown, home of the Baseball Hall of Fame Museum in upstate New York. Named after James Fenimore Cooper's father, this beautiful farming community is the supposed birthplace of baseball, according to the myth of Abner Doubleday in 1839.

Walking through the village streets, which seem to be paved with baseball history, you will notice one memorabilia store after another. In one such store adjacent to Doubleday Field, you can find an 8" × 10" photo of "The Shot Heard Round the World"—Bobby Thomson's winning home run in the 1951 playoff and a 16" × 20" print of Ebbets Field.

Ebbets Field was home for the Brooklyn Dodgers from April 9, 1913, until September 24, 1957. Of all of the ballparks that ever existed, none has been put on a pedestal more prominently than Ebbets Field. The demise of this grand playing field heralded the end of the Brooklyn Dodgers, and the greatest era in the history of Brooklyn. Home plate was moved from the cozy park to the country club at Dodgers Pines in Dodgertown, Vero Beach, Florida.

That visit to Cooperstown and those two finds were the beginning of one of the most fascinating and exciting hobbies imaginable to this writer—collecting baseball memorabilia.

Since the first edition of this handbook was published in 2000, collectors have experienced a few changes in the hobby. Exclusive signing contracts with dealers have increased the costs to obtain autographed memorabilia. Baseball shows have become cost-prohibitive for children and parents new to the hobby. Concerns about authenticity have authenticators present at baseball shows certifying that a player signature is real with an additional cost provided for this service. Authentication companies have become more prevalent in the hobby today and the process of authentication will be discussed in chapter five.

Back in 2000, collectors would obtain baseball player autographs in person, attend baseball shows, purchase online from auctions and eBay, trade with other collectors, use the mail approach with retired players and acquire autographs from reputable dealers. Over the past eight years, the proliferation of huge player contracts and the greater costs incurred by dealers has affected the state of collecting baseball memorabilia. In many instances the costs to obtain signed memorabilia has more than doubled. Dealers are now charging higher player signing fees with an extra charge to add HOF (Hall of Fame and the year the player was inducted), and fees for adding their accomplishments on photographs, baseballs, bats, hats, jerseys and equipment. Frank Robinson, a member of the Hall of Fame, has participated in signings at baseball card shows throughout his career, and will sign the following Items with these charges:

Flat Items (photos, book) 11" × 14" and baseball	$85
Flat Items over 11" × 14", hats and equipment	$99
Bat, jersey	$175
Inscriptions (HOF, 1982 or 586 home runs)	$30

Some of the players are under contract to conduct private signings and have become less accessible for their fans. In fact, in the April 11, 2008, *Sports Collectors Digest* there was a story that Sandy Koufax who has always been a difficult autograph for collectors (usually conducts two baseball shows each year), signed an exclusive deal with a New York based memorabilia company. The price list provided included the following items and their prices: Single-signed baseballs will cost $750, $900 for a 16" × 20" photograph and a Mitchell & Ness jersey will cost $1,600. The number of items mailed in will be extremely limited to 100–150. The signing will be private because that's the way Koufax wants it.

What has changed? The business of collecting baseball memorabilia, the unrealistic and excessive fees, the greed from players who are not being accessible and dealers who need baseball fans the most. For new collectors and children entering the hobby, collecting autographs at baseball shows has become cost-prohibitive.

PSA/DNA was founded in 1998 by Professional Sports Au-

An Ebbets Field print autographed by 46 players of the Brooklyn Dodgers.

thenticators in response to concerns of counterfeiting, forgery and not authenticated auto-graphed memorabilia. PSA/DNA has provided a four-step authentication process which has changed the hobby of collecting autographs and memorabilia, and this process will be discussed in chapter five. Some collectors would call this process an inexact science, but the majority of people in the hobby would agree that the idea of authentication has always been an opinion. Because of the concerns about authenticity, the process will make it safer and more enjoyable for all collectors. We know that baseball players sign different types of mem-orabilia outside the stadium, inside the stadium and conduct private signings, and because their signature may be different, a quick scribble of their name outside or inside the sta-dium compared to a neat written signature at a private signing, may make their signature questionable to authenticators. Expertise is a big part of authentication, and the companies that have the best authentication process and expertise will be most successful in the mar-ketplace.

Joe Orlando, president of PSA/DNA Authentication Services, responded to my con-cerns about the state of collecting and provided his own written perspective about authen-tication:

> Third party authentication plays a vital role in today's sports memorabilia market. Prior to the advent of third party authentication, there was an inherent conflict of interest in virtually every transaction. The seller, the person who has a financial interest in the sale of the item, was forced to become the expert as well. The buyer, in turn, was forced to simply accept the word of the seller. Today, having a third party expert involved can help the buyer and seller avoid sit-uations such as the one described above. It provides peace of mind to buyers and a more liquid product to sellers. In fact, most high-end or valuable autographs are extremely hard to sell without third party authentication in the current market.
>
> It is important to note that part of a third party expert's job is to be familiar with variations within an athlete's signature. Sometimes, those great differences are seen when you compare "private signing" signatures versus "at the ballpark" versions. In one case, the athlete is given ample time to place his full signature on a piece while the other version typically appears abbre-viated or rushed. A great example of this would be the clear difference between a Mark McG-wire autograph obtained at the ballpark during the late 1990s versus one obtained at a rare show appearance during his career.
>
> Baseball legends like Jimmie Foxx and Mickey Mantle showed varying signature styles throughout their lives. In fact, a great example of that could be seen firsthand when Mantle's family auctioned Mickey's personal items just a few years ago. Included in the auction was a contract from each year of his career, beginning with a simplistic version of Mickey's signature during his rookie campaign all the way to the more flamboyant style used towards the end of his career and during his post-playing days. The latter version is the one that most collectors would recognize.
>
> That being said, the expert has to evaluate the signature on its own merit and there are occasions when a signature may exhibit characteristics that vary so greatly from the typical sig-nature pattern known of a particular player that the expert or service cannot certify the item. While instances like these are rare, it can happen. There are cases where signatures that are technically authentic will not pass third party experts because of the great variance.

One thing no authentication service can guarantee is the authenticity of any signature they did not see signed themselves. Services such as, PSA/DNA and James Spence Authentications (JSA) can guarantee that they have an authentication process which they define and fully disclose, and follow through to provide peace of mind to buyers. Because of the changes in the way we collect baseball memorabilia today, a new edition has been written to provide new collectors, both children and their parents, and established hobbyists a cost-effective, easy and fun approach to begin collecting baseball autographs. Practical strategies will be provided to help authenticate a collection of baseball autographs and guarantee the authenticity of the player signatures.

In order to begin a collection of baseball autographs, the collector should formulate a plan of action regarding acquisition methods. The collection should include the collector's personal and financial goals, which will determine how to acquire autographed memorabilia. Since there is limited information in the field of collecting baseball memorabilia, the experienced collector will be reluctant to share their acquisition strategies and sources. The intent of this book is to provide the novice collector, as well as the general collector, with an inexpensive and direct approach to acquire autographs. Inclusive in this approach is the element of fun, parent-child interaction in an exciting hobby, and learning to network with other collectors.

Memorabilia

Sports collectors are searching to hold onto or collect specific items from childhood memories and experiences. There has been an abundance of baseball card brands on the market, and although the collector wants to collect one of everything, they have begun to realize it isn't practical to purchase everything. The collector today is focusing on vintage older cards and memorabilia. *The Washington Post* published a story on the hobby, indicating that sales now total $750 million a year. New collectors, as well as the established ones, are seeking attractive items to display in their home or on office walls. Restaurants in every major city in America use memorabilia and autographs as displays to attract people into their establishment. Baseball shows, private signings, and auctions have become popular ways to acquire autographed memorabilia.

Each summer, the Sports Collectors National Convention brings together collectors, dealers, baseball players, corporate executives and a new crop of young collectors from all over the country, most searching to collect autographed memorabilia.

The most appealing autographed memorabilia include baseballs, game equipment (bats, hats, jerseys, wristbands, batting gloves, shoes), photographs, index cards (the autograph can be used as a cut signature and attached to pictures), postcards, Hall of Fame plaque cards, programs, magazine covers, books, letters, contracts and documents, baseball cards (common players, inexpensive cards), tickets from historic games, player's canceled checks, and team promotional giveaways. To begin collecting baseball memorabilia there are six approaches to acquiring baseball autographs:

Baseballs, baseball cards, game tickets, and plates are among the appealing items for collectors to seek out.

1. An in-person request to a player.
2. Mailing a request and personal letter to the player.
3. Purchasing memorabilia at an auction.
4. Purchasing memorabilia from a reputable dealer.
5. Trading with other collectors.
6. Networking on a personal computer (e-mail, Internet) with other collectors.

Prior to determining which approach is most suitable for you to employ, it is beneficial to purchase a team media guide, subscribe to *Sports Collectors Digest*, and purchase R. J. Smalling's The *Baseball Autograph Collector's Handbook Number 14.*

Media guides are most valuable for collectors interested in collecting single-signed and team player memorabilia. First, they help the collector identify the roster of players, since the players' photographs appear in the guide. This will make it easier to identify the players in person when you seek their autograph. The media guide includes an alphabetical listing of the all-time players on the team, and the years they played. This information can be handy when you want dates, statistical data, and specific historic events added on memorabilia signed by the players. The guide will also inform you where the players stay on the road, and the team hotel and phone number will appear for each city. Meeting the players at the team hotel is one of the easiest ways to obtain their autograph. You can schedule a vacation or business trip and coordinate the dates with the information in the media guide. Should you make reservations early, you could stay at the same hotel and with luck meet the players of your favorite team in person. The guide may cost $10 to $15 at the stadium or can be ordered by calling the stadium business office, which will furnish the appropriate details for mailing.

Sports Collectors Digest is a weekly sports trade publication designed for collectors. A monthly calendar of scheduled baseball shows, player appearances, and events in the fifty states is included. A dealer directory with the company name and phone number helps collectors purchase the newest and vintage memorabilia available. Additionally, feature player stories and interviews, as well as a schedule of phone auction dates and a listing of all of the items available, make it easy for collectors to register and bid on items. Collectors are encouraged to subscribe to this publication.

R. J. Smalling's *The Baseball Autograph Collector's Handbook Number 14* is an essential reference for autograph collectors. This book provides the mailing addresses for virtually every player who has appeared in the major leagues. With the information provided in the book, you can send photographs and baseballs to be autographed by the players you may not be able to meet. The mailing addresses of players debuting from 1920 to 2006 are documented here. An address directory for the baseball Hall of Fame members is included as well. The Sports Market Report (SMR) offers in depth articles and lots of good information on collecting. You can subscribe to the magazine by calling (800) 325-1121 or visit www.psadna.com The aforementioned reference materials will guide the collector to begin to plan an approach to acquire autographs. Addresses are included at the end of this book in the "Directory of References."

The six approaches of acquiring baseball autographs are strategies that have been successfully employed to build a great baseball collection. Use the approach that best suits your goals — and above all, make collecting baseball memorabilia a fun and exciting hobby.

Suggestions for In-Person Autograph Requests

- **Arrive at the ballpark early before batting practice begins.** Approach the dugout area with your pen and material accessible, and always be polite and courteous with your request.

- **Place flat items like photographs on a clipboard.** This allows more support and players can sign more neatly on a hard surface.
- **Use the digital camera to document the player signature is authentic.** As players sign your items, quickly have your camera ready and take a few pictures documenting their signing. Notate the name of the player, the date the item was signed and the type of collectible provided. Keep this information stored on your personal computer. You may request to take a picture with a player as well and be ready to have someone assist you.
- **Children should approach the players with a baseball and request an autograph on the sweet spot of the ball.** Many players will sign anywhere unless directed to sign on the sweet spot (the area on the ball where the seams are closest together).
- **Strike up a pleasant conversation with a player and request a game-used piece of equipment (cracked bat, hat, baseball or batting glove).** After batting practice a player may return and furnish you with some type of memorabilia.
- **Many fans wait by the dugout area.** Head over to the bullpen area where you can find some of the pitchers congregating. This is a great area to obtain many autographs, and is usually not crowded.
- **When a player refuses to sign or ignores your request, never make a rude gesture or remark.** When the player has completed his practice, most often he will return to provide autographs to polite and friendly fans.
- **Purchase game tickets close to the field level.** Many players will approach the fans five to ten minutes prior to game time, and autograph memorabilia. Since your seats are there or nearby, the ushers will usually leave you alone.
- **Be reasonable with your expectations.** Never request more than two autographs on memorabilia at a time. Hand the player a photograph and baseball, and immediately say, "Thank you."
- **Be specific in your request with the player.** If a personalization or career achievement is desired, and you want this added on your memorabilia, clearly indicate this in your request.
- **Offer the player an extra baseball card or his photograph on a unique collectible.** He will appreciate your generosity, and may acknowledge you in the future.
- **When the visiting teams come to your town use the team media guide and identify the visiting team hotel and phone number.** Allow some time to visit the hotel and meet the players. For the more outgoing collector, call a player to make an appointment and be very specific and polite with your request. Some players will meet you in the hotel lobby before they either depart on the team bus, or leave early by taking a taxi to the stadium. When you meet the player in the lobby thank him for allowing you to meet him, and check to see if he needs a ride to the stadium. He may accept your offer of assistance, and a new friendship may begin.
- **Blending in with other hotel guests is important.** Sitting in the hotel lobby, reading

a newspaper or talking to guests makes you unobtrusive and less likely to annoy the players whose autographs you are seeking.

- **Be discreet in the hotel lobby.** Make your appearance and actions those of a guest. Act like you belong in this environment. Many players will sit in the lobby next to you. Prior to making an autograph request, strike up a conversation, which will make it easier to approach the player. In this manner it is assumed that the player has accepted your request, and you pose no threat to him.
- **Avoid wearing baseball hats and keep your memorabilia in a plastic bag when you enter the hotel lobby.** To make this a good experience, less attention should be directed to the collector. Conceal the items that you want autographed. Keep a low profile here.

The players usually report to the stadium four hours prior to the start of the game. Arriving at the stadium and meeting the players at the parking entrance is an excellent opportunity to acquire autographs. This is one of the best kept secrets. Most days, not many fans are present, the players will have a little time to sign some of your memorabilia, with additional writing added for their career achievements, and they will honor your request for personalizations. Again, be reasonable with your expectations. Depending on the number of collectors present, request up to two items to be autographed. As you can detect, the in-person approach to acquiring autographs is the most satisfying method and the best way to absolutely guarantee the authenticity of an autograph.

Over the past few years, baseball teams have functions like Dinner on the Diamond where many players interact with the fans after the game with food served in a fan friendly atmosphere on the field. A nominal fee is charged to the participants with a charitable donation made by the team for a particular charity. This is another great opportunity to meet the players and have lots of memorabilia autographed.

Acquiring autographs and memorabilia at a baseball card show is another great way of collecting and meeting the baseball players in person. Usually the promoter of a show will employ either former or present players to sign many types of collectibles for a nominal fee. Promoters often impose time limitations for player signings, so it is advisable to purchase tickets in advance and arrive early. Often collectors become aware of these in-person shows through newspaper advertisements and hobby publications. This is the perfect opportunity to converse with the player, have a picture taken with him, and request additional writing on the memorabilia signed. Promoters will be flexible with reasonable requests at most shows.

From 1970 to 1980 collectors could obtain autographs at shows from DiMaggio, Mantle, and Ted Williams for $10 to $25 on a signed ball. Their value today has appreciated to over $600 on a signed ball. The feeling in the hobby today is that the fees charged for the present star player will continue to appreciate over time. Baseball shows are the appropriate event to have valuable and rare items signed. The personal experience one has meeting

Baseball shows are the perfect occasion for a player to sign many autographs for the promoter. Bob Gibson signs a dozen baseballs.

the player and actually seeing the items being signed are remembered throughout a lifetime. Remember to bring a digital camera to a baseball show and document the player signing with photographs and a short video clip, and record this event on your personal computer. This will help you avoid concerns about authenticity.

Suggestions for Mail Autograph Requests

- **Purchase a dispenser pack of Care Mail self-sealing bubble mailers.** They should be 8½" × 11" or larger, to hold up to four baseballs. It is more cost-effective to purchase a box of 25 mailers from an office supply store.
- **Purchase a box of 6½ × 5½ sandwich bags to hold baseballs you include in the bubble mailers.** Some people feel the bags prevent smudging better than the paper wrap that comes with the balls. Never send a ball out with the box it came in. Remove the baseball from the box, discard the paper and place the ball in the bag.
- **Write a good letter that is sincere and to the point.** In the first or second paragraph, specify exactly what you want the player to do. Requests should be specific. If additional writing is desired, clearly state this in your request.
- **Always include a self-addressed stamped mailing envelope (SASE) when you send out baseballs, hats, books, or other types of small memorabilia.** Use Priority Mail,

which is usually the least expensive and quickest method of shipping, taking no longer than two or three days each way. Priority Mail envelopes and boxes are free at your local post office.

- **When you mail photographs, baseball cards or postcards, use a hard plastic insert (toploader), which you can purchase at memorabilia stores.** You can make your own hard cardboard material and include this in the envelope with your items. You want to prevent damage to your items.
- **Be considerate of a player's time and aware that they receive many requests.** Send the players only a couple of items to be signed and include an extra one for him to keep. Most retired players will sign memorabilia at no cost.
- **The postal service success rate is excellent; however, do not send valuable, one-of-a-kind items to the player.** Items can get lost or be damaged and you may not be able to replace lost collectibles. You may consider paying an extra fee to insure items with the current market value of your collectible included.
- **Provide thought-provoking ideas with your request.** You want your letter to stand out and make the player respond. Add unique and colorful graphics on your letterhead. Don't be surprised if you receive a written letter from the player.
- **The best way to make requests to present day players is at the team's address at the stadium.** Some of the players today feel that requests sent to their home intrude on their personal life, and they will ignore your request. Don't forget to include a self-addressed stamped envelope with the exact amount of postage for the return home.

For an unusual or special request write a personal letter to a player requesting permission to send him the item you want autographed. With his permission you could send him a bat, which would be sent in a tube, and have it insured. Include the exact amount of postage, attach a new address label on the tube, and have it returned Priority Mail. Most players will return it in a timely manner.

Auctions are another approach to acquiring autographed collectibles. These events are scheduled in hobby publications with photographs of all of the materials being offered. Collectors can call the company for a description of the lots or groupings of items before the auction begins. These auctions are conducted in person, by telephone or online, with the latter being more popular in the hobby today. Often quality material becomes available from collectors who had a personal relationship with the players, and many times, from the estate of the ballplayers. Today auctions feature the sale of unusual baseball memorabilia usually unavailable at hobby stores or baseball shows.

Suggestions for Auctions

- **Read the auction rules carefully prior to making a competitive bid.** Request a brochure or catalog, if one is available. The buyer (bidder) must register and obtain a username and password to bid online. Phone bids are accepted and some auctions today can take place beginning and ending after one month. The auction will end when the website indicates the bidding is closed.

- **Check to see if a buyer's premium is included.** Some auctions require the buyer to pay an additional 10 to 15 percent fee for the winning bid. This is also called a hammer fee.
- **Consult a knowledgeable dealer about the items you're interested in bidding on.** The dealer will provide ideas what an item may be worth, and may furnish you an estimate for your bid.
- **Every auction has bidding restrictions, so plan an approach that will encourage a winning bid.**
- **Establish a bid limitation for each item; an astute buyer will look for a bargain.** If you cannot be available for a phone auction, let the seller know the maximum you will bid. This is the ceiling bid.
- **Call for descriptions of the lots the day before the auction begins.** You want to be informed about items that you may bid on.
- **Buyers must register to bid in an auction.** Bids may increase by as much as 10 percent.
- **A bidder is obligated to honor all bids submitted; however, the seller can reject a bid for any reason.** Avoid the frenzy of the moment and never overbid on an item.
- **During an auction, a seller should be available at a designated time to answer questions from bidders.** Question the seller before you continue to bid.
- **Be aware that payment for a winning bid is due within 7 to 10 days, and postage and insurance will be added to the invoice.** You should be prepared for the expenses of a winning bid and comply with the rules.
- **Seller must adhere to a prompt closing time for a scheduled auction, and notify the buyer, as soon as possible, about their winning bid.**
- **Collectors can consign or sell items from their collection to an auction company.** When you consign items to be sold at an auction, don't be afraid to negotiate the fee requested by the auction house. Fees may vary from 10–15 percent; see if you can agree and only pay a 10 percent fee. The auction company gets paid from both the buyer (bidder) and seller (individual who consigns items from their collection).

Lelands, a leading auction dealer in New York City, represents individuals who have obtained vintage or rare collectibles from the personal collection of a player, and family members selling the collection through the player's estate. Some items that were purchased include Pete Rose's 1973 Most Valuable Player Award, which sold for $33,675; a baseball signed by Ty Cobb and Joe Jackson brought $14,375, and a Walter Johnson single-signed baseball was purchased for $10,114. The February 2008 Mastro Classic auction had a 1961 New York Yankees World Champions team-signed ball (26 signatures) including Mantle and Maris selling for $14,400. A Barack Obama single-signed ball sold for $2,760 and a single-signed Satchel Paige baseball was purchased for $1,440 (information provided in *Sports Collectors Digest*). The most valued items, which are more difficult to find, command the higher prices. Participation in an auction is very exciting, and the shrewd buyer will acquire autographed memorabilia for a reasonable price.

Purchasing Memorabilia from a Reputable Dealer

Another easy way to acquire autographed memorabilia is to purchase it from a reputable dealer. The best way to determine the integrity and honesty of a particular dealer is through their business practices. Guidelines for collectors making purchases at baseball stores should include the following:

- **Associate with reputable, established dealers who have a genuine interest in your concerns.** All of the items for sale should carry a guarantee of authenticity.
- **Dealers must provide a return policy for items purchased.** In the hobby a 14 day return policy is the general practice among many dealers.
- **Some hobby publications have instituted the following consumer protection policy: The dealers are required to provide a money-back guarantee on all autograph items purchased which may be proven to be non-authentic.** Should the dealer not comply, they will lose their advertising privileges in the publication.
- **Collectors should avoid purchasing any items that may be questionable, or they feel uncomfortable with.** The buyer should return an item found unacceptable.
- **When the collector considers purchasing a store-bought autographed item, it is not uncommon to request a letter of authenticity from the dealer.** Request a reasonable return policy to satisfy your concerns.
- **On one-of-a-kind autographed memorabilia, which is scarce, it is important to have the dealer explain the history, and how he obtained this piece.** A reputable dealer should have patience and explain the origin of the item in question.
- **Question other collectors on their relationship with a particular dealer.** Have they ever had a bad experience? Inquire as to how long they have been established in business. As a precaution, you may call the Better Business Bureau in your area to see if complaints have been reported.
- **After consulting with others, let your good judgment allow you to form a relationship with a reputable dealer.** Request that you be added onto his mailing list.

Reputable dealers can be a valuable source for collectors. They can help you locate quality items for your collection. Some of the local dealers conduct private signings with the players. This is an excellent way to acquire autographed memorabilia at a reasonable price, and have a guarantee of authenticity. Perhaps the dealer has a photograph of himself and the player at the actual signing event. This could be sent with mail-order purchases. The collector should be aware that the price of autographed memorabilia will vary in different areas. This is based on supply and demand factors — local interest, the price the dealer paid for an item, quantity of items, and knowing the value of an item.

A popular and easy way to acquire autographs is by trading with other collectors. Collectors have similar and different collecting themes, and can share their experiences to form a good working relationship. Many collectors have established a network of collectors to trade with all over the country. A common trait among these hobbyists is a general interest in acquiring autographs, a genuine concern of authenticity guarantees, and looking to find unique memorabilia to collect. Trading is a satisfying form of building a collection. Collectors receive items to fill their needs as they provide items to satisfy another collector's goals.

Suggestions for Trading with Other Collectors

- **A trading network can be established through the collector-to-collector section of a publication such as *Sports Collectors Digest.*** You can purchase advertising space in hobby publications. This is an easy way to meet other collectors with similar ideas and interests.
- **Trade duplicate material for other collectibles you need to enhance your own col-**

At baseball shows fans meet new collectors and begin to network.

lection. Always acquire two or more autographs of the same item using the aforementioned approaches. You can find other collectors with duplicate items who need some of your extra material.

- **Use of your personal computer with Internet access will attract a network of collectors.** You can purchase inexpensive advertising on the Internet to either trade or sell your duplicate memorabilia. Design a unique website that will attract other collectors.
- **Attend baseball card shows.** This is a recommended approach for the novice collector. Your participation at these events enables you to meet new collectors who may be interested in trading with you. At these events you will become familiar with the newest products.
- **Network with collectors locally and nationally.** Prepare a "want list" to mail out to those collectors whose ideas and opinions you value. Through your associations with other collectors, you can easily help each other accomplish your collecting goals.
- **Collectors can trade extra autographed materials with dealers who have a personal interest in collecting or selling the signed item.** Trading with dealers is an acceptable approach in the hobby.

As the hobby continues to make advances, it is imperative for everybody involved to adapt to technology. Use of your personal computer, with online services, is another exciting way to acquire autographs. Collectors have begun networking with others all over the world, seeking to acquire autographs using the Internet and e-mail on a daily basis. The Internet will enable you to browse the Web and locate new areas of interest. Collectors can visit reputable dealers on the Web, and see the prices of different types of memorabilia, check out special items, new inventory, and be informed about upcoming events and private signings. Online auctions have become common in the hobby. Online auctioneers check for authenticity and condition by conferring with hobby experts, and will stand behind their lots. Internet deals with individuals do not have a system to track the transaction, and are buyer-beware purchasing. Proceed with caution on the Internet.

Suggestions for Networking and Using Internet Services

- **Browse the Web to collect information about acquiring autographs.** Every major league team selling baseball memorabilia can be found on the Internet. To begin this search, you should type in the key word "baseball memorabilia." You will discover a wealth of information about the hobby. Go online to eBay to purchase autographs from the present day players to players in the Hall of Fame.
- **Consult your contacts and sources, and obtain their homepage address.** Some of your business can be conducted on the Internet. Eliminate telephone calls and use e-mail for product information and hobby questions.

- **Network with other collectors.** Prepare a list of items you wish to trade or sell, and a "want list" of items you need.
- **Develop a buddy list for direct online communication.** Both you and another collector can e-mail and respond continuously.
- **For the more outgoing collector, use the white pages that can be found on various websites to obtain the phone number and address of players whose autograph you would like to have.** Many players are listed and contacting a player over the telephone may be another way (with the player's permission) to acquire autographed memorabilia.

To learn more about *Sports Collectors Digest* you can e-mail: sports@krause.com

Parallel Collectible Hobby

It is possible for collectors to acquire baseball autographs from antique, art, coin, stamp, and comic book dealers. The items may appear tempting to purchase, but the buyer should proceed with caution. These dealers are not considered experts in acquiring autographed items, and have their interest in another area. The collector assumes the risk of buying an item that is not authentic and should pose the following questions to the dealers:

1. Will you furnish a written guarantee of authenticity?
2. Will you put in writing the origin and how the item was obtained?
3. Will you provide a 14 day guarantee on your return policy (in writing)?

Unless the dealer is willing to agree to all of these conditions, avoid making this purchase.

Flea markets are another area where the inexperienced collector should exhibit caution. Flea market browsers and collectors can find items at bargain prices; however, it is advised not to purchase autographed materials here. Only purchase items that haven't been autographed, such as baseball photographs, post-cards, baseball plates and other unusual collectibles (oddball memorabilia).

As a hobby, collecting baseball memorabilia is fun and exciting. It enables the collector to establish an approach that is challenging and satisfying. The thrill of meeting one of your heroes in person and acquiring his autograph on a baseball, will be memorable forever.

2. Collecting Baseballs: Single-Signature and Team Baseballs

The collector market has experienced a major increase in products that are autographed. The most appealing item, which is sought by collectors, is the autographed official major league baseball. Baseball cards, photographs, and equipment are also signed, but the autographed baseball has become the most popular and valuable collectible to display. Collectors should purchase the official major league baseballs at the stadium, hobby stores, sporting goods stores, and through advertisements in hobby publications. It is wise and less expensive to purchase baseballs in bulk — sold in quantity of twelve baseballs per box. You and a friend can purchase a few boxes of baseballs, share the expense of the purchase, and save a significant amount of money. Additionally, you are prepared to acquire the player's signature at any given time.

Here are some of the tools you will need to begin your collection.

Baseballs

Major league baseballs have the league and the name of that league's president stamped on them — in black for the National League, and blue for the American. In addition, official league baseballs bear the inscription "ROA" (Rawlings Official American League) or "RON" (Rawlings Official National League).

The age of a baseball can be determined by the signature of the league president stamped on the sweet spot of the ball, and purist collectors strive to have that signature correspond to the period during which the autographing player played. For example, a 1996 Dodgers team ball should be inscribed with National League President Leonard Coleman's signature instead of that of his predecessor Bill White, who was league president from 1989 to 1994. A Roger Maris signed ball, which is highly sought out by collectors, could be purchased on either an American or National League baseball with American League President Bobby Brown's signature and with National League President Charles Feeney's signature.

22

A baseball collection is a practical and cost-efficient approach to obtain player memories and their accomplishments. Pictured is a collection of New York Yankees single-signed and team baseballs.

Maris had passed away in 1985 and would've signed baseballs prior to his death with the aforementioned presidents. Obviously, if you can't find a ball from the period of time during which the players played, you can use whatever is available. The following table lists all the league presidents and the dates they served.

American League	*Tenure*
William Harridge	May 27, 1931–January 31, 1959
Joseph Cronin	February 1, 1959–December 31, 1973
Leland MacPhail, Jr.	January 1, 1974–December 31, 1983
Bobby Brown	January 1, 1984–July 31, 1994
Gene Budig	August 1, 1994–December 31, 1999

National League	*Tenure*
John Heydler	December 10, 1918–December 11, 1934
Ford Frick	December 11, 1934–October 8, 1951
Warren Giles	October 8, 1951–December 31, 1969

National League	Tenure
Charles Feeney	January 1, 1970–December 11, 1986
A. Bartlett Giamatti	December 12, 1986–March 31, 1989
William White	April 1, 1989–February 28, 1994
Leonard Coleman	March 1, 1994–October 31, 1999

The president's name on older balls is important in determining the period during which the ball was autographed, either by an individual player or by a team, or even the authenticity of the autograph. If you see a Babe Ruth autographed baseball with Gene Budig's name inscribed on it, you know it has to be a forgery, since the Babe was long gone by the time Budig became American League president. Knowing the dates each league president served is one way to detect a forged signature. Another factor to consider in determining authenticity is the type of writing material used when the player was alive. Collectors can utilize the services of companies that specialize in authenticating autographs, documents and other collectibles. Some hobby stores may have the Rawlings Official American and National League baseballs available, and it may be more expensive to purchase than the Selig baseballs.

In 2000, Commissioner Bud Selig eliminated the American and National League presidents' positions to unify the leagues. The new baseball that became available to the teams and hobby outlets throughout the United States that is presently being used is inscribed as follows:

Rawlings

Official

Major League Baseball

Allan H. Selig

Commissioner

Writing Implements

The table below shows the correct writing tool to be used for specific kinds of collectibles. All can be purchased inexpensively at office supply stores.

Collectible	Writing Tool
Baseball Card, Ticket or Stub	Fine or Extra-Fine Point Sharpie, Blue
Photograph, Poster, Print, Bat	Fine or Extra-Fine Point Sharpie, Blue
Hall of Fame Postcard, Magazine	Blue or Black Sharpie

Collectible	Writing Tool
Book, Program, Plate, Jersey	Blue or Black Sharpie
Uniform, Baseball Glove	Paint Pen or Sharpie

It is important to use the correct writing tool for a baseball, helmet, postcard, bat, and game ticket.

Collectible	*Writing Tool*
Batting Glove	Blue or Black Sharpie
Hat, Shoes, Black Bat	Silver or Gold Paint Pen
Helmet, Bat	Paint Pen or Sharpie
Baseball	Medium or Fine-Tip Ballpoint Pen

Ballpoint pens, either medium or fine-tip with blue or black ink, are the only writing implements that should be used on baseballs. Some collectors prefer to use a blue ballpoint for an American League ball, and a black ballpoint for a National League ball.

The Sanford Sharpie is a permanent marker that can be purchased in either fine or extra-fine point. Never use a permanent marker (Sharpie) on a baseball. It will ultimately bleed into the ball. Also, it makes it difficult to distinguish the letters of a signature.

The Pen-Touch gold or silver permanent marker is especially good for hats, helmets, shoes, and black bats. It comes in three sizes and dries quickly.

Collectors should have concerns about the writing instrument used when purchasing autographed baseballs from dealers and other types of vendors. The ballpoint pen, which is commonly used by collectors today, was prominent in the 1940s. Felt tip pens became popular in the 1960s, Sharpies in the 1970s, and the Pen-Touch permanent marker in the 1980s. Knowledge of the period when writing materials were used can be a good detection of forgery. Some factors you should consider when investigating the authenticity of autographed materials include:

1. Was the player living when the ink was available?

2. How can it be determined that the signature is genuine, not a ghost-signed autograph? During the 1950s, it was a common practice for clubhouse personnel to answer fan mail requests, and furnish autographs. Be wary of merchandise from this era.

3. If at all possible, when obtaining a specific autograph, try to have a reproduction of that signature for comparison.

4. Know the players' signing preferences. It was reported in a national newspaper that Mark McGwire will not autograph bats. An inexperienced collector purchased one from a Florida dealer, and tried to authenticate the bat through McGwire's agent. Unfortunately, the collector was informed it was a forgery.

Collectors must educate themselves to the fact that a small criminal element is selling forged autographs. You can learn quickly by attending baseball card shows and see the quality collectors and vendors in the hobby. Former players have been signing at these shows since the 1970s, and the demand has continued today. Every weekend there are shows all over the country with the retired and the present day players participating in the signings.

The aforementioned information has been provided to make the new collectors and the general collectors aware of the concerns for authenticity. Avoid purchasing expensive or questionable autographed baseballs and other types of memorabilia prior to conducting your own research on these items. Remember, this is a great hobby, and security measures have been provided to eliminate a small element of dishonesty.

Authenticating services have been used at private signings where collectors are receiving money-back guarantees for mail-order purchases. A word of caution is provided for collectors looking to buy cheap autographs for players more difficult to find. Collectors should be very careful in buying Mark McGwire autographed baseballs and other items. McGwire has not conducted a private signing or attended an autograph show in the past ten years. He doesn't sign in bulk and will not charge a fee to sign. You could pay $50 to $75 for his autograph on a baseball before he broke the home run record. Now a single-signed baseball goes for $350 to $500. Should you find an inexpensive autograph at a show, it is probably a fake signature. He will only conduct a rare public or private signing. Remember, sometimes a bargain is expensive.

Game-Used Baseballs

This type of baseball can be obtained at a game under the following scenarios:

1. During pre-game practice the player can toss a ball to the fans.
2. During batting practice the fans could collect a souvenir.
3. When the game begins fans could catch foul balls.
4. Fans can catch the home run baseball at the game.

Some of these home runs can be historic, and will be sought out by the player(s). On August 23, 1998, unaware that Barry Bonds had hit his 400th career home run, the fan who caught the ball was approached by collectors. One collector offered the fan $5,000 for the ball. At the same time the stadium security ushered him to the Giants clubhouse to negotiate a trade with him. The fan was approached by Orel Hershiser (Giants pitcher), who wanted to know what he would like to trade for the baseball. The individual had no idea what to request, but indicated that he was offered $5,000 for the ball, and Hershiser agreed to match the offer. Collectors should be aware of career achievement events when they attend baseball games.

Another record-breaking, historic home run that created lots of attention in the 2007 season was the ball Bonds hit for number 756 which was bought in an auction. The baseball was purchased by fashion designer Marc Ecko for $752,467, and he polled fans to determine whether he should mark it with an asterisk symbol. This symbol reflected that the accomplishment may be questionable. Bonds has been linked to using performance enhancing drugs to break the previous all-time home run record established by Hank Aaron. In 2008, the Hall of Fame accepted Bond's record-breaking baseball with the asterisk notated.

Game-used baseballs may appeal to a specific type of collector, one that is interested in historic events. It was reported in *Sports Collectors Digest* that the game baseballs used in games 2,130 and 2,131 for Cal Ripken's record streak (special baseballs produced for the two games) were sold by the umpires to retail outlets. This type of baseball is generally donated to the Baseball Hall of Fame Museum, to be displayed as an accomplishment for a historical event. It is more difficult to authenticate, unless the collector can substantiate that the ball was obtained during a game. During McGwire's chase of Maris' record specially marked baseballs were used when McGwire was batting. The record-breaking baseball was delivered to Cooperstown the following day.

Suggestions to Obtain Game-Used Baseballs

- **Collectors should use photographic equipment to authenticate their presence at the game.** Have your picture taken when you catch a foul ball. Make a short video clip with a digital camera and provide the date and year the ball was caught, and the name of the stadium.

- **When a player hands you a baseball, have a picture taken of the two of you together.** You can use a small handheld video camera to capture the moment.
- **Take a picture of the player handing you a ball, and request his autograph.** Try to photograph the player while he signs the baseball. Document the date and player who provided a game-used baseball.
- **At a historic baseball game, when you catch a game-used baseball, request from a team official (in writing) a short sentence indicating your presence at the game.** You can request their signature, title, and place the date on the paper. You should save the ticket stub as a way to indicate your presence. Display the game-used baseball and game ticket stub with the letter attesting to your presence in a display type of case. A wood base and card display holder can protect and store the baseball and ticket stub.
- **Only purchase game-used baseballs from a reputable dealer who can produce a written letter authenticating the item being sold.** It would be more desirable for the letter to be on team stationery, or the personal letterhead of the baseball personnel.
- **When you purchase game-used baseballs from other collectors, you must request proof of authenticity.** Never accept oral representations as fact; get the proof in writing or avoid purchasing the item.
- **As a collector you may be interested in the following types of game-used baseballs —** All-Star Game, World Series, no-hitter game (also a perfect game), statistical record-breaking events, which include home runs, strikeouts by a pitcher, most wins by a pitcher, etc. Also, Major League Baseball produces special baseballs for historic events. Any collector who obtained a game-used baseball when a player hit his 3,000 career hit, 500th career home run, a pitcher won his 300th game or a pitcher throwing a no-hitter should save the game stub and find a way to have the ball autographed.
- **Attend historic baseball games and request prior to the game a game-used baseball from the team personnel, such as the batboy or a player.** Arrive at the stadium early, and get close to the field level. When you have a one-on-one opportunity to interact with a player or team personnel make your courteous request. Nothing ventured, nothing gained.

Special Event Baseballs

The Rawlings company makes the official major league baseball and also produces the official league baseballs for the All-Star Game and the World Series. It produced the baseballs for Cal Ripken's pursuit of Lou Gehrig's consecutive games streak, and in his game numbers 2,130 and 2,131 a special baseball was used. Also, the Jackie Robinson commemorative baseball was used on opening day in 1997 to commemorate the 50th anniversary of his breaking the color barrier. These commemorative baseballs that are produced for special events are available at hobby stores and through vendor advertisements in hobby publications.

The 1994 World Series baseball was the only special event baseball that wasn't game-used. That series was canceled due to the baseball strike.

Suggestions for Use of Special Event Baseballs

- **Purchase the All-Star Game baseball for a particular year, and request a single signature on the sweet spot from one of the players.**
- **A more creative approach would be to collect as many players as possible from either the American or National League on a single baseball.** This is a real challenge for the hobbyist.
- **The Ripken record baseball is available at hobby stores.** Cal Ripken, Jr., has been considered one of the best players in the autograph market. He was easily obtained during spring training and would usually sign for about 45 minutes near the end of the game. He would sign one autograph for everybody at a particular area.
- **The Robinson commemorative baseball is used for autographs which can be single-signed and as a team baseball.** The players you could request to sign this type of baseball would be living teammates, like Duke Snider, Carl Erskine, etc. You might want to add many of his teammates on this baseball (team ball). Also, you can request the signatures of former players who played opposite Robinson. Some collectors had requested Johnny Sain, a former Braves pitcher, and he was a popular autograph guest, to add on this baseball — "1st pitch to Robinson" — with his name inscribed on the baseball (Sain was the first pitcher Robinson faced in the majors). This is a fun way of researching players from the past and meeting them in person at autograph shows. Collectors can purchase these commemorative baseballs which have been signed in the manner above at baseball shows and at hobby stores.
- **A common practice for World Series collectors is to obtain single-signed baseballs.** These specially designed baseballs frequently appear for sale on home shopping programs on television and in *Sports Collectors Digest*. Collecting a World Series team baseball from the winning team is extremely popular and valuable. It can be obtained in person, but can take plenty of time to complete.
- **The collector of a special event baseball wants to signify their connection to the event in some manner.** Since they cannot attend an All-Star or World Series game, being able to purchase the special event baseball is an important element in their collection. It makes their collection historical, which is an important goal.

Single-Signature Baseballs

The element that has made the hobby mature is the autographed single-signature baseballs. Many hobbyists are determined to collect one autographed baseball for each popular player or Hall of Famer. This specialized area of collecting has shown an amazing increase in value. Collectors find acquiring the single-signature of a player on the sweet spot of a baseball very appealing. The sweet spot is the shortest distance between the two seams of the baseball. Request the player to sign here, although some players will sign anywhere on the baseball. Collectors should use the official major league baseball, which should correspond with the appropriate league the signing player has played in. When approaching Tony Gwynn of the San Diego Padres, for example, you would use the National League baseball. For players who have represented both the American and National Leagues, you could use either baseball. Today collectors use the Rawlings Official Major League Baseball with Selig inscribed on it. The star player or the more popular player signing the baseball will add the greater value. Factors that determine the value of a single-signed baseball include the following:

1. Name recognition and accomplishment of a player.
2. Principles of supply and demand based upon regional and national interest.

A single-signature baseball collection has become the most popular and desirable for the hobbyist. Always request a signature on the sweet spot of the baseball.

3. Player appearance, and those who refuse to participate in shows or private signings, and deceased players who never appeared at shows or private signings (scarcity).

4. Condition of the acquired autograph — baseball signatures which are smudged, faded or in poor condition will diminish the value of the autograph.

Some players with name recognition that many collectors will purchase on a single-signed baseball include Mickey Mantle, Joe DiMaggio, Ted Williams and Stan Musial. The availability of the latter group is plentiful due to many signings. Based upon supply and demand factors, players like Mark McGwire, Ken Griffey, Jr., and Randy Johnson, who never conduct signings, will be more difficult to obtain and be more expensive to purchase. The availability of signatures of the more popular deceased players will usually be limited on single baseballs, causing a strong demand and high expense in obtaining them. Collectors can develop a theme area to concentrate on acquiring single-signature baseballs.

Suggestions to Acquire Single-Signature Baseballs

- **Select a collection theme or an area of interest.** Themes include a Hall of Fame collection, Rookie of the Year recipients, 500 home run hitters, players with 3,000 hits, 300 game winning pitchers, pitchers throwing no-hitters, CY Young Awards, All-Star players, Most Valuable Players (MVP) and historic events (Don Larsen will sign a single baseball and add "Perfect Game" 10/8/56).
- **For the serious collector, purchase baseballs in bulk, one or two dozen at a time.** Keep a large supply in your automobile, and be prepared when traveling to ballparks or baseball shows. Also, having the baseballs with you will be beneficial when you find the whereabouts of teams, players, and retired players.
- **Use baseball reference books to obtain statistical data for collecting with a historical perspective.** The National League Green Book and the American League Red Book provide each team roster and club information, home run records, lifetime grand slams, pitching records from the previous season and lifetime records. Statistical data on hitting, pitching, fielding and team stadium information is very concise. This book is an excellent reference source. You should request the player to add the event, and the date it occurred on single-signature baseballs. Collectors could request Bobby Thomson to write "The Shot Heard 'Round the World, Oct. 3, 1951." Kerry Wood, the Cubs rookie phenom, set a rookie record and tied a major league record by striking out 20 Astro batters on May 6, 1998. Collectors frequently garner his signature on a baseball with his addition of the record. Collectors will request Wood add 1998 Rookie of the Year (ROY) on a baseball.
- **Attend special events like the Hall of Fame Induction Weekend at the museum in Cooperstown, New York.** Many former inductees participate in the festivities in late July or at the beginning of August. Autograph sessions are conducted throughout the

village during the weekend. Usually a free signing is scheduled for children only. Each year 30 to 40 players attend, and many collectors purchase single-signature baseballs. Because of the popularity of this event, it is recommended that you call early to make hotel arrangements for the following year.

- **Check the newspapers and sports publications for a listing of baseball card shows.** Many of the shows include a signing session for a couple of hours. Active and inactive players participate, and for a nominal fee collectors can acquire single-signature baseballs.
- **Collectors can initiate a single-signed baseball collection for the American or National League teams playing in their regional area.** You can pursue the players with lesser appeal, and those more difficult to obtain.
- **It is easier and less time consuming for many collectors to purchase single-signature baseballs of the more popular players from reputable dealers.** This is a good way to make a new contact who has the ability to obtain the signatures of the higher profile players. Request to be included on the dealer mailing list.
- **It is easier to collect new players (rookies) at the beginning of their career when the demand isn't as great.** All-Star players like Derek Jeter and Alex Rodriguez were easily obtained during their rookie season, but are more expensive to purchase today. They are less accessible to in-person autograph requests.
- **The value of a single player signature, in most instances, will exceed the value of many signatures on a baseball.** Single-signature collections are preferred by most collectors.
- **Use specially designed baseballs, such as the All-Star Game, National Hall of Fame logo balls and World Series baseballs, which can be purchased in most hobby stores, to design a special event collection of single-signature baseballs.** These baseballs will cost a little bit more, but will make your collection interesting.
- **Try to develop a collection of individual players with certain Hall of Fame credentials.** Seek out players like Craig Biggio, Lance Berkman, Chase Utley, and Jim Thome, all of whom conduct signings from time to time.
- **For team collectors, you can design a single-signature baseball collection of your all-time favorites.** You can incorporate retired players and active ones. Some collectors have more than 100 single-signed Brooklyn Dodgers and New York Yankees baseballs.

Team Baseballs

A creative and interesting approach to collecting is acquiring the signatures of an entire team on a single baseball. A team baseball collection requires the starting players, pitchers, and the bench players to complete the ball. It is customary for the manager's signature to be reserved for the sweet spot, and a team baseball should have 20 to 25 signatures to be complete. It is more of a challenge to collect an entire team at the ballpark, but some collectors will endure an entire season to complete this collection. A signed team baseball collection will have greater value when the team wins the World Series. Otherwise, the collection doesn't provide the greatest value. As a comparison, a single-signature baseball collection of the identical team baseball will have a significantly greater value as a collectible. Many ball clubs sign dozens of team baseballs during the season and use them in a promotional manner as giveaways. These baseballs will become available and can be purchased at baseball shows, online auctions and through reputable dealers.

A factor that will determine the value of a team baseball is the key signatures on the baseball. Two examples of team baseballs from different periods are provided. First, the collector of a 1961 New York Yankees team baseball (World Champions) would have the following key signatures on the baseball: Mantle, Maris, Berra, Ford, Howard, Kubek, and Tresh. This baseball has been valued at $14,000 to $20,000 from purchases at auctions and the condition of the signatures will affect the value. The collector of a 1997 Florida Marlins team baseball (World Champions) would have the following key signatures on the baseball: Alou, Bonilla, Brown, Counsell, Hernandez, Johnson, Leyland, Renteria, and Sheffield. This baseball has been priced at $750 to $1,000. Some reasons why the 1961 Yankees team baseball is expensive include: three players inducted into the Hall of Fame (Berra, Ford, and Mantle), historical significance of Roger Maris setting a new record at that time with 61 home runs, and the age of the baseball (scarcity).

Suggestions for a Team Baseball Collection

- **Use the official American or National League baseball for a team collection consisting of twenty to twenty-five signatures, with the manager on the sweet spot.** Baseballs not recognized as the official baseball could reduce the value of a team baseball by 50 percent or more.
- **Only use a ballpoint pen and the same color ink for a team collection.**
- **Purchase a team media guide and become familiar with the entire roster.** This book enables the collector quick and easy access to the players.
- **Group the players in the following manner — starting players, bench players, and pitchers.** Focus on one group at a time when acquiring autographs. It doesn't hurt to add the coaches, general manager or owner on the baseball.
- **Another type of team baseball collection is an all-time team collection of retired players from a different period of time.** Many teams will schedule an old-timers day event and game where many of the players participate in autograph signings. Some promoters will put together an old-time theme show of living players from a particular era.
- **Attend reunion baseball shows where many players from a special or championship team sign for a few hours.** The 1969 New York Mets players conduct this signing each

year and usually 15 or more players appear. Some of the players from the 1998 New York Yankees "World Championship Team" conducted a reunion baseball show immediately after the World Series was completed.

- **Attend team Fanfest events.** Many teams request the players to sign at the stadium to induce fans to purchase tickets. At these events there will be a group of players signing for about one hour, and another group signing afterwards. This event will take place on the weekend when many fans can participate. Fanfest events are usually scheduled during spring training.
- **Commemorative baseballs are the official league baseball, which should be used by the collector to acknowledge an accomplishment by a group of players.** Some collector themes include signatures of the living members of the "500 Home Run Club," "3,000 Hit Club," and "300 Game Winners"; and a collection of Most Valuable Player Award recipients can be grouped together. Collectors can purchase commemorative, signed baseballs, which are unique due to a limited production and a scarcity of these signatures.
- **Use the Rawlings Official Commemorative Baseball, which has produced a special baseball for the All-Star Game and World Series.** The World Series and All-Star Game Baseball has a special logo with the signature of the commissioner replacing the league president. The All-Star Baseball has the logo of the host city. It may be more cost efficient to purchase autographed commemorative baseballs, because of the expense and amount of time it would take to collect these signatures in person.

Some factors to consider when purchasing a team baseball include the following:

1. Check to see if the baseball is the official league ball. Beginning in 2000 the new Selig inscribed baseball was the official baseball for both leagues.

2. Determine if the signature is acceptable. Some players write a shortened version of their name, which appears incomplete. Bobby Bonilla signs baseballs by writing "BO" instead of Bobby Bonilla.

3. Determine whether or not the signature is legible.

4. Check to see if the condition of the baseball is acceptable. Assess the appearance of the ink, and are any signatures fading?

5. For a complete baseball, count the number of signatures on the ball, which should have about 25 players, and see if the manager is on the sweet spot.

6. Only purchase team baseballs signed with a ballpoint pen and the same color ink. Remember, it is more difficult and time consuming to put together a team-signed baseball. It is more cost-effective to purchase a team-signed ball at a baseball show or from a reputable dealer.

3. Unorthodox Collecting

The baseball collector has become a specialist, not only in seeking the customary memorabilia, but in opening up new modes of collecting. Reaching beyond the usual baseball memorabilia and single-signed baseballs, many collectors, both new and established, are searching for items commemorating historical events. Eager to experience new records and great memories, they are looking for oddball (unusual) memorabilia to collect. They want to connect their childhood memories of the players with the materials they collect. In their quest to document the history of the game on some type of memorabilia, the collector has found a method of unorthodox collecting.

The unorthodox collector wants to recall the events of the game that have now become milestones in our lives. Mark Allen Baker, in *Team Baseballs*, indicated for example that some such hobbyists are interested in building a collection of signatures of not only individuals affiliated with the game, but also prominent people who are only indirectly associated with baseball. In the latter, of interest are single-signature baseballs of presidents of the United States, and signatures and memorabilia of celebrities and who have personified the game of baseball in the movies they have appeared in. These celebrities have a relationship with baseball, and are another challenge for collectors.

Baseball's relationship with the presidency began in 1910 when President William Howard Taft threw out the first ball to begin the season. Taft is credited with beginning a baseball memorabilia tradition that day when he signed his name on an official National League baseball at the game at Pittsburgh's Forbes Field. Every U.S. president since 1910 has made the ceremonial first pitch which has become the standard for baseball on Opening Day. The baseball that Taft signed in 1910 was purchased in Mastro Auctions' in March 2001 for $39,708.

The Baseball Hall of Fame Museum owns a collection of presidential autographs that includes Taft, Calvin Coolidge, Woodrow Wilson, Theodore and Franklin Roosevelt, Warren Harding, Herbert Hoover, Dwight Eisenhower, John F. Kennedy, Richard Nixon, Gerald Ford, Jimmy Carter, George H. Bush, Bill Clinton and George W. Bush. Since the approaches employed by collectors to obtain presidential signatures are more limited, the demand and value is greater. A Richard Nixon baseball was purchased at an auction in 2006 for $2,530. A John F. Kennedy single-signature baseball was auctioned for $37,700 in 2005. (from *Sports Collectors Digest*). George H. Bush has participated in private signings and collectors can purchase his autographed baseballs, commemorative bats and commemorative jerseys.

From time to time collectors have been able to meet presidents at golf events, celebrity (charity) tennis events, on the campaign trail, and at private receptions — where you make a contribution to their campaign, and receive an invitation to dine with the president. At the event you and the president are photographed together (maybe you can request his signature on an item). Collectors could use the mail request approach, and find President Gerald Ford was receptive to signing baseball memorabilia until 2002. President Clinton responded to mail requests in the early 1990s, but he unfortunately signed baseballs with a black Sharpie. During the 2008 Florida Presidential Primary, Hillary Clinton made a victory appearance in Fort Lauderdale and similar to President Clinton she signed a baseball with a black Sharpie. When she signs memorabilia she adds her middle initial to programs and baseballs, and writes: Hillary R Clinton. President Clinton is an avid baseball fan and he received a copy of *October Baseball* from the author in April 2008. He responded with a personal letter, thanking the author for the book and provided his signature on the letter. For collectors there is a connection between baseball and presidents. Below is a chart of Presidential single-signed baseballs and the purchase price from auctions from 2001–2008 (from *Sports Collectors Digest*).

Presidential Single-Signed Baseballs, Purchase Price, Auction and Date

Herbert Hoover	$63,654	Lelands.com	April 2006
Franklin Roosevelt	$42,012	Lelands.com	December 2006
William Taft	$39,708	Mastro Auctions	March 2001
Calvin Coolidge	$39,000	SCP/Sotheby's	June 2008
John F. Kennedy	$37,700	Robert Edward	April 2005
Woodrow Wilson	$33,000	SCP/Sotheby's	June 2005
Warren Harding	$26,000	Hunt Auctions	February, 2005
Theodore Roosevelt	$17,250	SCP/Sotheby's	December 2004
Harry Truman	$16,698	Mastro Auctions	December 2006
Ronald Reagan	$5,676	Mastro Auctions	December 2006
Dwight Eisenhower	$3,744	Lelands.com	November 2007
Richard Nixon	$2,530	Hunt Auctions	May 2006
George W. Bush	$752	SCP/Sotheby's	September 2007
Bill Clinton	$565	SCP/Sotheby's	September 2007
Jimmy Carter	$392	Universal Rarities	June 2006
George H.W. Bush	$330	American Memorabilia	September 2006
Gerald Ford	$256	Premier Auctions	June 2007

According to hobby experts John F. Kennedy signed baseballs have always been the most desirable for collectors. These balls are very difficult to find and there may be less than 20 that can be genuine. The limited amount of Kennedy balls (scarcity) will continue to increase the value over time.

President Clinton and Secretary of State Hillary Clinton signed baseballs with a black Sharpie.

The unorthodox collector uses movie posters, scripts, plates, magazine covers, photographs of the celebrities, baseballs, and other unusual collectibles to connect the signature of the celebrity to the event. The movies have always portrayed the game of baseball in a positive manner, and the collector has added the signatures of movie stars like Kevin Costner (*Bull Durham, Field of Dreams, For the Love of the Game*) and Robert Redford (*The Natural*) to their collection. This type of collection is unique, and not common for many collectors. The unorthodox collector is looking for different ways to accumulate items recalling baseball memories. Some auctions today feature signed and professionally framed photographs of actors in baseball movies (Tom Hanks wearing a baseball uniform in the movie *League of Their Own*).

Combination (Combo) Signatures

Equally important for this type of collector is an area of connecting the heroes of the game — pitcher and catcher of the winning team or the losing pitcher with the opposing batter (the hero of the game), and placing two or more signatures on a baseball. This type of collecting is called "combination or combo signatures," and is related to an historical collection. When acquiring combo signatures of two players, request that each player sign on the sweet spot of the baseball. Some collectors will ask that the players add the event and date.

Suggestions for Collecting Combination (Combo) Signatures

- **Prior to beginning this type of collection research an area of interest.** Start with teams of interest and players that could be grouped together. Imagine having a baseball signed on the sweet spot by Ruth and Gehrig (very rare, but they do exist). For the Cincinnati Reds collectors, the Big Red Machine theme could include the combination of Rose, Perez, Morgan and Bench on a single baseball. For a collection of Atlanta Braves, a signed baseball with the addition of Maddux, Glavine and Smoltz would be interesting and they may be grouped together on one of the panels of the baseball. This would be a unique collection and be easier than completing a team ball.
- **Use a good ballpoint pen, either blue or black ink, but the same color ink is most desirable for both signatures.** Always use the same ink color for two or more signatures (important for team baseballs). Display in a cube or wood base ball holder.
- **Purchase the official major league baseballs, and use the appropriate American or National League baseball when the event occurs in the same league.** If you cannot purchase the aforementioned balls, use the Selig Official Major League baseballs. When an historical event occurs, and the players are from different leagues, you can use either the American or National League baseball. In the 1960 World Series, Bill Mazeroski (Pittsburgh Pirates) hit the game-winning home run off Ralph Terry, the New York Yankees pitcher. To acquire these player signatures, you could use either league baseball or the Selig Official Major League baseball, but request Terry first. He appears on the celebrity golf circuit, and will sign a single-signature baseball (but will not sign the ball if Mazeroski's signature appears). Mazeroski will sign in person at baseball shows, and hasn't been predictable with mail requests since he was elected to the Hall of Fame in 2001.
- **A combination baseball could have the signatures of two or more players.** You could include up to three signatures on the sweet spot of the ball. For three to five signatures request the players to sign on one of the panels. In the early 1990s, collectors would request Mantle, Snider and Mays, three great New York centerfielders, to sign on the sweet spot. You can purchase a Snider, Mantle and Mays combination baseball from reputable dealers and online auctions.
- **Select themes of interest — historic events, most valuable players of the World Series, player accomplishments, and team firsts.** On April 5, 1993, the Florida Marlins' inaugural season opening game, Charlie Hough recorded the Marlins' first win, and Bryan Harvey the first save. On a baseball you could request both signatures and have the

players inscribe "1st win, save 4/5/93." Also, for an inaugural team you could request individual players to add accomplishments—first hit, first home run, etc.—and date the baseball. Scott Pose had the Marlins first team hit in their inaugural season and Benito Santiago had the first team home run. You could request Mike Lowell, the 2007 World Series MVP to add this on a baseball.

- **Focus on historic events from past memories and include recent happenings.** A popular combo baseball includes the signatures of Don Larsen and Yogi Berra (they appear together at baseball theme shows). Don Larsen has thrown the only perfect game in World Series history, and Yogi Berra was his catcher that day. Request the players to write "Perfect Game," and the date 10/8/56. During the 1998 season, David Wells of the Yankees also threw a perfect game. Collectors could include a combo baseball with the likes of Wells and Sandy Koufax, or others with this achievement. Have one of the players add "Perfect Game" on the baseball.
- **Team baseball collectors could develop a Hall of Fame combo baseball with the following signatures on one of the panels: St. Louis Cardinals theme—Musial, Schoendienst, Gibson, Brock and Ozzie Smith.** All of the players appear on the baseball show circuit. Design your own favorite combo baseball team theme.
- **A combination baseball theme can acknowledge either the highs or lows, and include baseball records—home runs, hits, runs batted in, strikeouts, World Series game-winning home runs, and costly errors.** Some of the heroes and players who made mistakes will appear together at theme shows. Bill Buckner (Red Sox) and Mookie Wilson (Mets) both played in the 1986 World Series and participate in these baseball shows. It was Buckner's error that allowed the Mets to become the 1986 World Champs. One of the game umpires retrieved the baseball and had it donated for a charity auction. Charlie Sheen, an actor, purchased this game-used baseball for approximately $93,500. Because of the historical significance of these events, many of the players involved appear at various functions throughout the year. To successfully combine a combo signature on a baseball, it is recommended that you approach the less fortunate player first, and add the hero afterwards. Otherwise, many players will refuse to sign because it presents an unpleasant memory. Be tactful and polite when you approach these players.
- **Create your own combo theme.** Find a creative approach to combine two or more players on a single baseball. This is less time consuming than constructing a team baseball, and as much fun. At a live, silent auction for the Joe DiMaggio Hospital in 2008, a newspaper advertisement listed the players who would appear. From the list, collectors could add two or more combo signatures from the same team. One collector had the signatures of some New York Yankees from the 1960s—Phil Linz, Tom Tresh, Al Downing, and Stan Bahnsen on the same panel of a baseball.
- **Oddball combo baseball themes.** Include the signatures of the American League and National League presidents on the same baseball (use either baseball) or the signatures

A combination baseball theme of Brooklyn Dodgers, New York Giants and New York Yankees is popular with collectors because of the teams' rich histories.

of baseball commissioners, like Bud Selig and Fay Vincent, both of whom are receptive to signing the same baseball. A challenge for the unorthodox collector would be a combo baseball signed by Fay Vincent and Pete Rose. It would be interesting if both individuals signed the same baseball. Commissioner Vincent banned Rose from participating in baseball and being considered for induction into the Baseball Hall of Fame. Also, eccentric or controversial baseball owners would be an interesting combo baseball theme — in particular, Rupert Murdoch of the Dodgers (sold the team in 2004) and George Steinbrenner of the Yankees, two owners who will pay millions of dollars to win a championship.

Oddball Memorabilia

Baseball fans and collectors have an assortment of items they have saved, ranging from game day programs, yearbooks, newspaper headlines, periodicals, ticket stubs, and promotional giveaways (which include team pin sets, player bobbleheads, collectible plates, team hats from past eras, replica jerseys, fotoballs of the face of a player appearing on the baseball, batting helmets, team pennants, and much more). During the 2008 season, the Pittsburgh Pirates had the following giveaways: Willie Stargell bobblehead, Roberto Clemente collectible plate, Dave Parker bobblehead and a Freddy Sanchez replica batting jersey. Many of these treasures are stored in a closet, and referred to as oddball memorabilia. Dealers often purchase many cheap-seat tickets and receive for free the promotional giveaways that they will profit from.

The collector is searching for other unique items, rather than a baseball, to have autographed: team ticket stubs or unused tickets from significant events such as the World Series, All-Star or playoff games, games of achievement where a pitcher has thrown a no-hitter, and games where a record is broken. Imagine having a ticket stub or program from the September 8, 1998, St. Louis Cardinals home game, when Mark McGwire hit his 62nd home run, a new major league record at the time. The modern collector should preserve these items in excellent or mint condition using plastic inserts that prevent fading and tearing. Also, at the appropriate time, the collector should acquire the autograph of the player who has a connection to the game ticket.

During the 1995 All-Star Game, Jeff Conine of the Florida Marlins pinch hit the game-winning home run and was chosen the game's Most Valuable Player. He was photographed receiving the MVP trophy, and a photo card was produced and given away as a promotional item at a game during the Marlins' next homestand. Each fan attending the game received an 8" × 10" photograph card, which many had him sign. The most popular item related to his achievement, which collectors acquired, was the 1995 All-Star Game baseball. At his signing, most collectors requested the addition of "1995 All-Star M.V.P."

Old game programs with a player featured on the cover, World Series or All-Star game programs, and periodicals — including *Sports*, *Sports Illustrated*, *Time* and *Life*— have featured many baseball players on the covers of their magazine. Of recent interest to collectors is the *Sports Illustrated* Sportsman of the Year issue with a baseball player appearing on the cover. Some of the players you can find include Sandy Koufax, Orel Hershiser, and Cal Ripken, Jr. These magazines are very desirable to collectors who want the cover autographed. The magazines can be purchased unsigned at flea markets, libraries, hobby stores, baseball card shows, and through hobby publications for a reasonable price. An unsigned August 2, 1963, *Life* magazine with Sandy Koufax appearing on the cover could cost $60 to purchase. The value of magazines, like other memorabilia, is determined by the factors of age, condition, name recognition and scarcity (older magazines are very rare).

Game day programs acquired by fans and collectors are an oddball collectible. Every month a new program cover is printed, and some collectors have an entire collection of programs for many years. These souvenir programs are usually purchased at the stadium to keep score in. Many collectors refuse to write on the scorecard, but have the cover autographed

by a player prior to or after the game. Acquiring an autograph will increase its value. Also, an attractive program cover design will add value to the program. Should you keep score, write neatly, as it does present some history of the game. Programs should be stored in plastic holders, and to be considered in excellent condition should have no wear and tear. An easy way to purchase other team programs is by visiting their website on the Internet.

Another affordable type of collection is team yearbooks. Collectors usually purchase this publication at the stadium each year. The cost is nominal, and yearbooks can be ordered through the mail as well. To be officially classified as a yearbook, it must contain the photographs of the 25 player roster, managers and coaches, and include player biographies and statistical information. This can be helpful in recognizing the players in order to acquire their signature. Collectors can purchase a collection of yearbooks from the 1960s to the present at an affordable price. The yearbooks from the 1950s are most costly due to age and scarcity. The greatest value in any yearbook collection are the ones that have the cover signed. Like other collectibles, yearbooks should be preserved in plastic holders and kept out of the sunlight.

As a collector, especially a novice to the hobby, one of the most important books that should be utilized is *The Baseball Encyclopedia*. Obtain the latest edition at your local bookstore. Baseball books, as a collectible, are very desirable. It is easy to obtain used books in good condition at a very low price. As more and more collectors pursue this route and obtain used baseball books, the price will begin to escalate. The uniqueness for this type of collection is acquiring autographs on the cover or inside at the beginning of the book. Some collectors who purchase books about their favorite team will have many players sign the inside of the book. Factors that determine the value of a used baseball book include condition, age, scarcity, recognition, and edition. Listed below are some books to include in a baseball collection. You can find these books at baseball card shows, flea markets, and in bookstores.

A Biographical Dictionary of the Baseball Hall of Fame, John Skipper, 2000—Great reference information on the members of the Hall of Fame, 2000.
The Boys of Summer, Roger Kahn, 1971—Classic book about the Brooklyn Dodgers of the 1950s.
The Cincinnati Game, Lonnie Wheeler, 1988—Great book for a team collector.
Dodgers—The First 100 Years, Stanley Cohen, 1990—Excellent book for a team collector, and for acquiring autographs.

A different oddball item that has interested collectors is the commemorative first-day limited edition envelope. These envelopes, known as first-day covers, recall an historical baseball event. When the event takes place, an employee of the post office in that city will hand cancel the stamp on the envelope. Back in 1939, at the opening ceremonies for baseball's 100th birthday celebration in Cooperstown, New York, the legends of baseball—Babe Ruth,

Opposite: **Old magazines, All-Star, World Series and old game programs are popular displays.**

Ty Cobb, Walter Johnson, Honus Wagner, Tris Speaker, Cy Young, and others — were on hand to sign the envelopes with the first commemorative stamp. These stamps were postmarked and canceled that day at the Cooperstown Post Office. This was the beginning of first-day covers, which have since become a popular collectible. It is interesting to note that over 350,000 stamped envelopes were canceled that day in Cooperstown. You can purchase this particular first-day cover at hobby stores, from dealers at baseball card shows, and could pay from $20 to $30 for an unsigned cover. The signed ones, which are rare, will appear at auctions from time-to-time. Another good place to find these commemoratives is at flea markets and through some stamp dealers. As with most oddball memorabilia, acquiring a signature related to the event will increase the value of the item.

Suggestions for an Oddball Memorabilia Collection

- **Figurines, statues, and plates can be found in gift stores at a reasonable price.** Purchase single player items that you can have autographed. Sometimes you can receive a better price if you purchase two or more items.
- **Check the promotional team giveaways for your major league team.** Photos, prints, collectible player plates, mini-bats, hats, helmets, replica jerseys and commemorative items are excellent for acquiring player autographs. Look in the newspaper, media guide and game programs which provide the dates of team giveaways. You can call the stadium to inquire about special event giveaways or check the team websites.
- **Visit flea markets, hobby stores, and baseball shows where you can find inexpensive, unique oddball memorabilia.** Check all of the dealer tables to compare items and prices. At times, you can only negotiate prices that may seem unreasonable!
- **For the new collector entering the hobby, initiate a bobbing-head doll (ceramic player statues) collection of all the major league teams.** It's an inexpensive collection, and attractive decor in a memorabilia room. In addition, every team provides a bobblehead of some of the players (present and past) at special event giveaways during the season. The bobblehead promotion is provided to the first 15,000 fans arriving at the stadium and you should arrive early to avoid missing out on this unique item.
- **Network with other collectors who are looking to find oddball memorabilia.** Check hobby publications and home computer online services. You can find interesting websites with an array of oddball items to purchase. This is a great way to also trade items with other collectors.
- **Visit art galleries where you can find player portraits, stadium art, and limited edition paintings which may be signed or unsigned.** You can also find limited edition lithographs numbered and usually signed by the artist and the player.
- **Visit antique stores where you can find stadium equipment — original seats, turnstiles, scoreboard signs, stadium bricks, dugout or bullpen benches, clothing, etc.**
- **Purchase cut signatures and canceled player checks, which can be matted and framed**

Plates and steins are unusual items that collectors seek.

with unsigned photographs. Cut signatures and canceled checks are another option of acquiring the signatures of players more difficult to find (discussed in Chapter 9). Cut signatures are more affordable to purchase than signed prints and photographs.

- **Player fotoballs with the face of a player printed on the baseball have become a common oddball item for many collectors.** These baseballs are great for acquiring signatures. The addition of these player printed baseballs makes a great display in a memorabilia room.
- **Collect newspapers of historical events — record-breaking moments which are captured on headlines make valuable collectibles, and appreciate over time.** A concern for newspaper collectors is that the pulp in the paper has a high content of acid which will cause a yellowing over time.
- **Newspapers should be stored flat in acid-free types of holders.** Because of the acidic content in the paper, it becomes brittle and deteriorates. A 100 percent cotton rag matted board may preserve the newspaper. You may consider professionally framing historical and record-breaking events captured in your newspaper collection.
- **Acquire the signature(s) of the player(s) who are connected to the historical event.**

Also, call the newspaper and check whether a commemorative display piece will be printed. Historic events will be featured in a special newspaper display in many baseball cities.

• **Purchase commemorative items of historical significance with a limited edition of signed and numbered items.** In most instances the number of items signed commemorates the significant event. You may find a series of 715 signed photographs of Hank Aaron's record-breaking home run. Considering the amount of items the players sign during their lifetimes, a limited edition series which is numbered has greater value.

• **Create your own oddball memorabilia and have it signed by the appropriate player.** During spring training in 1997, a collector approached Cal Ripken with a handheld iron and requested his signature on the shiny side. Ripken began laughing and signed the item with a blue Sharpie. Everyone present laughed at the "irony" as Ripken is known as baseball's "Iron Man."

Other Oddball Memorabilia

Collectors have continued to explore other memorabilia to include in their collection. Below is a listing of inexpensive items that can be purchased at hobby stores, at baseball card shows, and through hobby publications.

• Major league baseball Beanie Babies, Beanie Bears and BamBinos player series.
• Silk cacheted covers, limited edition of historic events and individual players. In creating these classy little collectibles, an artist first designs a painting of the event or player. The painting is then transferred, on silk and in color, to envelopes that have been stamped and postmarked by the post office in the city where the event occurred.
• Major league baseball mini-helmets include the team color and logo.
• Baseball cartoon-art paintings, limited edition with team color and logo.
• World champion team photo plaques.
• Cereal boxes, limited edition with historic event and player(s) on cover.
• Autographed signs with player advertising food or beverage product.
• Team pocket schedules with player(s) appearing on the cover. Some collectors acquire the schedules of all major league teams.
• Player and stadium plates and figurines — a neat item to have signed.
• Commemorative magazines, such as *Sports Illustrated*, which make a special commemorative issue for historic events.
• Player buttons, World Series pins, and press credentials from past years.
• Commemorative player street signs with player name and record printed as the street address.

Opposite: **Odd memorabilia — mini-bats, books, mini-helmets, yearbooks and magazines with popular players appearing on the cover.**

4. The Hall of Fame
Baseball Collection

The pinnacle of a memorabilia collection is the Hall of Fame baseball collection, and different collectors approach this project in different ways. Some search for all types of memorabilia on a single player, including cards, baseballs, commemorative Hall of Fame baseballs, bats, jerseys, hats, Hall of Fame Plaque Cards, books, posters, bobbleheads, mini-helmets, plates, figurines, and other oddball items. Other collectors search for items related to the living members of the Hall of Fame. The prominent theme a majority of collectors will pursue is a single-signed baseball collection of the living inductees of the Hall of Fame.

Some seek to acquire single-signed baseballs of the deceased members which will be more costly to purchase. Multi-signatures of the Hall of Famers on a single baseball and recently issued commemorative Hall of Fame induction baseballs with the face of the player stamped on the ball have become popular items. The single-signed baseball collection is most preferred by collectors and generates the greater value.

Each baseball should be signed on the sweet spot, which is the shortest distance between the two seams of the ball. A multi-signature baseball collection is unique with 20 to 25 players on a single baseball, but does not generate the greatest value. Collectors may include this type of collection to create an all-time theme of Hall of Famers, as a historical baseball. Some prefer a combo Hall of Fame theme — such as players of the same team — as another type of collection. Whatever design you employ, a Hall of Fame baseball collection continues to be a great investment and memorable experience for the hobbyist.

For collectors, it is possible to design a collection of the living inductees and obtain their signatures in person, through mail requests, or trading with other collectors. One can also purchase these signed baseballs from reputable dealers, participate in live online and telephone auctions, and use the Internet and online services from your home or office computer.

Prior to beginning a Hall of Fame collection you should formulate a plan of action. What approach should you use to obtain this collection? Consider the factors of time and cost for acquiring each single-signed baseball. Purchase resource books, such as *The Baseball Encyclopedia*, which will furnish statistical data and other pertinent information on every living Hall

Opposite: **A single-signed Hall of Fame baseball collection has become prominent in the hobby.**

of Famer. You can also go to www. baseball-almanac.com and www.baseballhalloffame.org These websites have the most current information regarding the members of the Hall of Fame. You will quickly find the data very useful when you approach the players at in-person signings.

Starting a Hall of Fame Collection

- **Use a cost-efficient approach that best suits your needs.** At baseball card shows or private signings, baseball cards, photographs, and baseballs are the least expensive items to purchase. Hats, jerseys, and bats are more expensive. Negotiate with the dealer and see if you can receive a better price if you purchase a dozen or two dozen baseballs.
- **You can purchase new baseballs and ball holders at baseball card shows and at hobby stores to protect the signature from smudging.** Hobbyists should place the baseball in the ball holder as soon as they acquire the player signature. Keep the displayed baseballs at home away from sunlight so the signature doesn't fade.
- **A single-signed baseball collection has great appeal, and the value of the signatures will appreciate over time.** A single-signed Hall of Fame collection is a worthwhile investment. In the past five years, some Hall of Fame player signatures have doubled in value.
- **Use only the official major league baseball, either the American or National League ball to correspond with the player(s) and team(s) they represented.** Purchase the Selig Official Major League baseballs if you cannot find the American or National League ball. Use reference books to check the appropriate league the players represented before you attend a baseball signing.
- **At in-person events and through mail signings, ask the players to add any significant career achievement — wins, home runs, awards, nickname, birth name, etc.** It is a common practice for collectors to request that the baseballs be signed on the sweet spot with HOF (Hall of Fame) and the year the player was inducted added on the ball.
- **Network with other collectors.** Check to see which players refuse signing mail requests, and avoid this approach. Other collectors will share their good and bad experiences.
- **Some players will respond to mail requests.** Be aware of the enormous amount of mail the players receive, and don't be too concerned when your items haven't returned in a month or more.
- **For mail requests, compose a brief and neat letter, and only send a couple of items in the appropriate size bubble mail bags.** Include a self-addressed stamped mailer with your items so the player doesn't incur a cost returning your items to you.
- **The post office furnishes free Priority Mail bags and boxes.** Request priority postage stamps, which will deliver your items in two or three days to its destination. You may

want to insure one-of-a-kind memorabilia that you cannot replace. For more expensive items, like a bat or jersey, send the player a letter requesting permission for the items to be signed. Some have been receptive to these requests. Again, have these items insured, and include a name and address label with postage stamps.

• **Certificates of authenticity are worthless, unless a reputable dealer will provide a money-back guarantee on any signed item that may be questionable to the collector.** Authenticating services have intervened and include a recognizable hologram which may become a future hobby standard. Some vendors have photographed the players signing memorabilia and include a copy of the picture with the purchased items (provides assurance for collectors unable to see the item signed).

• **Purchase hobby publications which provide information on in-person and private signings throughout the country.** You will be furnished with a fee schedule of all items being signed, and the address and phone number of the sponsoring dealers. It is less costly to mail your own items. Specify what you want written on the baseball or other items.

• **Plan a visit to the Baseball Hall of Fame Museum during the induction weekend (end of July or beginning of August).** Call the National Baseball Hall of Fame Museum to get the exact date of the next induction. You should make hotel arrangements at least one year in advance. Try to make reservations at the Otesaga Hotel in Cooperstown, New York (Hall of Famers frequently stay here). You can acquire signatures from the 30 to 40 players who usually attend this event. Signing sessions will be conducted throughout the weekend for a nominal fee. Many players congregate in the hotel lobby. Be discreet and polite when you approach the players, and request only one autograph from each player. This is a great time to acquire many free autographs.

Below is a profile for beginning a Hall of Fame baseball collection. Each player should be identified with the notation HOF and the year inducted. You should ask the player to add this on the baseball. The player profile might include career achievement information that you could also ask the players to inscribe on a baseball, and the best approach to obtain their signature. Unfortunately, at baseball shows today, an extra fee is assessed for the players to add HOF and the year they were inducted, and for adding their accomplishments on a baseball.

You will be advised which players to avoid for mail requests, as well as some of the older players who are unable to participate in baseball shows due to health reasons. An approach to obtain their signatures will be provided. Some factors that determine the value of a single-signed Hall of Fame baseball collection include the following:

1. Supply and demand where players appear at many signings will lower the value of the signed baseball.

2. Players with legendary status and appeal will be more expensive (Ruth, Gehrig, DiMaggio, and Mantle).

3. Players who make rare appearances or an occasional private signing will be more expensive to purchase.

4. Age and health as it relates to players not appearing at baseball shows will increase the value of the signature. Decreasing supply increases the value of a player autograph.

5. Untimely death will increase the value of signed items immediately. A player who made few appearances prior to passing away will generate a rapid increase in autograph costs.

The list below is intended to assist the collectors and make collecting fun. It can provide an exciting in-person approach to acquiring autographs. The players are presented in alphabetical order. Those who have passed away are so noted. The best approach to add these players to your collection is by purchasing items from reputable dealers and buying from online auctions.

Hank Aaron, HOF 1982

Hank Aaron is known for breaking Babe Ruth's all-time home run record, and compiling 755 home runs during his 23-year career. He received the Most Valuable Player Award in 1957. The best approach for getting his signature is in person at a show. He refuses to add "HOF 1982," but will write "#755" under his name when you make this request. He will only accept charitable donations for mail requests to sign baseballs, and he may sign one item in person at the park or at the hotel. The availability of his signature is plentiful, and trading with other collectors is another good approach to obtain his on a baseball.

Luis Aparicio, HOF 1984

Luis Aparicio was the 1956 American League Rookie of the Year. Your best approach is to have him sign a baseball in person at a show. Mail requests could be risky, since he lives in Venezuela. Luis is very approachable, and will add "HOF 1984" under his signature. He makes many show appearances, and collectors should check the *Sports Collectors Digest* monthly calendar of shows.

Ernie Banks, HOF 1977

Ernie Banks was the 1958 and 1959 Most Valuable Player, and a member of the elite 500 Home Run Club, blasting 512 homers. Mr. Congeniality, Mr. Cub, and a fan favorite, Ernie is very approachable at the hotel, on the golf course, or at a baseball event. He will write "HOF '77" under his name, and "Mr. Cub" upon request. Spend a few minutes in conversation with Ernie, and you will feel good about this hobby. Collectors can obtain his signature on a single-signed baseball and include him on a "500 Home Run Baseball."

Opposite: **An autograph of the legendary Babe Ruth is a highly sought after single-signature on an official major league baseball.**

Johnny Bench, HOF 1989

Johnny Bench was the Rookie of the Year in 1968, and the Most Valuable Player in 1970 and 1972. The best place to get his signature on a baseball is at a baseball show. Depending on the length of the lines, he may or may not write "HOF 1989" below his name. He appears at golfing events throughout the year, and refuses to sign any baseball memorabilia. He will only sign the golf program at golfing events. A good approach to obtain his signature on a baseball is to purchase one from a reputable dealer. He never responds to mail requests.

Yogi Berra, HOF 1972

Yogi Berra was the Most Valuable Player in 1951, 1954, and 1955. He is very approachable and will sign in person at the ballpark, and will appear at baseball shows. He will add "HOF 1972" and his awards on a baseball, and collectors can include him on an all-time New York Yankees theme baseball. Since he has established a Berra Family Corporation selling baseball memorabilia, he doesn't accept mail requests. You can visit his website: www.yogi.berra.com, and purchase his collectibles.

Wade Boggs, HOF 2005

Wade Boggs is the only player in the major leagues to accumulate 200 hits and score 100 runs in seven consecutive seasons. He was selected to eight consecutive All-Star games and is a five-time batting champion. A lifetime .328 hitter and a member of the 3,000 Hit Club, he collected 3,010 hits. He actively participates on the baseball show circuit and has been responsive to mail requests.

Lou Boudreau, HOF 1970

Lou Boudreau was the Most Valuable Player in 1948. He was a popular signer throughout his career. Boudreau passed away on August 10, 2001. The best way to obtain his signature is from a reputable dealer and from online auctions. Boudreau was always a fan favorite.

George Brett, HOF 1999

George Brett was a dominant player for 21 seasons with the Kansas City Royals, and a three-time batting champion. A lifetime .305 hitter and a member of the 3,000 Hit Club, he accumulated 3,154 hits. He was the 1980 Most Valuable Player with a .390 batting average. George is a willing signer during spring training at the Royals complex, and best approached at baseball shows. As a member of the Hall of Fame, he will actively participate on the baseball show circuit. Collectors should avoid mail requests.

Lou Brock, HOF 1985

Lou Brock is a member of the elite 3,000 Hit Club and acquired 938 stolen bases during his career. Best approached on the baseball show circuit, he is congenial and will add "HOF 1985" after his signature. You can request his signature on a single baseball, and include him on a separate special achievement baseball — as a member of the 3,000 Hit Club with the other recipients. Since he hasn't been responsive to mail requests, the in-person approach seems to be the best way of obtaining his autograph.

Jim Bunning, HOF 1996

Inducted in 1996, Jim Bunning pitched a perfect game for the Phillies against the Mets on Father's Day in 1964. Prior to his reelection as senator from Kentucky, he was accepting mail requests. Now, the best way to get an autographed baseball would be the in-person approach at a show, where he will make appearances from time to time. Jim will add "HOF 1996" on a baseball, and collectors can also purchase these baseballs from reputable dealers.

Rod Carew, HOF 1991

A most consistent player and seven-time batting champ, Rod Carew is another member of the 3,000 Hit Club. He was the Rookie of the Year in 1967 and the Most Valuable Player in 1977. He is a willing signer who is best approached on the baseball show circuit. He is congenial and approachable, and will add writing to a baseball if you ask. Collectors should avoid mail requests.

Steve Carlton, HOF 1994

A four-time Cy Young Award winner in 1972, 1977, 1980, and 1982, Steve Carlton was a great pitcher and is a member of the 300 Win Club, but was not a fan favorite during his playing days. Fortunately, this all changed after he was inducted into the Hall of Fame. Carlton now participates in the baseball card circuit, and will sign a baseball with "Steve 'Lefty' Carlton" and add "HOF 1994" upon request. Since he attends many shows, his memorabilia is easy to purchase at hobby stores, but he hasn't been responsive to mail requests. Collectors should include him on a separate special achievement baseball with the other 300 game winners.

Gary Carter, HOF 2003

Gary Carter was a great catcher and a three-time Gold Glove winner. He belted 324 home runs and collected 2,092 hits in his 19-season major league career. He is remembered for his clutch 10th inning single in Game Six of the 1986 World Series that sparked a dramatic Mets comeback victory, and leading to a World Series championship. He participates on the baseball show circuit and at golf events, and will add HOF 2003 and 1986 World Series Champs under his name.

Orlando Cepeda, HOF 1999

Orlando Cepeda played most of his 17-year career with the San Francisco Giants. Cepeda was the 1958 National League Rookie of the Year, and the 1967 Most Valuable Player. He has a career .297 batting average, with 379 home runs, 2,351 hits, and 1,365 runs batted in. Cepeda was also nine-time All-Star and frequently attained batting averages above .300. Cepeda willingly signs at multicultural events during the baseball season. He actively participates on the baseball show circuit, and this is the best approach to obtain his autograph on memorabilia. Signed baseballs can easily be obtained from reputable dealers.

Joe DiMaggio, HOF 1955

Known as "The Yankee Clipper" and the player with the longest hitting streak of 56 consecutive games in 1941, Joe DiMaggio was a legend in his own time. He was the Most Valuable Player in 1939, 1941, and 1947. A lifetime .325 batter, he compiled 2,214 hits and 361 home runs. Amazingly, he struck out only 369 times in his entire career. He usually participated in only a couple of baseball shows each year, and in recent years was under contract with dealers to conduct private signings. He was very involved with the Joe DiMaggio Children's Hospital in Hollywood, Florida, but wouldn't provide in-person autographs at the functions he attended. The best approach to obtain his signature on a baseball is to purchase one from reputable dealers and through participation in auctions — in-person, telephone, and online purchasing. In life and in death DiMaggio has been considered the greatest player, and the most challenging autograph to collect. DiMaggio passed away on March 8, 1999.

Larry Doby, HOF 1998

Larry Doby was the first African American player in the American League, and made his debut for the Indians on July 5, 1947. He played 13 seasons in the major leagues, and was a six-time All-Star. Doby had been active on the baseball show circuit, and the show promoters were charging an extra fee for writing "HOF 1998." Collectors should avoid mail requests. Doby was participating in many shows around the country, and a single-signed baseball can be easily obtained from hobby dealers. Doby passed away on June 18, 2003.

Bobby Doerr, HOF 1986

Bobby Doerr is another fan favorite, and very approachable on the baseball show circuit. He is responsive to mail requests, and both in person and through the mail he will add "HOF 1986" below his name. Doerr played his entire career with the Red Sox, and had many fielding records. In fact, in 1943 he had a two-month errorless streak, handling 349 chances. You can expect your mail request signed and returned in a timely manner.

Dennis Eckersley, HOF 2004

Dennis Eckersley was a starting pitcher the first half of his 24-year big league career winning 197 games, and threw a no-hitter in 1977. Over the last 12 years of his career he saved 390 games, led the Oakland A's to four American League West titles, and earned both the Cy Young and MVP honors in 1992. He is an active participant at baseball shows and his signature is readily available from reputable dealers.

Bob Feller, HOF 1962

"Rapid Robert" Feller was considered the fastest pitcher in his career during which he won 266 games. Feller won twenty or more games six times, and in 1940 he earned 27 victories. He is very active on the baseball show circuit and easy to approach. You can find him at different team events during the season, and he will sign baseballs and other items free, prior to and after the game. For mail signings he does request a nominal fee. His signature on a baseball is easily obtained from dealers.

Rollie Fingers, HOF 1992

Rollie Fingers was a great relief pitcher with the Oakland Athletics and the Milwaukee Brewers, and one of the few relief pitchers to receive a Cy Young and Most Valuable Player Award in the same season (1981). Rollie has always been a willing and congenial participant on the baseball show circuit. At a baseball show he will add below his signature "HOF 1992, 1981 Cy Young & MVP." He is not responsive to mail requests.

Carlton Fisk, HOF 2000

Carlton Fisk became the 13th catcher to be inducted into the National Baseball Hall of Fame on July 23, 2000. He played 24 seasons behind the plate (2,226 games) more games than any catcher in history. He was an 11-time All-Star, with 376 home runs and 2,356 hits. He hit the most memorable home run in Game Six of the 1975 World Series, a 12th inning blast off the left field foul pole, giving the Red Sox a 7–6 win over the Reds. The best approach to collect his signature is at baseball shows.

Whitey Ford, HOF 1974

Whitey Ford has been a fan favorite and popular guest on the baseball show circuit. He collected 236 career wins and was victorious in ten World Series games with the New York Yankees. He commonly signs "Whitey Ford" but may write "Edward Whitey Ford" and has included either "HOF 1974" or "Chairman of the Board" when collectors have requested this. He appears with other Yankee Hall of Famers at theme shows and is easy to approach. Responses to mail requests have not been consistent.

Bob Gibson, HOF 1981

A great pitcher with a blazing fastball and 251 career wins, Bob Gibson excelled in the World Series as a clutch performer and was the Most Valuable Player in 1968. The best way to get his signature is either to attend a baseball card show where he is a willing participant or to purchase a signed baseball from a reputable dealer. He is not receptive to mail requests and has been known to ignore collectors at the hotel or stadium.

Rich "Goose" Gossage, HOF 2008

Rich Gossage was an intimidating relief pitcher in both the American and National leagues for 22 seasons, compiling a 2.14 earned run average with the Yankees for seven seasons. He earned 124 wins, 310 saves and a 3.01 career earned run average in 1,002 games and 1809.1 innings pitched. A nine-time All-Star and 1978 Rolaids "Relief Man of the Year," Gossage joins Fingers, Eckersley and Sutter as relievers in the Hall of Fame. As a new member of the Hall of Fame he is an active participant on the baseball show circuit and will participate in signing events at the Hall of Fame.

Tony Gwynn, HOF 2007

Tony Gwynn played his entire 20-year career with the San Diego Padres. He won a National League record-tying eight batting titles and was selected to 15 All-Star teams. One of the greatest hitters in major league baseball history, he had a .338 career batting average, and a member of the 3,000 Hit Club collecting 3,141 hits. Gwynn hit over .300 in 19 consecutive seasons and his devotion to the San Diego community earned him the name "Mr. Padre." The best approach to acquire his signature on baseball memorabilia is at a baseball show. Mail request should be avoided.

Catfish Hunter, HOF 1987

Jim "Catfish" Hunter was nicknamed "Catfish" by the Athletics team owner Charlie Finley because he was an avid fisherman. Commonly signing "Jim 'Catfish' Hunter," he was a congenial participant on the baseball show circuit. Hunter passed away in September 1999 from amyotrophic lateral sclerosis (Lou Gehrig's disease). The best way to obtain his signature is from a reputable dealer or hobby publication.

Monte Irvin, HOF 1973

Monte Irvin played most of his career with the Newark Eagles in the Negro Leagues, where he won the 1946 batting title. One of a few Negro League players who made it to the major leagues, Monte became a star with the New York Giants. He is active on the baseball show circuit and will sign in the following manner: "Monford 'Monte' Irvin" with "HOF 1973" added, and "Monte Irvin" as per your request. He is very friendly, also responsive to mail requests, and may request a nominal donation for a charity. Collectors should be able to obtain his signature on a baseball at hobby stores.

Reggie Jackson, HOF 1993

Known as "Mr. October" for his clutch performances around World Series time, Reggie Jackson is also a member of the 500 Home Run Club, and the 1973 Most Valuable Player. You can acquire his signature at baseball card shows, but he is not responsive to free mail requests. You should add him on a 500 home run ball with the other players, and obtain a single-signed baseball. At the park he can be very moody, or completely ignore his adoring fans. He is a regular participant at New York Yankee theme shows.

Ferguson Jenkins, HOF 1991

Ferguson Jenkins, commonly signing as "Fergie Jenkins," was a consistent, durable pitcher who garnered 284 career wins, the 1971 Cy Young Award, and six consecutive 20-win seasons. Associated mostly with the Cubs, he is also remembered for pitching against the 1969 Miracle Mets. He actively participates in baseball card shows and will add career honors on a single baseball. He has a pleasant disposition and is the only player who normally writes the exact date of his induction into the Hall of Fame — "7/21/91." Collectors should find it easy to obtain his autograph in person, at the park, at his hotel, or on the show circuit.

Al Kaline, HOF 1980

A most consistent player who played his entire career with the Tigers from 1953 through 1974, Al Kaline's 3,007 hits make him a member of the 3,000 Hit Club. He is an active participant in the baseball show circuit and is willing to add "HOF 1980" below his name. Should you be a theme collector, you could add him on a 3,000 Hit baseball with the other members. Mail requests have been very unpredictable, and is an approach you should avoid. You will find his signature on a baseball easy to obtain from reputable dealers.

George Kell, HOF 1983

An outstanding third baseman during the 1940s and 1950s with a lifetime batting average of .306, George Kell was the American League batting champ in 1949, and batted over .300 nine times. Kell had his best seasons with the Detroit Tigers. He is most responsive to autograph requests and is a fan favorite. It is best to approach him on the baseball show circuit, and he will add "HOF 1983" on a baseball. Collectors have had success with mail requests.

Harmon Killebrew, HOF 1984

A powerful home run hitter who belted 573 home runs, Harmon Killebrew is another member of the 500 Home Run Club. He hit 40 or more home runs in eight seasons, was the American League home run leader for many years, and won the 1969 Most Valuable Player Award. He also led the Minnesota Twins to the 1965 World Series. He is active on the baseball show circuit, and on single-signed baseballs he will add "573 HRS, HOF 1984" below his name. Collectors could acquire his signature along with others on a 500 home run baseball. Mail requests have been unpredictable.

Ralph Kiner, HOF 1975

Ralph Kiner was a home run–type batter who during ten seasons accumulated 369 home runs and posted a home run to at-bat ratio of third all time, trailing only Mark McGwire and Babe Ruth. After his playing career, he became a popular television broadcaster for the New York Mets. Kiner has always been a prolific signer at the team hotel and ballpark, and actively engages in baseball shows. He will add "HOF 1975" below his name if you ask him, and requests a nominal donation for a charity for mail requests. He has always been a fan favorite, and his signature is easy to acquire.

Sandy Koufax, HOF 1972

An overpowering pitcher for the Dodgers, Sandy Koufax's career was shortened by elbow injuries. He was the Nolan Ryan of the 1960s, with four no-hitters during his career. He received the Most Valuable Player Award in 1963, as well as the Cy Young Award in 1963, 1965, and 1966.

During the 1980s, he was a pitching instructor at spring training in Dodgertown, and was a responsive signer. When he resigned from the team in 1988, he became more reclusive and avoided public appearances. In the 1990s he participated in two or three baseball shows (each year) and occasionally conducted a private signing. He is very reserved and likes his privacy, so the best approach is to attend a baseball show or purchase a signed baseball from a reputable dealer or at a private signing. He does appear at Dodgertown in Vero Beach, Florida, from time to time, and will obligingly sign 10 to 15 autographs before leaving. He will not furnish additional writing on a baseball, and mail requests should be avoided.

Tom Lasorda, HOF 1997

Although Tom Lasorda pitched for three years in the major leagues, compiling an 0–4 record, his 1997 induction into the Hall of Fame was based on his managerial prowess. During his twenty years as manager, he led the Los Angeles Dodgers to 1,599 victories, including two National League Championships in his first two seasons (1977 and 1978). Always a colorful personality and dynamic motivator, his teams won two World Series Championships (1981 and 1988). The best approach to obtain his signature is on the baseball show circuit. He appears at the Dodgers Fantasy Camp in November and February, and you can acquire his signature during spring training, as he signs daily at Dodgertown in Vero Beach,

Florida. Lasorda has been responsive to mail requests; however, it may be a couple of months before you receive your signed items.

Bob Lemon, HOF 1976

A consistent pitcher with the Indians, Bob Lemon helped guide them to the 1954 World Series, and managed the New York Yankees to the 1978 World Championship. He won 207 games during his career, and was a responsive signer and fan favorite at baseball shows. He responded to mail requests and added "HOF 1976" below his name. Lemon passed away on January 11, 2000.

Al Lopez, HOF 1977

Al Lopez was a steady catcher, playing in over 1,900 games. His claim to the Hall of Fame was his great ability as a manager, leading the 1959 White Sox to the World Series. He wasn't active on the baseball show circuit, and conducted a private signing only occasionally. Mail requests were unpredictable, an approach that should've been avoided. His signature on a baseball is most easily obtained from dealers who conducted private signings with him. Since he seldom made appearances, his signature on a baseball is expensive. Lopez passed away on October 30, 2005.

Juan Marichal, HOF 1983

As a pitcher for the San Francisco Giants, Juan Marichal amassed 243 wins, was selected to the All-Star team eight times, and in his 1960 major league debut pitched a one-hit shutout against the Phillies. He had an unusual high leg kick and tied Sandy Koufax in 1963 with the most wins in the majors — 25. The best approach to obtaining his signature is on the baseball show circuit. Mail requests have gone unanswered, so this isn't a good approach. Collectors can find his signature at hobby stores.

Eddie Mathews, HOF 1978

A slugging member of the 500 Home Run Club, hitting 512 home runs in his career, Eddie Mathews led the National League in homers in 1953 and 1959, and participated in three World Series. Mathews played most years with the Braves — Boston, Milwaukee, and Atlanta. He participated in many baseball shows, especially 500 Home Run theme shows with the other members. At the baseball shows, he responded to requests, and added below his name, "HOF 1978, 512 HRS." Mail requests were unpredictable. Mathews passed away on February 18, 2001.

Willie Mays, HOF 1979

The "Say Hey Kid" had all of the tools — running, hitting, hitting with power, fielding, and throwing. He is another member of the 500 Home Run Club, with 660 home runs, and a member of the 3,000 Hit Club, with 3,283 hits. He was the Most Valuable Player in 1954 and 1965. He actively participates in the baseball show circuit, and collectors could request his signature on theme baseballs — one for the 500 Home Run Club and another baseball for the 3,000 Hit Club. Unfortunately, at baseball shows, dealers charge an additional fee for him to write "HOF 1979" below his name. Mays is not a fan favorite at the baseball shows. He isn't very friendly and doesn't interact with his fans. Mail requests should be avoided. Single-signed baseballs can be purchased from hobby stores.

Bill Mazeroski, HOF 2001

Bill Mazeroski played 17 seasons with the Pittsburgh Pirates and won eight Gold Glove Awards, and earned the reputation as one of the greatest fielding second baseman in the history of the game. He collected 2,016 hits in his career and achieved hero status in the ninth inning of Game Seven of the Pirates 1960 World Championship against the Yankees, when he became the first player ever to hit a World Series winning home run. He actively participates on the baseball show circuit and mail requests haven't been predictable.

Willie McCovey, HOF 1986

Willie McCovey was known as "Stretch," and was the 1959 Rookie of the Year and the 1969 Most Valuable Player. He is a member of the 500 Home Run Club, amassing 521 home runs during his career with the San Francisco Giants. McCovey is a responsive participant on the baseball show circuit, and this is the best approach to obtain his signature on a baseball. Mail requests should be avoided. Collectors should include McCovey on a 500 Home Run baseball.

Paul Molitor, HOF 2004

Paul Molitor was a consistent contact hitter for 21 seasons and a seven-time All-Star. A lifetime .306 hitter and a member of the 3,000 Hit Club, he accumulated 3,319 hits (eighth on the all-time list). It is best to approach him on the baseball show circuit and you can obtain his signature on memorabilia at hobby stores.

Joe Morgan, HOF 1990

A versatile second baseman and a key member of "The Big Red Machine," Joe Morgan was the Most Valuable Player in 1975 and 1976, and played in nine All-Star Games. He is responsive to autograph requests and participates on the baseball show circuit. He is very congenial and approachable at the stadium, especially during spring training. He is an active golfer, and you can find him on the links during the off-season participating in celebrity events. These events usually take place on weekdays, so the crowds are small, and collectors have an excellent opportunity to meet him and collect signatures. Joe Morgan travels extensively and works on the ESPN and NBC Sports Networks, so mail requests should be avoided. The best approach is to catch him at baseball shows and "The Big Red Machine" theme shows.

Eddie Murray, HOF 2003

A consistent and productive hitter for 21 seasons, Eddie Murray is the third player to have collected both 3,000 hits and 500 home runs. He accumulated 3,255 hits and 504 home runs. Murray had .287 lifetime batting average and had 1,917 runs batted in. He participates in many baseball shows, especially 500 Home Run theme shows with the other members. Avoid the mail request approach.

Stan Musial, HOF 1969

Stan Musial became known as "Stan the Man" because when he played against the Brooklyn Dodgers the fans were amazed by his hitting prowess and how he seemed to own the Dodgers. His nickname grew originally from the terror he inspired in Brooklyn pitchers and their fans, who often were heard to question, "Who is that man?" A member of the 3,000 Hit Club and the Most Valuable Player in 1943, 1946, and 1948, Musial established many records, ending his career with 3,630 hits and a lifetime batting average of .331. He is a fan favorite, very amiable and approachable. In past years he had been receptive to mail requests; however, he recently formed Stan the Man, Inc., which sells his baseball memorabilia with his career highlights on them. His company provides a certificate of authenticity with Stan Musial's signature on the certificate (most dealers do not give you a player's signature on the certificate of authenticity). You can obtain his autograph through the baseball show circuit or by ordering signed memorabilia directly from his company. He has been very obliging and will accommodate his fans.

Hal Newhouser, HOF 1992

Hal Newhouser was a great pitcher for the Detroit Tigers and the Most Valuable Player in 1944 and 1945, winning 29 games in 1944 and 25 games in 1945. In 1946 he won 26 games and over his career won 207 games in 17 seasons. Since his induction into the Hall of Fame in 1992, he had been active on the baseball show circuit, and a congenial and approachable individual. He had been receptive to mail requests, and charged a small fee. Newhouser passed away in November of 1998, and collectors can obtain his signature on a baseball from reputable dealers and through hobby publications.

Phil Niekro (Knucksie), HOF 1997

A knuckleball specialist with 318 wins over 24 years, Phil Niekro was the mainstay for the Milwaukee and Atlanta Braves, and he also pitched for the Yankees and Indians. He won 23 games in 1969, 20 in 1974, and 21 in 1979, collecting five Gold Gloves and five All-Star appearances along the way. His 3,342 strikeouts place him eighth on the all-time list.

Niekro actively participates in baseball shows, and he will sign "HOF 1997" on your baseballs. You should consider acquiring his signature on a 300 Win baseball. Collectors should avoid mail requests.

Jim Palmer, HOF 1990

A great Baltimore Orioles pitcher and three-time Cy Young winner, in 1973, 1975, and 1976, Jim Palmer piled up 268 wins in 19 seasons. He was a popular player among Orioles fans, and he still makes public appearances, plays in golf tournaments, and is accessible to collectors. On a single-signed baseball he will add "HOF 1990, 268 wins." You can find him at the ballpark, and it is easy to obtain his signature on your items.

Tony Perez, HOF 2000

Tony Perez played 23 seasons and was a fixture on "The Big Red Machine" team of the 1970s. He was a clutch hitter with 2,732 hits, 379 home runs and had 1,652 runs batted in. He hit three home runs in the 1975 World Series, including a key two-run shot in Game Seven that helped propel the Reds to a World Championship. He is a responsive participant on the baseball show circuit and this is the best approach to obtain his signature on a baseball and other collectibles.

Gaylord Perry, HOF 1991

Winning 314 games in 22 seasons and the Cy Young Award in both the American and National leagues, Gaylord Perry was consistently accused of throwing an illegal pitch (spitball), which he denied. He makes appearances in different cities, participating in baseball card shows and theme shows, such as "The 300 Win Club," to which all of the 300 game winners are invited. Some collectors feel he isn't receptive to mail requests, and this is an approach you should avoid.

Kirby Puckett, HOF 2001

Kirby Puckett played his entire 12-year career with the Minnesota Twins. He was a consistent player with a .318 lifetime batting average and collected 2,304 hits. A team leader, Puckett led the Twins to two World Series titles in 1987 and 1991. He was selected to 10 consecutive All-Star teams and was a six-time Gold Glove winner. He was an active participant on the baseball show circuit. Puckett passed away on March 6, 2006. The best approach to obtain his signature is from reputable dealers and online auctions.

Pee Wee Reese, HOF 1984

A great shortstop for the Brooklyn Dodgers and the hub for their success, "The Little Colonel" played 16 seasons and accumulated 2,170 hits. Reese passed away on August 13, 1999. The best way to obtain his signature is from a reputable dealer or hobby publication.

Cal Ripken, Jr., HOF 2007

During his 20 seasons with the Baltimore Orioles, Cal Ripken Jr. was known as "The Iron Man of Baseball" because of his incredible work ethic. He played in 2,632 consecutive games (major league record), breaking Lou Gehrig's record of 2,130. He is a member of the 3,000 Hit Club amassing 3,184 hits, 431 home runs, 19-time All-Star and was the Most Valuable Player in 1983 and 1991. He has his own memorabilia company and will appear on the baseball show circuit a couple of times each year. Collectors can purchase different items from reputable dealers and online auctions.

Phil Rizzuto, HOF 1994

Another great shortstop who played for the New York Yankees, Phil Rizzuto was known as the "Scooter" and was the American League Most Valuable Player in 1950. In 1950 he had his best season, batting .324 with 200 hits and 125 runs scored. He later became highly visible and recognizable as the Yankees play-by-play announcer who used the expression "Holy Cow." Phil was easy to approach and friendly at the hotel or at the ballpark. He participated on the baseball show circuit and signed as "Phil Scooter Rizzuto" with "HOF 1994" and "Holy Cow" added below his name. Collectors can purchase his signature on a baseball from a reputable dealer. Rizzuto passed away on August 13, 2007.

Robin Roberts, HOF 1976

A consistent pitcher for most of his career with the Phillies, Robin Roberts had 286 wins, and in six consecutive seasons he won 20 or more games, recording 28 wins in 1952. He is active on the baseball show circuit, and like most other Hall of Famers will sign mail requests for a small fee that is donated to charity. He is very responsive to requests, and will add "HOF 1976" below his name. Collectors should find it easy to obtain his signature from dealers or through mail requests.

Brooks Robinson, HOF 1983

During his 23 seasons with the Baltimore Orioles, Brooks Robinson became known as the "Human Vacuum Cleaner" because of his incredible fielding talent at third base. He was also an exceptional hitter who was a clutch performer in the World Series and collected 2,848 hits in a magnificent career. He has a great personality, and collectors will find it easy to obtain his signature on a baseball in person, at baseball shows or at the stadium. He will address autograph requests through the mail, and solicit a donation for his personal charity.

Frank Robinson, HOF 1982

Frank Robinson had a 21-year playing career during which he became a member of the 500 Home Run Club, collecting 586 homers, as well as 2,943 hits. He won the Most Valuable Player Award in 1961 with the Reds, and in 1966 he was awarded the Triple Crown and named Most Valuable Player with the Orioles. Collectors have indicated that he isn't a fan favorite, and can be difficult when it comes to in-person requests. You should avoid the mail request approach; the best approach is by attending baseball shows or by purchasing a signed ball from a reputable dealer.

Nolan Ryan, HOF 1999

Nolan Ryan pitched 27 seasons with the Mets, Angels, Astros, and Rangers. He is a member of the 300 Win Club, collecting 324 wins and seven no-hitters. He is the major leagues' all-time strikeout leader with 5,714. Nolan earned 61 career shutouts and in 1973 set an all-time single-season mark with 383 strikeouts. Collectors can purchase autographed memorabilia through the Nolan Ryan Foundation in Alvin, Texas. He has been an active participant at baseball shows and should be available for private signings. He recently became the President of the Texas Rangers and will participate in team signing events at the stadium. Autographed baseballs can be bought through hobby publications and from reputable dealers.

Ryne Sandberg, HOF 2005

A consistent second baseman with tremendous power, Ryne Sandberg was the Most Valuable Player in 1984, a 10-time All-Star and he earned nine consecutive Gold Glove Awards. He collected 2,386 hits and 282 career home runs, and in 1990 belted 40 home runs. The best place to obtain his signature is at baseball shows and from reputable dealers.

Mike Schmidt, HOF 1995

A great player and power hitter for 18 seasons with the Phillies, Mike Schmidt is a member of the 500 Home Run Club, blasting 548 homers during his career. He was the Most Valuable Player three times (in 1980, 1981, 1986), and a clutch performer and fielder, winning 10 Gold Gloves (1976–1984, 1986). His popularity has increased since his induction into the Hall of Fame. The best approach to obtain his signature is at baseball shows. He will add his career honors below his name and also write "HOF 1995." A good place to meet him is at golfing events or at the ballpark. A word of caution: When there is a large crowd, Schmidt will hurry his signature, and it may appear illegible and sloppy. So it is best to get him alone with a small crowd, or attend a baseball show.

Red Schoendienst, HOF 1989

During a 19-year career, mostly with the Cardinals, Red Schoendienst was an extremely productive hitter. He batted .342 in 1953, collecting 193 hits. In 1957 Red tallied 200 hits and led the league in that department. Collectors have requested his signature as follows: "Albert Schoendienst," "Albert 'Red' Schoendienst," or "Red Schoendienst," which he has obligingly signed. The mail request approach should be avoided, and he is an active participant at baseball shows. He is easy to approach and will add "HOF 1989" below his name.

Tom Seaver, HOF 1992

A dominating pitcher who spent most of his career with the "Amazing Mets," Tom Seaver was the 1967 Rookie of the Year and received the Cy Young Award in 1969, 1973, and 1975. He is a member of the 300 Win Club, collecting 311 wins with a career 2.86 earned run average. Tom Seaver was a fan favorite during his playing days and is still a congenial and approachable individual. He can be found regularly on the baseball show circuit or at Hall of Fame induction events in Cooperstown, New York. He usually participates in 300 Win theme shows, and mail requests should be avoided. He has been broadcasting games for the New York Mets, and you may catch him at the stadium or team hotel.

Enos Slaughter, HOF 1985

North Carolina native, Enos "Country" Slaughter had an outstanding 19-year career, mostly with the Cardinals and Yankees. Admired for his hustling style and great fielding, he batted .300 and collected 2,383 hits in his career. He had been a responsive signer, a regular participant on the baseball show circuit, and a fan favorite. Slaughter was receptive to mail requests, and collectors requested his signature as follows: "Enos Slaughter" with "HOF 1985" added, or "Enos 'Country' Slaughter" with "HOF 1985." He appeared at the Yankees Fantasy Camp in Fort Lauderdale and at team special events. Slaughter passed away on August 12, 2002.

Ozzie Smith, HOF 2002

A great defensive shortstop who played most of his career for the St. Louis Cardinals, Ozzie Smith was known as "The Wizard of OZ." He was a 13-time Gold Glove winner and set major league shortstop records for assists, double plays and total chances. He accumulated 2,460 hits and 500 stolen bases. He is an active participant on the baseball show circuit and participates in signing events at the Hall of Fame induction each year.

Duke Snider, HOF 1980

Because of his magnificent career with the Brooklyn and L.A. Dodgers, "The Duke of Flatbush" has been grouped with the other great center fielders like Willie Mays and Mickey Mantle. He played 18 years with a .295 career batting average and 407 home runs. He hit 40 or more homers in five consecutive seasons and led the Dodgers to the World Series six times. Duke is a fan favorite, and has been a regular participant in baseball shows and makes appearances each year at Dodgers Fantasy Camp in Vero Beach, Florida, usually in November and February. He commonly signs "Duke Snider" and has been receptive to requests to write his birth name "Edwin Donald Snider" or "Edwin Duke Snider" and adding "HOF 1980" below his signature. However, at public appearances he will not add "The Duke of Flatbush," apparently because of his contract with a sports company. He will sign many items for the fans and is a real gentleman.

Warren Spahn, HOF 1973

A great pitcher whose career was mainly with the Braves, Warren Spahn is yet another member of the 300 Win Club, with a total of 363 victories. He was a Cy Young Award winner in 1957 and led his team to the World Series in 1948, 1957, and 1958. He was a responsive signer, and participated at baseball shows, and very congenial and easy to approach. Spahn charged a small fee for signing mail requests and honored requests such as "363 Wins" and "HOF 1973." He attended many events with the other 300 Win members and was a regular at the Hall of Fame induction ceremonies. Collectors should consider adding his signature on a baseball with other pitchers with 300 career wins, and on baseballs with other Hall of Famers. Spahn passed away on November 24, 2003. Collectors will find it easy to purchase signed memorabilia from hobby stores.

Willie Stargell, HOF 1988

A consistent and solid performer with the Pirates for 21 seasons, Willie Stargell was a team leader who earned the Most Valuable Player Award in 1979. His lifetime batting average was .282, with 2,232 hits and 475 home runs. He was a regular participant in baseball shows and worked with the Pirates organization. He was available during spring training or at the stadium during the regular season. Stargell passed away on April 9, 2001. He was a fan favorite and should be easy to include in your collection.

Bruce Sutter, HOF 2006

Bruce Sutter pitched as a relief pitcher for 12 seasons, compiling an outstanding 2.83 earned run average and 300 saves. He became the fourth reliever enshrined in the Hall of Fame, following Hoyt Wilhelm (1985), Rollie Fingers (1992) and Dennis Eckersley (2004). Sutter was the first player never to start a game to be inducted in the Hall of Fame. He learned a new pitch, a split-fingered fastball that made him one of the game's top relief pitchers. He is an active participant on the baseball show circuit and easy to approach.

Don Sutton, HOF 1998

Don Sutton pitched the majority of his 23 years with the Dodgers, and collected 324 wins. He finished in the top ten in strikeouts (3,574), starts (756), and shutouts with 58. One of 20 pitchers to win 300 or more games, he won 21 games in 1976. From 1969 to 1978 he consistently won 14 or more games each season. Sutton, a four time All-Star, is currently a broadcaster for the Atlanta Braves, and can be sought out by collectors at the stadium and golf events. He is very friendly and personable, and has become an active participant at baseball shows. He has been responsive to mail requests.

Earl Weaver, HOF 1996

The great Baltimore Orioles manager who led his team to four World Series was adored by his fans and his players alike. He had a knack for generating excitement and charging up his team when he got into it with the "men in blue" (umpires). Earl has always been responsive to collectors and is an active participant on the baseball show circuit. He can be approached at the Orioles spring training camp at Fort Lauderdale Stadium, or on the links in the Miami Lakes area. His signature on a baseball should be easy to collect.

Hoyt Wilhelm, HOF 1985

Hoyt Wilhelm pitched as a relief pitcher in both the American and National leagues for 21 seasons, compiling an outstanding 2.52 career earned run average and 227 saves. He was one of the first pitchers to throw a knuckleball, and he earned 143 wins overall. He was an active participant in baseball shows, a congenial guest, and was easy to approach. He was responsive to mail requests, and collectors would send him a small fee, which he donated to a charity. Wilhelm passed away on August 23, 2002.

Billy Williams, HOF 1987

Billy Williams hardly ever missed games with the Cubs from 1962 through 1970. After being named Rookie of the Year in 1961, he went on to play 18 seasons with a .290 lifetime batting average, 2,711 hits and 426 home runs. He was a clutch performer and won the batting title in 1972 with a .333 average. An active participant on the baseball show circuit, Billy also works as the Cubs bench coach, and can be found with the team during spring training and the regular season. Billy is approachable at the team hotel when the Cubs are on the road, and will sign a few items, adding "HOF 1987." He charges a small fee for mail requests, but collectors should have no trouble getting his signature in person.

Dick Williams, HOF 2008

Dick Williams joins a select group of 18 managers who have been elected into the National Baseball Hall of Fame. He managed six teams in his 21-year managerial career that ended in 1988. He won the World Series with the Oakland A's in 1972 and 1973, the American League pennant with the Red Sox in 1967 and the National League pennant with the San Diego Padres in 1984. He was able to help underachieving teams with his hard-nosed style and he won 1,571 games during his career. He participates at baseball shows and has responded to mail requests.

Ted Williams, HOF 1966

A magnificent outfielder who played his entire 19-season career with the Boston Red Sox, Ted Williams was known as "The Splendid Splinter." A member of the 500 Home Run Club, Williams ended his career with 521 home runs. He had a .344 lifetime batting average, with 2,654 hits, and was the Most Valuable Player in 1946 and 1949. He was the last player to bat .400 or more, hitting .400 in 1952 and .407 in 1953. Williams had been active on the baseball show circuit during the 1980s, but a stroke had prevented him from signing baseballs, and he had become less involved in baseball shows. He would usually appear at two special theme shows — 500 Home Run Club shows at Atlantic City, New Jersey, held each year — but had limited his signing to flat items (pictures) and 500 Home Run prints. He was very involved in the Ted Williams Museum in Citrus Hills, Florida, and conducted a Hall of Fame gala event each year. The best way to obtain his signature was through his son John Henry Williams, who had formed a company in Hernando, Florida, selling baseball memorabilia and signed baseballs. Williams passed away on July 5, 2002. Collectors can also obtain his signature from reputable dealers.

Dave Winfield, HOF 2001

Dave Winfield became the first player to enter the Hall of Fame as a Padres player when he was inducted on August 5, 2001. He played 22 seasons, a 12-time All-Star, a consistent player with a .283 lifetime batting average, a member of the 3,000 Hit Club collecting 3,110 hits, 465 home runs and seven-time Gold Glove winner. He is very approachable at baseball shows and participates in 3,000 Hit Club theme shows.

Early Wynn, HOF 1972

Early Wynn pitched for 23 seasons in the American League with the Washington Senators, Cleveland Indians, and Chicago White Sox, and is a member of the 300 Win Club. He won 20 or more games during five seasons and collected 49 shutouts in his career. He had been an active participant in baseball shows over the years. Wynn passed away in April 1999. The best way to obtain his signature is from a reputable dealer or hobby publication.

Carl Yastrzemski, HOF 1989

A clutch hitter and an excellent fielder with the Boston Red Sox for 23 seasons, Carl Yastrzemski is a member of the 3,000 Hit Club, with a career total 3,419 hits, 452 home runs, and a lifetime .285 batting average. In 1967 he won the Triple Crown and was the Most Valuable Player. "Yaz" won six Gold Gloves and was named to 18 All-Star teams. He is an active participant at baseball shows, so the best place to get his signature is at these shows or to purchase a signed ball from a reputable dealer. He is not responsive to mail requests.

Robin Yount, HOF 1999

Robin Yount played his entire 20-year career with the Milwaukee Brewers. He was a consistent player with a .285 lifetime batting average, and a member of the 3,000 Hit Club amassing 3,142 hits. Yount was the Most Valuable Player in 1982 and 1989. In 1980 he led the league with 49 doubles, and in 1982 was the league leader with 210 hits. The best approach to acquire his signature on baseball memorabilia is at a baseball show. Mail requests should be avoided.

Collectors attending baseball shows today are collecting the signatures on baseballs of the Hall of Famers of the future — Alex Rodriguez, Frank Thomas, Manny Ramirez, David Ortiz, Derek Jeter, Mariano Rivera, Ken Griffey, Jr., Craig Biggio, Tom Glavine, Greg Maddux, John Smoltz, Mike Piazza and other up-and-coming stars. Players of the past waiting for the call for their induction into the Hall of Fame include Jim Rice, Steve Garvey, Andre Dawson, Rickey Henderson, Gil Hodges, Roger Maris, Tony Oliva, Ron Santo — all great players who deserve consideration.

Unfortunately, an objective method for induction into the Baseball Hall of Fame hasn't been determined. The method of election is a screening committee of baseball writers who are elected by the Baseball Writers' Association of America. Each committee member can vote for ten eligible candidates appearing on the ballot, and may vote for fewer players if they are unable to objectively select ten. The players have to be retired from the game for at least five years. The players on the ballot have to receive 75 percent of the votes to be elected, and the committee of writers uses integrity, sportsmanship, character, and attitude as criteria, as well as ability and achievement (contribution to the team(s) on which the player played). A player who may have avoided the press and refused interviews could be overlooked. This committee has never elected ten players in any given year.

Another method of election is the Baseball Hall of Fame Committee on Baseball Veterans. This voting committee is comprised of former baseball players who are members of the Hall of Fame. To be considered eligible to be elected by the Baseball Veterans, a major league player will have played in at least ten seasons and be retired as a player at least 23 years. Also, players who started their careers after 1945 should have obtained 100 or more votes in one or more elections conducted by the Baseball Writers' Association of America.

The Baseball Veterans elected Phil Rizzuto, who had many friends on the committee but could never gather enough votes from the writers' committee. Bill Mazeroski never collected enough votes from the Baseball Writers' Association of America, but was elected to the Hall of Fame in 2001 by the Baseball Veterans as well. As the rules for election into the Hall of Fame have been cemented for years, unfortunately, Thurman Munson will never be inducted. When great players have untimely deaths, and should be considered for induction into the Hall of Fame, the members of the rules committee must consider revising their rules.

Over the past eight years, the revelations of widespread use of performance enhancing drugs by the players was disturbing to baseball fans and to Commissioner Selig, who requested Senator George Mitchell to investigate this critical problem. The Mitchell Report uncovered 83 players (the report didn't even scratch the surface, more players are using performance enhancing drugs) including Roger Clemens and Barry Bonds, among the more well known players using steroids. After reading the Mitchell report Selig indicated that he would take action. Will the Hall of Fame react to this problem that will affect great players who may not be inducted by the Baseball Writers' Association of America in the future?

The rules for election into the Hall of Fame for the players who have been retired at least five years include the voting will be based a player's integrity, character, sportsmanship, player's record and playing ability. Applying integrity and character to future elections in the Hall of Fame will make the great players like Bonds, McGwire, Sosa, Palmeiro and Clemens suspect. For the players who used steroids to help enhance their performance or prolong their career, some baseball insiders feel the records attained by steroid users should be either removed from the books or the records should be notated with an asterisk symbol to suggest the accomplishment was questionable during the steroids era.

Barry Bonds will go to trial in March 2009 on federal charges of lying to a grand jury about his use of performance-enhancing drugs. Should he be guilty of all of the charges, will his records be stricken from the books?

Hall of Fame Memorabilia

Collectors should consider vintage items (rare, game-used equipment belonging to a player) to add to their collection, and where possible have these items signed at baseball shows and other in-person meetings. You can find the signatures of some deceased players on baseballs for a reasonable price. Here are some other considerations for initiating a Hall of Fame collection.

- **Begin a single-signed Hall of Fame baseball collection.** It is possible to include all of the living members in this extremely popular type of collection, and is a wise investment. Besides having fun, you begin to network with other collectors in person and online.
- **You can acquire the following players on a single-signed baseball for under $50 and initiate a quality Hall of Fame collection:** Dennis Eckersley, Bob Feller, Rollie Fingers, Ferguson Jenkins, Ralph Kiner, Juan Marichal and Robin Roberts. You can meet these players at baseball shows and acquire signed baseballs at hobby stores, online auctions and purchase or trade with other collectors.
- **You can purchase the following deceased players on a single-signed baseball for under $100: Richie Ashburn, Lou Boudreau, Buck Leonard, Johnny Mize, Billy**

Single-signed Hall of Fame baseballs of Warren Spahn, Whitey Ford, Mickey Mantle, Ernie Banks, Al Lopez and Eddie Mathews.

Herman, Ray Dandridge, Rick Ferrell, Hal Newhouser and Luke Appling. You can obtain these baseballs from hobby stores, auctions, and purchase or trade with other collectors.

- **When you purchase items belonging to the players it should be validated in written form.** Vintage memorabilia furnished by a player may include a baseball, bat, hat, jersey or tangible awards (Most Valuable Player trophy or other accolades). You want the dates they received the awards in written form. A letter of authenticity is acceptable.
- **Vintage unsigned memorabilia which can be purchased from hobby stores should be brought to baseball shows and validated by the signing player by requesting some notation on the item.** Call the show promoter in advance and make it clear what you want added on the item. Request a letter of authenticity signed by the player attending the show and you can expect to pay an additional fee for this service.
- **You may consider purchasing rare vintage signed memorabilia from historic games that can be validated with letters from the players and from the estate or family members of deceased players.** It is essential to receive letters authenticating the item

Single-signed Hall of Fame baseballs of Luis Aparicio, Don Drysdale, Pee Wee Reese, Hoyt Wilhelm, Bob Doerr and Willie McCovey.

in some way (request a written statement from everybody). Never accept oral representations as fact.

- **For interest, appeal and value you could include the following special theme baseballs: 300 Win Club on a single baseball; 500 Home Run Club on a single baseball; 3,000 Hit Club on a single baseball.** You might include some of the present great players who have accomplished this. They include the following players: Ramirez, Griffey Jr., (will have over 600 home runs in 2008) and Sosa for the 600 Home Run Club; Maddux and Clemens for the 300 Win Club; Bonds and Griffey for the 3,000 Hit Club. Cal Ripkin for 3,000 hits. In October 1999, two of these elite clubs had new members: The 3,000 Hit Club added Tony Gwynn and Wade Boggs; the 500 Home Run Club, slugger Mark McGwire.

- **Commemorative Hall of fotoballs are another unique collectible to add to your collection.** The player's name and face appears on these baseballs, which acknowledge a specific milestone or event applicable to the player's career and the game of baseball. This is another creative approach to collecting.

Single-signed Hall of Fame baseballs of Steve Carlton, Leo Durocher, Phil Rizzuto, Earl Weaver, Tom Lasorda and Larry Doby.

Establish Your Own Hall of Fame Collection

Below are easy ways to successfully accomplish the in-person approach for autograph acquisition with the members of the Hall of Fame.

1. Participate in a team Fantasy Camp where you can be instructed for usually one week by a group of Hall of Famers. Most major league teams conduct this camp either in Florida or Arizona (each year from November through February, prior to spring training). Call any major league baseball team to get more information about their Fantasy Camp.

2. Play in a celebrity golf event with Hall of Famers. You pay an entry fee which usually includes a dinner reception and autograph session. Many of these events include a memorabilia auction.

3. Volunteer for celebrity charity events where you provide service and interact with the players. The sponsors seek free assistance and allow opportunities for acquiring autographs at the conclusion of the event.

4. Schedule a trip to the National Sports Collectors Convention each year during the summer. Many Hall of Famers and future inductees make signing appearances during the

four-day gala event. Autographed memorabilia and game-used equipment take center stage among collectors. Check hobby publications for show schedule and information about hotel lodging.

    5. Establish a network base locally and nationally, collector-to-collector, trading duplicate single-signed baseballs that you both may need. This is an easy way to meet collectors and learn more about the hobby.

5. The Sleaze Factor

Collecting baseball autographs and memorabilia is a challenging and rewarding experience. The novice entering the hobby and general collectors must establish guidelines and develop a set of high standards and principles for the acquisition of baseball autographs. Ethical behavior acquired early by collectors will improve the integrity of the hobby.

Concern about forgery has the hobby officials — promoters, dealers, sponsors, players, and collectors — asking how is it possible to collect baseball autographs safely. The hobby is searching for high ideals, accepted practices, and collector ethics — a system of acceptable behavior which encourages trust and honesty. Collecting autographs involves the interaction of dealers, show promoters, professional players and collectors all developing acceptable practices, standards and mutual respect for each other.

Unfortunately, there is a small unsavory element in the hobby that deals in forgeries of hard to find or rare autographed baseball memorabilia. Some of the more common forged signatures on baseball memorabilia include players like Babe Ruth, Joe DiMaggio, Mickey Mantle, Ted Williams, and Mark McGwire. Some dealers claim to purchase memorabilia from reputable sources, but could unknowingly purchase inauthentic material. Without knowledge of the origin of signed items, the collector has to be careful with all purchases. Acquiring autographed memorabilia can be very risky.

The seller (dealer) owes the collecting community honesty and integrity in their business dealings. When an item is found to be inauthentic, the dealer must rectify the problem with a money-back guarantee. This is a serious problem because some dealers are purchasing items from people they don't know. Although the signed items may be legitimate, there are no contracts, proof or origin of the signing. The dealer cannot guarantee the authenticity of the signing since they haven't seen the items signed in person. What's to prevent a professional forger from developing their own system to sell signed items to dealers?

Another problem that exists is that some offensive dealers hire runners (children and or adults who stalk the players, using cell phones to provide tips about the players' whereabouts). This slimy element will cut in line, attempt to get many signed items, and use a tactless and deplorable approach. Fortunately, some of the players are aware of this problem, seeing the same group each day during their stay in town. They realize that some opportunistic dealer is exploiting their signature on an item. Some of the players are turned off by the actions of a few unethical individuals, and refuse to sign for anybody. Consequently, the honest collectors suffer from this element. An approach is presented below to identify the problem and encourage hobby ethics, raising the odds that the autographs you acquire are authentic.

The Problem

A handful of dealers are purchasing autographed memorabilia from unknown sources, people they don't conduct business with on a regular basis. Since the dealers haven't seen the items signed, and cannot make a strong claim about their origin, how can they guarantee that the autographed material isn't forged? The second problem is that some dealers have employed runners—a group of individuals who lack a code of ethics and use deceptive tactics to obtain autographs. At most, these unsavory characters may receive only a few signatures, not enough for a dealer's business to thrive on. What's to prevent these runners from employing forgery? Since this is very possible, suggestions to deal with the problem are provided below.

Suggestions for Avoiding Forged Memorabilia

- **Collectors should use the in-person approach for autograph acquisition.** Not only do you have the opportunity to meet the player, you are absolutely certain the signature is authentic.
- **Use a digital camera and take a picture of your items being signed.** Ask another hobbyist to take a picture of you with the player at the signing and display the items that were autographed. This should guarantee that the signature is authentic.
- **Dealers need to embody the highest standards, professionalism, and hobby ethics.** They should avoid purchasing signed items from people they don't know, and eliminate using runners.
- **A code of ethics should be established by dealers.** Dealers should only purchase signed items from other reputable dealers and collectors they have had associations with over a long period of time. The dealers owe the collecting community honesty and integrity.
- **Establish a dealer-to-dealer network that can provide only authentic autographs.** Purchase autographs from dealers who attend in-person signings and conduct private signings. Many dealers purchase signed memorabilia from the promoters of baseball shows.
- **Deal with reputable established businesses.** When signed items are purchased and may be questionable to the buyer, look for a money-back guarantee policy. Buyers should avoid purchasing any questionable signatures. Dealers should follow the same advice when buying from a collector. If the signature doesn't appear authentic, pass on it.

- **Dealers must have a good reputation in the community.** They shouldn't apply deceptive tactics to receive free autographs, especially autographs that they intend to profit from. Is it ethical to trick a player into signing a free autograph that they have no intention of keeping? Collectors are turned off by this and quickly learn which dealers to avoid. Also, when questioned about the history or origin of a signature, the dealers should be able to verify how they obtained the autograph. Avoid dealers who will not provide this information.
- **The dealers and show promoters should develop a network with a paper trail authenticating the autographs that were signed at the event.** The show promoters can develop a system of verification that they can pass along to the collectors. Some promoters who conduct private signings will include a stamped ticket identifying the player signing, the date of the event, and address where the signing took place. In this manner the collector has some information (history) about their signed memorabilia. Many promoters will include this information with all mail order purchases. Some promoters have provided their own photograph of the player(s) conducting a signing with mail order purchases.
- **Both dealers and collectors should develop an organized filing system to identify their signed memorabilia.** Use a computer and index card system as a record-keeping tool so you can catalog your items for future use. Having a written system stored in some manner can make it easy to describe how you acquired autographed memorabilia.
- **The hobby officials — sponsors, promoters, and dealers — should develop a universal authentication service.** A cost effective and creative approach can be instituted and implemented. Authenticating services are available for dealers who conduct private and in-person signings. In this manner the signed items you purchase at baseball shows and through mail orders is professionally documented. You know the signatures are real. With this system, it may cost the collector a little more to purchase signed memorabilia, but you know the autograph is authentic.
- **Become familiar with hobby sources who will utilize authentication services.** At shows, you are more at risk when you purchase signed items from vendors who cannot authenticate the signed collectibles. Collectors should never buy an autograph whose origin cannot be verified.
- **It would be unique for dealers to include a certificate of authenticity signed by the autograph guest.** Unfortunately, most are signed by promoters or other hobby officials at the signing. This could be an innovative idea and future hobby standard.
- **Documenting and authenticating the signed memorabilia will eliminate the need for a return policy.** Once collectors have total assurance that the signatures they've purchased are real, they won't be overly concerned about a return policy. This is a good way to network with local collectors and make new contacts who have the same concerns.

- **Develop a sticker or universal hologram to place on the signed item.** The amount of time and effort employed to create a secure autograph system will promote consumer confidence and trust, and continue to improve the hobby in the future. The Bob Feller Museum provides a sticker on signed baseballs and mail order purchases.
- **Network with other collectors from other states.** These contacts will attend shows in person and purchase signed items for you. When the occasion arises you will reciprocate and send them signed memorabilia. This system will enable collectors to establish a good collection. Also, by your presence at these events, both of you can verify and authenticate the autographed items. This is called a collector-to-collector network.
- **Purchase signed memorabilia from hobby publications that have a money-back guarantee policy.** The advertisers have an agreement with the publication to help the consumers buy with confidence and security. Should the signed item not be acceptable, you need to return it in the same condition and receive your money back. Proceed with extreme caution when purchasing autographs online. This can be risky without a guarantee.
- **A couple of memorabilia companies have developed a letter of authenticity with a hologram.** The extra cost for this service should be nominal and passed on to the consumers. The collectors want to know that the autographs they collect are real, and this is a small price to pay for security.
- **Professional memorabilia authenticators now have a process using DNA combined with ink to validate autographs.** It involves the use of a DNA pen, special sticker and laser scanner. Soon authorized dealers will have the laser scanner available to verify authenticity.
- **Network with other collectors in person, as well as by computer.** The local contacts you meet at shows can benefit both of you. You can help each other obtain signed items you both need. Networking with collectors in other areas by means of a computer will enable you and your new contacts to acquire new items. You and your friends can e-mail each other on a daily basis. This is a good way to keep each other informed about hobby issues and which guests will appear at hobby shows. It is also a good way to assist one another, learn new collecting methods, and have fun interacting.
- **Purchase signed memorabilia from home shopping television networks that provide a money-back guarantee policy.** The advertisers have an agreement with the network to help the consumers buy with confidence and security. Should the signed item not be acceptable, you need to return it in the same condition, and you will receive your money back. Proceed with extreme caution when purchasing autographs by mail order. Only deal with companies that provide a money-back guarantee.
- **Collectors should conduct their own research.** Investigate the appearance of an autograph before you purchase one at a private signing. After seeing the same autograph you may be able to detect distinct characteristics in the player's signature and writing

style. For older players, you must consider their age and health, which can make their signature appear different.

- **Use good judgment.** Purchase autographs from reputable sources that you can trust. Should you not have positive feelings about a particular dealer, sever the relationship. Also, should you find a signed item at a bargain price, let your sound judgment determine whether or not you should make the purchase. Always request a money-back guarantee return policy.
- **State licensing regulations for the hobby industry.** To protect the consumer, the promoters, dealers, and sponsors should be required to be certified as hobby operators. Educational training with testing and fingerprinting procedures is being considered by state lawmakers.
- **The hobby needs to improve its image about forged autographs.** The media has reported the negative aspects of the hobby, and put collectors on notice. As collectors begin to understand that authentic autographs cost more than forgeries, legitimate dealers will see an increase in their business. Eventually, the unsavory dealers will become extinct.
- **Dealers who adhere to strict authenticating procedures will generate more consumer interest.** The hobby professionals with good business practices and a concern for the consumers will continue to be the hobby leaders. Collectors want to be assured what they purchase is authentic signed memorabilia.

Professional Sports Authenticator (PSA/DNA) is the leading third-party authentication service for baseball memorabilia and autographs. *PSA/DNA* was founded in 1998 to address the concerns of forgery, counterfeiting and the questionable practices of an unsavory group of individuals involved in autographed memorabilia. *PSA/DNA* has developed a four-step authentication/identification process which has enhanced the hobby of collecting autographed memorabilia, and has made it more enjoyable and safer for collectors. A nominal fee is charged for this service and the cost for authenticating autographs for current players and the members of the Hall of Fame is on the PSA/DNA website. The process is presented below, courtesy of Professional Sports Authenticator.

Step 1: **Examination**—A physical examination is provided when an item is received. The most important characteristics are checked for letter size, spacing, flow and other features necessary to examining any signature, including, the type of ink that was used. For example, a Babe Ruth autograph in a black permanent marker would be counterfeit, since these markers weren't available when Ruth was alive. Sometimes, the collectible is checked with the use of a Video Spectral Comparator (VSC), which examines the autograph using sophisticated color and infrared imaging, magnification, coaxial lighting, and in-screen side lighting. The VSC reveals erasures, obliterated signatures, differences in ink type and high-tech tampering.

Step 2: **Anti-Counterfeit Tagging**—In-the-presence autographs and vintage autographs deemed genuine by the experts are marked with both overt and covert anti-counterfeit tagging. Invisible ink laced with synthetic DNA sequence/combination, specific to PSA/DNA and detectable only under a specially calibrated laser, is applied to the object. A non-destructive label bearing an alphanumeric serial number is applied to the item in a discrete location or on the Letter of Authenticity.

Step 3: **Certification** — A certificate or a detailed Letter of Authenticity is issued with your item. Each links your collectible to PSA/DNA, giving it maximum monetary potential in the market. Letters of Authenticity include the date, certification number and a photo of your exact submission on watermarked paper.

Step 4: **Documentation** — All PSA/DNA authenticated autographs and memorabilia can be verified online at *www.psadna.com* under "Cert Verification." To check an item's authenticity, enter its alphanumeric serial number, and the screen will display all the pertinent information relating to the item.

This is the best-known Bath Ruth single-signed baseball that was authenticated and graded a 9.5 and privately sold in 2005 for $150,000 (courtesy Professional Sports Authenticator).

Recommendations to Improve the Hobby

Below are suggestions to improve the relationship between the dealers, collectors, and autograph guests (hobby participants), and modify some of the negative hobby practices.

- **Include a printed sticker that can be placed on a cube baseball holder.** The sticker can include the name of the autograph guest, date, where the event took place and it could be signed by the autograph guest (this would be the ideal hobby standard for a certificate of authenticity). A small label with the aforementioned information should be placed on signed items such as, photographs, books, bats and jerseys.
- **Promoters can use authenticating services at baseball shows and private signings throughout the country.** Only authenticators could mark the signed baseballs, and collectors should be encouraged to only purchase signatures with this special marking. Collectors could have their signed items validated by the authenticators who use laser scanners.
- **The authenticator witnesses the signing of an item and it is guaranteed as being genuine and guaranteed for life.** Signed-in the presence authentication services are appearing on the baseball show circuit. An additional fee is provided for this service.
- **Many reputable dealers and auction companies are using authentication services to**

encourage collectors to purchase items that they haven't seen. With more online auctions, collectors are protected and buying with confidence.

- **Dealers should eliminate an extra fee for the players to provide additional writing on the signed items.** They should understand that many collectors want their awards and achievements included on their memorabilia. And many players include additional writing at free signings. The hobby needs to attract new collectors and children who may not be able to afford the extra costs for autograph acquisition. Unless collecting becomes cost-effective, many children will leave the hobby.
- **Show promoters shouldn't allow dealers with questionable business practices to purchase tables at baseball shows and sell their merchandise.** Promoters know which dealers have an excellent reputation. However, a way to deal with hobby issues is to have the participants at these shows complete a survey. From their responses, the promoters can detect the general concerns of the collectors.
- **Dealers who utilize the services of runners to obtain free autographs should be banned from the hobby.** The hobby has to take some action against this unethical element. The hobby publications should print the names of unethical dealers.
- **Dealers should include some time at the end of baseball shows for the collectors to take pictures with the autograph guest.** When collectors use their camera and request a player's picture during the signing, they are not being considerate of others waiting in long lines.
- **The hobby participants should develop workshops on hobby issues and ethics to better serve the novice and the general collecting community.** Include a session with the autograph guest — speaking engagement and question and answer time. This is a good opportunity to attract new collectors and children into the hobby.
- **The hobby is interacting with the law enforcement officials.** The officials are willing to pursue the forgers (small criminal element) and make the necessary arrests. A combination of educated collectors, authenticity-oriented dealers, and the involvement of law enforcement will only strengthen the autograph industry.
- **The hobby sponsors — promoters, dealers, and distributors — should develop interactive baseball shows for children.** Sponsors should include speakers, games, hobby events — collecting baseball cards, flipping cards, trading, etc.— and include free player autographs. The sponsors can also include giveaways, like baseball items that can be autographed. The goodwill gesture will bring a new generation of children into the collecting community.
- **Collectors who focus on expensive and older memorabilia (vintage) should develop a network of hobby experts who can help them authenticate their purchases.** You should confer with the experts prior to buying expensive items. Make sure you receive a money-back guarantee policy from the dealers. Some of these items can be game-used equipment from retired and deceased players.

The hobby needs to continue to police itself and insure the legitimacy of their products. Authenticity of autographed memorabilia must become the hobby standard. Innovative ideas should attract a new group of children into the hobby. Both collectors and dealers should educate themselves. Through books like this, the business of collecting autographed memorabilia will encourage great collections and promote a code of ethics for the hobby participants. Finally, new collectors should become familiar with baseball shows, attend player signings, and use the services of dealers, who can become very helpful.

Suggestions for In-Person Player Signings at Baseball Shows

- **Purchase signing tickets in advance or arrive early before the player appears.** With time limitations or a limited number of tickets being sold, it is advisable to purchase tickets a week or more before the signing. When you cannot be present for a signing, mail your items to the dealer with a check and a self-addressed stamped mailing envelope (SASE), and you will receive your items back as soon as possible.
- **Use your own preferred writing tools for the items you want signed.** A silver paint pen shows up better on a black bat than a blue or black Sharpie. A good blue ballpoint pen should be used on baseballs. Sometimes the show promoters use writing tools that may be different from your own. Be prepared.
- **Feel free to make requests for additional writing on your items.** The players should be proud of their accomplishments, and include this on your memorabilia. Always be polite with your request and say "Thank you."
- **Should you have an extra collectible of the player offer it to him.** This is a good gesture, and the player will appreciate your offer. Sometimes the autograph guest will offer you an extra signature and talk to you after the show.
- **A good way to authenticate the player signing your items is to photograph him signing your collectibles.** Have your camera ready as he signs your items. You can scan the picture and store it in your home computer.
- **Visit all of the dealer tables before you make a purchase.** Look for similar items and compare prices; search for unique items that you may want to include in your own collection. You should inquire about a money-back guarantee policy and avoid the dealers who won't provide one.
- **Volunteer to work at baseball shows.** This is a great way to assist other collectors and meet hobbyists with similar interests. You have the opportunity to see the newest hobby products. Some of the show promoters will enable you to have some of your memorabilia signed at no charge.
- **Baseball shows offer participants an opportunity to practice good sportsmanship.** Collectors should wait patiently in long lines for their items to be signed and have respect for one another. Being polite and courteous should always be the acceptable hobby standard.

- **The hobby participants (dealers and promoters) should always look for ways to improve their business practices.** They must be fair and honest in their dealings. Good practices will enhance more business. Collectors value dealers who have integrity and good character.
- **The major league baseball teams should encourage player signings by the entire team each season.** A baseball show can be arranged at a convention center or at the stadium. It should be mandatory for the entire team roster of players to be present. This exchange is important since the community of collectors and baseball fans consistently support their teams. This would be the best time for collectors to establish a team collection. Many teams today schedule a signing event at the team stadium prior to spring training and encourage the fans to purchase tickets for the season and individual games.

Major league baseball has been concerned with its image, and continues to explore ways to attract fans to the baseball games. The team executives have to encourage the players to become more fan-friendly, to become more visible during the baseball season. It would be a great gesture for the players to conduct free signings at baseball shows. This would truly make collecting baseball autographs a positive experience. As the hobby continues to address these concerns, new collectors will emerge and acquire authentic autographs.

6. The Autograph Craze

When you meet a ballplayer at an event or a different arena, most often when you tell your friends whom you've met, they will be inquisitive and ask, "Did you obtain his autograph?" This seems to be the general question asked about meeting a recognized player in person. Why is this such a common question? The collector seeks to acquire someone's autograph because it is a unique experience. It can reinforce pleasant childhood memories of the times when you and your parents attended baseball games together. Some of the players were your childhood heroes. And the player's signature can help you recall memorable moments — specific games, a game-winning home run, a career achievement, or a catch that saved the game. How often have you heard someone tell you they met a celebrity in person, but didn't have the necessary tools (writing implement and paper) to request their autograph? Simply put, they weren't prepared to acquire an autograph. Collectors need to research historic events like knowing the members of the 500 Home Run Club, 3,000 Hit Club, pitchers who've thrown no-hitters, pitchers with over 300 wins, Rookie of the Year, players who've earned Most Valuable Player Awards, players who've earned the Most Valuable Players Awards in consecutive years (in the history of the game, only 11 players have accomplished this, and you will learn the names of the players in this chapter). By doing your homework prior to attending historic events, you are prepared to collect novel items and experience the autograph craze.

An autograph is an exciting opportunity to preserve special moments or historic events. Most collectors have developed an autograph craze — a euphoric condition or frenzy, to experience the joy of success through their association with the game. By collecting player autographs you share in their accomplishment, as it is a reflection of time, and for that moment your signed memorabilia re-creates memories. Collectors who acquired Cal Ripken's autograph on a baseball will share in his record-breaking triumph, and also recall that the greatest consecutive games streak of all time finally concluded at 2,632 games when Ripken decided to take the day off on September 20, 1998. As collectors stare at their autographed Ripken memorabilia they have formed an association with it. They remember for many years seeing Ripken's name in the box score of their newspaper — every game. And finally, seeing Cal Ripken tip his hat on television, and the crowd at Camden Yards applauding with admiration for an amazing record. Being the classy person that he is, Ripken trotted around the field that evening and shook hands with his fans. Although many high profile players are inaccessible and avoid the collectors, Ripken joins in the autograph craze and will sign for almost an hour. He has always been a fan favorite and was inducted into the Hall of Fame on July 29, 2007.

Sometimes collectors get too caught up in the autograph craze and exhibit inappropriate and aggressive behavior when meeting players. On September 1, 1998, Mark McGwire had completed batting practice at Pro Player Stadium in Miami, Florida. As he walked over to his dugout area, a crowd of collectors were pushing and shoving to establish a good position close to him. He approached two fans readying himself to catch two baseballs which he would sign. As McGwire signed the baseballs, a couple of rude people tossed baseballs at him and almost hit him. Realizing that the crowd was out of control, McGwire headed back to the field, ending his signing session.

In previous chapters, suggestions have been given for standards of acceptable behavior for in-person player signings. It's imperative for collectors to exhibit responsible behavior. Unfortunately, there is usually a small unpleasant element that hinders the opportunities for collectors to acquire the signature of the more high profile players. Collectors must realize that the players they seek out are human beings. They should be granted the same degree of politeness and respect that is accorded other people.

Factors that contribute to the autograph craze include the following:

1. Name recognition and superstardom status.
2. Accessibility to in-person and mail request approaches.
3. Hall of Fame memorabilia collecting.
4. Rookie of the Year recognition, and future All-Star status.
5. Hall of Fame status seems inevitable.
6. Retired players considered legends.

Name Recognition

The limited supply of autographed memorabilia for the most popular players will usually cause the greatest demand for the signed item. The autograph craze has been influenced by the condition of supply and demand. Usually super-stardom qualities have created more of a demand for a player's signature than can be met. Although Babe Ruth signed frequently, the demand has always been great for any of his autographed collectibles. When the demand exceeds the supply, it will increase the price for autographed items. The same can be said for Ted Williams. Williams was an active participant on the baseball show circuit during the 1970s through the 1980s. During the 1990s he suffered a stroke which prevented him from signing baseballs. Even though his autograph on single-signed baseballs is plentiful, collectors could pay from $350 to $500 for a single-signed baseball from a reputable dealer. Because many collectors want to keep a Ted Williams signed ball, the cost will continue to escalate in the future. Despite the higher prices for living and deceased superstars, some collectors are determined to add these great players to their collection.

Obtaining the signatures of every living Hall of Famer, and current greats — including Maddux, Smoltz, Glavine, Griffey Jr., Manny Ramirez, Chipper Jones, and Jeter — is a realistic goal. For a collector it is very possible to acquire their signature on a collectible, free of charge. This book offers good suggestions to help the reader learn how to acquire the signatures of the greatest players. In addition, you will have fun and learn more about the hobby. Of interest to collectors, Ken Griffey Jr. became a member of the 600 Home Run Club on June 9, 2008 and Manny Ramirez joined the 500 Home Run Club on May 31, 2008.

To determine whether the acquisition of signatures of the greatest players is a realistic goal, you must consider cost. The easiest way to acquire signatures on your memorabilia is by attending baseball shows, buying from reputable dealers, online auctions, trading with other collectors and purchasing autographs from a private signing. At these events you will incur costs to build your collection. Again, based upon the factors of supply and demand, some autographed items will be more expensive. You need to determine if this fits your budget prior to establishing collecting goals.

Accessibility

Collectors should find acquiring player signatures easy to accomplish using an approach like the in-person signing, mail request, or trading with other collectors. Being accessible is applicable for both the collector and the ballplayers you seek out. You may feel it is more cost-effective to acquire free signatures, but you must consider the following factors:

Time Constraints

Consider that the time you wait in line for a free autograph can be an hour or more at times. Do you have an abundance of free time to pursue the players using the in-person approach? Can you take off from work for a couple of hours? When you consider how you may be limited by time, you may feel it is more practical to purchase autographed items at baseball shows and at private signings. Establishing a good working relationship with the hobby professionals will enable you to accumulate harder to find player autographs when you cannot be available to attend baseball shows. A reputable dealer will find the items you may need and help you build an outstanding collection.

Preparation Concerns

When you use the mail request approach, are you prepared to acquire autographs in the appropriate manner? Do you have the correct size bubble mail bags, large enough to include your items with the return mail bag? Did you include a plastic insert to protect your photograph or baseball cards? Are the baseballs out of the box and placed inside plastic sandwich bags? Have you written a short and direct letter for your request? And don't forget to include postage on your return mail bag. Preparation is very important, and it is easy to become frustrated when you're not prepared. Before you plan to make a mail request, you should purchase the necessary materials from office supply stores and hobby stores. This process can be time consuming, but by being prepared and having your items nearby, the goal of collecting will be more exciting as you receive your signed items in the mail.

Establishing an autograph collecting goal will help you determine whether using an approach is most beneficial for you. The time you invest waiting in line at baseball shows, the post office, and purchasing the necessary materials at various stores may not be suitable for some collectors. If time constraints and preparation concerns aren't issues, you should be accessible to acquire free autographs using the in-person and or mail request approach.

A challenge for most collectors is acquiring the signatures of the more reclusive players in person. Hall of Famers like Hank Aaron and Sandy Koufax will participate in one or two shows each year, and conduct an occasional private signing. Willie Mays, another Hall of Famer, conducts one private signing each year, participates at in-person baseball shows, and doesn't sign in person should you meet him at the stadium in San Francisco. These players are more difficult to obtain in person, and you should expect their signatures on signed items to be more expensive. Collectors will find most Hall of Famers accessible at many events, especially charity functions. It is a good idea to volunteer at these events where many players participate, and you should find it easy to acquire free signatures.

Use your own creativity to find a way to obtain their signatures on your own memorabilia. Begin with a personal letter, indicate that you need their signature to help complete your collection, and make a reasonable request. Should you be traveling in their city, mention this in your letter and give them your telephone number. You will find that some players will respond to your request and include their phone number when they respond. Retired players appear to be more responsive for these requests.

Hall of Fame Memorabilia Collecting

A new interest for collectors is a Hall of Fame theme collection of historical items that may end up in the Hall of Fame. Collectors can consider unique items of record-breaking appeal, or new records in a player's career, similar to the ones that are included in the Baseball Hall of Fame Museum. Items can include the highs and lows of the game, and team records. It can be a baseball signed by the record breaker or the pitcher contributing to the new record. Suggestions for collecting themes are indicated below. Use your own creativity, and design your own collection.

Most Valuable Player Award in Consecutive Years, by Position

In researching this new area of collecting, it is interesting to note that only 11 players in the history of baseball have been selected for the Most Valuable Player Award in back-to-back seasons. Seven players are inducted in the Hall of Fame and the other four players have Hall of Fame potential, and most players have a different position on the field. Before you read ahead, can you name the players who were selected Most Valuable Player in Consecutive Years? Four of the players are deceased and played in the 1930s, 1940s, 1950s through the1960s. It is possible to add the remaining seven players on a single baseball as a theme collection and a very unique one. This would be a Hall of Fame theme collection. The position, the players, team and years selected MVP is represented below:

First Base	Jimmy Foxx	Philadelphia A's	1932–33
First Base	Frank Thomas	Chicago White Sox	1993–94
Second Base	Joe Morgan	Cincinnati Reds	1975–76
Third Base	Mike Schmidt	Philadelphia Phillies	1980–81
Shortstop	Ernie Banks	Chicago Cubs	1959–60
Catcher	Yogi Berra	New York Yankees	1954–55
Right Field	Roger Maris	New York Yankees	1960–61
Center Field	Mickey Mantle	New York Yankees	1956–57
Center Field	Dale Murphy	Atlanta Braves	1982–83
Left Field	Barry Bonds	San Francisco Giants	2001–2004
Pitcher	Hal Newhouser	Detroit Tigers	1944–45

Autographed Hall of Fame Theme on Baseballs or Other Memorabilia

- Cal Ripken with "**2632**" on baseball for record of consecutive games played.
- Barry Bonds adding "**73**" on baseball, the new home run record.
- Barry Bonds adding "**762**" on baseball, all-time career home run record.
- Frank Robinson and Carl Yastrzemski Triple Crown Winners
- Pete Rose usually adds "**4256**" on baseball, all-time hits leader.
- Ryan Minor. Orioles rookie prospect, replaced Ripken on September 20, 1998. His baseball shoes were sent to the Baseball Hall of Fame Museum. Collectors could request his signature on a baseball with "**9/20/98**" added.
- Bonds, Aaron, Mays, Sosa and Griffey, Jr., on baseball, all-time home run leaders.
- Lee Smith, Cubs and Cardinals closer, all-time saves leader with **478 saves**.
- Trevor Hoffman. Padres closer, set a National League record with 53 saves. Collectors should request "**53 Saves**" added on baseballs. The all-time saves leader has 554 saves through the 2008 season.
- Al Leiter threw the first no-hitter in Marlins history on May 11, 1996. Collectors could request the addition of "**Marlins 1st No-Hitter 5/11/96**" on a baseball. And a few collectors

have the whole game ticket from his no-hitter signed by Leiter. These items represent what the Hall of Fame wants to add to their collection.

- Kerry Wood. Cubs pitcher and 1998 Rookie of the Year, set a new National League record with 20 strikeouts on May 6, 1998. At a private signing some collectors requested the addition of "**20 Ks 5/6/98**" which he included. When collectors meet him in person they can also request "**1998 ROY**" (rookie of the year).
- Craig Biggio. Astros star player, became the second player in history to accomplish at least 50 doubles and 50 stolen bases in the same season. He recorded **51 doubles**, **50 steals**, which can be added on your items. Tris Speaker was the other player to achieve this record.
- Barry Bonds became the first player in major league history to accumulate 400 career home runs and 400 stolen bases. Request the addition of "**400–400**" on your items.
- Manny Ramirez **20 career grand slams** and Willie McCovey **18 career grand slams** (all-time leaders in grand slam totals).
- Chris Hoiles. Orioles catcher, hit two grand slams in a game on August 14, 1998, and surrendered his bat to the Baseball Hall of Fame. You can ask him to notate **two Grand Slams in game**.
- Fernando Tatis. Cardinals All-Star prospect, entered the record books on April 23, 1999, when he hit **two grand slams in the same inning**. Innovative collectors should request this amazing feat on baseballs and photographs. Who was the pitcher who served up both home runs? Chan Ho Park, Dodgers pitcher, is credited with serving up both grand slams and his name appears in the record books at the National Baseball Hall of Fame.
- Mark McGwire and Sammy Sosa each clouted more than **60 round-trippers in back-to-back seasons** setting new major league records.

As the hobby continues to mature, the hobbyist searches to find interesting ways to develop a creative approach to collecting. This type of collection is unique with a historical perspective of the game of baseball. When new events, or records with statistical data are witnessed, you should identify the event in written form and include as much information as you can. Store this information on your computer and include the player, date of event, and brief description with numerical data. This will make it easy for you when you approach the players and make this kind of request, adding a new record on your memorabilia.

As a collector, you can focus on players who may be establishing a new record — individually or a team record. Usually, the Baseball Hall of Fame Museum will add game equipment when new records are established. It includes game-used baseballs, hats, bats, jerseys, baseball shoes, and so on from the record holders. As you become more accomplished as a collector, you can also develop this type of collection.

When you approach the players you meet, you can always make requests for additional writing. Make your request in a polite manner, and be certain about the facts you want added on your memorabilia. Players will sign a multitude of autographs during their lifetime; however, the number of baseballs signed with historical data will be significantly less. Consequently, the value of memorabilia with historical signatures will be worth more. As you probably can detect, a unique or unusual collection of autographed memorabilia is a more valuable collection. Cultivating ideas is what makes collecting baseball memorabilia exciting and fun.

Rookie of the Year Recognition

Hobby publications such as *Baseball Weekly*, *Baseball America* and *Baseball Digest* will make fans and collectors aware of the up-and-coming hot baseball prospects (rookies) each season. Scouting reports have rated the top 100 prospects in numerical order to familiarize these players to the baseball fans. Some collectors look at these players as future greats, and have begun to speculate on a Rookie of the Year Collection. It can be initiated early in the season when there is less demand, and it will be much easier to obtain their signatures on your memorabilia.

In 2006, when Hanley Ramirez reported to the Marlins spring training camp in Jupiter, Florida, the collectors could obtain his signature easily each day during his rookie season. At the end of the 2006 season, he was elected the National League winner of the Jackie Robinson Rookie of the Year Award with a .292 batting average with 46 doubles and 17 home runs. The Marlins have signed him to a six-year contract and he's considered one of the best shortstops in the big leagues. He has become a fan favorite and now makes appearances on the baseball show circuit.

When these players are selected as Rookie of the Year their autographs are more in demand, and long lines form to obtain their signature. As the lines grow long, some of the players begin to limit their signing appearances to baseball shows and private signings. Suddenly, the price for signing your memorabilia begins to escalate. Many promoters will charge an extra fee for the additional writing on your items.

During the 1995 season, the media was promoting Hideo Nomo, a Japanese rookie pitcher for the Dodgers. Nomo, a 27-year-old veteran in Japan, had a good season and was selected as Rookie of the Year (many believed that Chipper Jones of the Atlanta Braves was more deserving). Nomo would sign daily at spring training for about 20 fans and suddenly walk away. When he became the Rookie of the Year it was more difficult to obtain his signature in person, and the dealers were selling single-signed baseballs from $75 to $100. Nomo was providing fewer free signatures which caused the escalated price, and unfortunately the collectors were taken advantage of.

Collectors will increase the value of autographed memorabilia when they are willing to pay unreasonable fees. Conversely, there is a limit that collectors will pay. The hobbyist should realize a signed item is only worth what someone is willing to pay for it. Don't get caught up in the autograph craze and be taken advantage of. Some Rookie of the Year Award recipients have quickly fallen from the star status to mediocrity. As an example, collectors will find the price of a single-signed Hideo Nomo baseball steadily dropping due to his poor pitching during the 1997 and 1998 seasons. Be patient when you consider purchasing signed memorabilia from the Rookie of the Year Award recipients. Below are suggestions for developing a Rookie of the Year Collection that collectors can initiate.

Rookie of the Year Collection

- **Collecting one autographed baseball (single-signed) for each Rookie of the Year.** In a polite manner, request the player to add ROY (rookie of the year) and year the award was furnished. This specialized collection should appreciate in value.
- **You can establish an all-time Rookie of the Year Collection.** Include the award recipients from the American and National leagues, and use either league baseball to add their signatures. A unique collector can acquire 20 or more player signatures on a single baseball.
- **You can develop a league Rookie of the Year Collection.** It is not as demanding as acquiring the signatures from both leagues, but also is a lot of fun. Use the correct official league baseball — Rawlings baseball with "ROA" for the American League or the Rawlings baseball with "RON" for National League inscribed on the baseballs. If you cannot find the aforementioned league baseballs, use the Selig Official Major League baseball.
- **Create a team Rookie of the Year Collection.** Use baseball books as resources to assist you. You will find that this award was instituted in 1947, and many of the retired players will sign your items in person and through mail requests. From 1992 to 1996 the Dodgers had five consecutive Rookie of the Year winners — Eric Karros, Mike Piazza, Raul Mondesi, Hideo Nomo, and Todd Hollandsworth. Collectors can initiate this type of collection during spring training when many award winners are available after team practice.
- **When you initiate a Rookie of the Year Collection be creative and speculate early in the season.** Make your own predictions based upon reading articles and scouting reports. It is always easier to acquire rookie player autographs when they are unknown. Collectors who speculated on Chipper Jones of the Atlanta Braves may not have correctly chosen the Rookie of the Year, but Jones is an All-Star and will become a future Hall of Famer. Don't be afraid to approach the rookies for their signature on a baseball or other items — it makes collecting unpredictable at times, and exciting during the baseball season.

Hall of Fame Status

The serious collector should set realistic goals for themselves. On a piece of paper list your goals and the approach suitable to meet your collecting needs. In other words, develop a plan of action. Some collectors are acquiring autographs to have fun and shouldn't be concerned with this type of collecting. Choosing a realistic goal for collecting autographs will enhance your enjoyment of the hobby.

Many collectors have established a collecting goal to acquire the signature of every living Hall of Famer on a single-signed baseball. Many players categorized as having Hall of Fame status perform consistently each season, and barring any unforeseen accident, they should be inducted into the Hall of Fame in the future. Now is an excellent opportunity to find an approach to obtain their signatures on your items.

For current players, especially the more popular ones, you should mail your memorabilia to the stadium and avoid sending items to their homes. The players receive many mail requests, and it could take two or more months before your signed items are returned. With mail requests, you must exhibit plenty of patience. Again, speculate on the quality players, the perennial All-Stars. You should acquire their signature at the stadium or other in-person meetings. Besides baseball shows, you can acquire their signatures from private signings, trading with other collectors and purchasing items from online auctions. Once they become members of the Hall of Fame it will be more costly to acquire their signatures on your items.

As for the factors that have contributed to the autograph craze, you must consider your time, preparation concerns, and the expense of purchasing signed memorabilia. If time constraints and preparation issues are obstacles for a collector, then purchasing signed memorabilia may be the best approach for the serious collector. Cost is another factor that must be included in a collector's plan of action. You should include the cost for signed items at baseball shows and private signings, postage, telephone calls, travel expenses, and purchasing materials used for mail requests. Also, purchasing vintage, game-used equipment will be more expensive. As you assess these concerns, you will decide the most appropriate approach.

Below is an example of the memorabilia that collectors will seek out for a notable player like Nolan Ryan, a 1999 Hall of Fame inductee.

Nolan Ryan Memorabilia

- Cut signature on an index card
- Signature on a baseball card or photo card adding HOF 1999
- Action or portrait 8" × 10" color photograph
- Single-signed official American or National League baseball adding HOF 1999 and achievements

- fotoball with his face appearing on the baseball
- Commemorative baseball noting his career no-hitters
- Induction Day Hall of Fame 8" × 10" photograph card with career statistics
- All-Star game baseball
- All-Star game ticket
- Baseball hat from the teams he appeared on
- Magazine covers including *Sports Illustrated* or *The Sporting News*
- Commemorative or game-used baseball bat
- Mini-helmet from the teams he played on
- Game-used baseball shoes
- Prints, programs, posters and other flats
- Authentic game-used jersey (rare) or store-bought jersey
- Oddball memorabilia, other unique hobby collectibles — plates, bobbleheads, pennants, newspaper headlines and photos, and buttons.

Retired Players Considered Legends

Collectors have vivid memories of childhood experiences, especially the times spent with their parents at the ballpark. Some collectors can recall a specific game or event when these legends made the game bigger than life itself. Many remember Ted Williams hitting a home run in his final at-bat, as well as Roger Maris' record home run ending the 1961 season. And how can we forget watching Mark McGwire blast his 70th home run in his final at-bat, and ending the 1998 baseball season. The collector and their children witnessed that momentous home run on television, and when McGwire retires, the future generation of collectors will recognize him as another legend.

The retired players who have been classified as legends include Joe DiMaggio, Ted Williams, Stan Musial, Willie Mays, Duke Snider, Mickey Mantle, as well as many other great deceased players. Some of the legends only participate in baseball shows or private signings. They refuse to accept mail requests, and make limited in-person appearances. Memorabilia and game-used equipment can be purchased at hobby stores, trading and buying with other collectors, and from participation in auctions. Collectors can initiate another creative approach by developing a commemorative baseball collection. Below are helpful suggestions.

Suggestions for a Commemorative Baseball Collection

- **Purchase commemorative Hall of Fame player fotoballs.** The players appear on the baseballs and they include the date of their induction into the Hall of Fame. Call the Baseball Hall of Fame Museum for more information and refer to hobby publications.

You can find these baseballs in some of the baseball memorabilia shops in your local area.

- **Individual player commemorative baseball relevant to an accomplishment.** Have the player add the accomplishment and the date. Bob Gibson, a great pitcher for the Cardinals, had the most strikeouts in a postseason game. On October 2, 1968, he struck out 17 Tiger batters in the World Series. You can request his signature with "**17Ks — 10/2/68**" added.

- **You can have a commemorative baseball relevant to the game.** Devise a category, like pitchers with 3,000 or more strikeouts, and have the players who have achieved this sign on the same baseball. This is a unique type of multi-signature collection. You will utilize different approaches to obtain many signatures. The approach you use to acquire autographs can include in-person signings, private signings, and collector-to-collector networking using e-mail on your personal computer and communicating with other collectors by means of a telephone.

- **Purchase commemorative baseballs relevant to a special achievement.** You will find these baseballs to commemorate players who hit more than 500 home runs, pitchers who won 300 or more games, or players who hit 50 or more home runs in a season. Use your own ingenuity and create another theme. Other themes can include Stolen Base Leaders, Most Valuable Managers (Managers of the Year), Most Valuable Fielders (players with best fielding percentage in each league), and other collector-designed achievement categories.

- **Acquire commemorative baseballs relevant to historic events.** At many theme baseball shows, the players who were involved in the historic event appear together. You can purchase a commemorative baseball with Ralph Branca and Bobby Thomson signing, and Thomson will add "**The Shot Heard Round the World, 10/3/51.**" As you become more resourceful, you can make up your own themes of historic events. A couple of examples follow to help you initiate this type of collecting. In the 1993 World Series, Joe Carter (Blue Jays) hit the game-winning home run off Mitch Williams (Phillies) as the Blue Jays became World Champs. You could have both players sign on the sweet spot of a baseball and add the date or the event. In the 1997 World Series, Edgar Renteria (Marlins) drove in Craig Counsell for the winning run and World Championship. You could request both players to sign on the baseball and add "**Marlins 1st World Championship, 10/26/97.**" In their fifth season, the Marlins became the youngest expansion team to win the World Series. It is really easy to come up with a commemorative theme relating to historic events. As a collector, let your imagination take over.

- **Produce a commemorative baseball with your own legends.** On a single baseball you could add players like Musial, Mays, Snider, and other retired legends. The best way to obtain their signature is at baseball shows, private signings, network with other collectors in other cities, and check the baseball show schedule in hobby publications. *Sports Collectors Digest* will furnish information on player appearances, mailing instructions for player autographs, mail-order fees, and provide the phone number to speak directly with the show promoter. You will also be advised to either include a self-addressed stamped mail bag or pay an additional fee for postage and handling.

- **Commemorative baseballs can acknowledge strange events.** The peculiarities of the game of baseball sometimes involve an unpleasant interaction between players or umpires. Most collectors will remember the spitting incident with Roberto Alomar in the 1996 playoffs. But do these baseball aficionados remember the name of the umpire? Fortunately, both men have rectified their differences and will sign your items. And do you remember when Juan Marichal intentionally plunked John Roseboro with his bat during a game? Both players resolved their differences and appeared together at baseball shows. Collectors can create their own theme of weird happenings.

- **Collect commemorative baseballs with a numbered limited edition.** Some Hall of Famers who conduct a private signing with promoters will include a limited number of signed baseballs to commemorate a career achievement. For example, Ernie Banks could sign 512 baseballs to commemorate his career home run accomplishment. He could write near his name "**1 of 512**," "**2 of 512**," etc. Collectors could expect to pay an extra fee for a limited edition signed baseball. When you meet the members of the 500 Home Run Club at baseball shows, you should request their home run total added on your items. Some dealers will not charge an extra fee for this.

- **Design a commemorative Most Valuable Player Collection.** This award is provided in both the American and National leagues. Collectors should use the correct baseball when they obtain the signatures from the players in person. Steve Garvey, a popular autograph guest at baseball shows, played his entire career in the National League (Dodgers and Padres). When he signs a baseball or other item, you should request the addition of "**1974 M.V.P.**" (Most Valuable Player). Garvey is very receptive to collector requests, and many feel he deserves to be inducted into the Hall of Fame.

- **Design a commemorative Cy Young Award Collection.** The best pitcher in each league is recognized each season. You should request the players to add the year and Cy Young Award on your items. Rollie Fingers, a great relief specialist and Hall of Famer, was awarded both "**1981 Cy Young and Most Valuable Player.**" With your request he will add this on your baseball and other items.

It is very important for serious collectors to do their homework. You have learned in this book that most players have signed for many years, and in the past couple of years, collectors have been requesting additional writing on their signed memorabilia. Obviously, this type of collecting should increase the value of your collection. As a collector, you should purchase resource books which furnish you with statistical data. For the aforementioned commemorative baseball collection, you should research the players you may meet in person or through mail requests and develop a record keeping system — index card file or use the word processor on your computer to create files with this information. Notate their career achievement, awards acquired, and the year it was presented. Remember, planning and preparation are essential to construct a quality collection.

Suggestions for Coping with the Autograph Craze

- **Prevent impulsive buying.** When dealers charge unreasonable fees for hot prospects, avoid purchasing signed items immediately. At some point the supply will match the demand, and bring the prices down. You should exhibit plenty of patience when you consider purchasing items from players with very little experience. Remember, inconsistency and poor performances will affect the value of signed memorabilia.
- **When you purchase autographed memorabilia, you should request an unconditional guarantee of authenticity.** This guarantee assures the buyer that the dealer will accept a returned item due to uncertainty or authenticity concerns. The buyer must return the items in the same condition immediately.
- **Be careful when you consider purchasing Rookie of the Year signed items.** These items can be expensive, and many Rookie of the Year players experience the sophomore jinx. These players have an off season with average or below average performance. Consequently the demand is not as great as the large supply. When the dealers face this situation and need to move their merchandise, the price for these signed items should decrease. Take a wait-and-see attitude to determine the status of these rookies.
- **Players with superstar qualities can be less accessible to collectors.** Some of these players refuse to appear at baseball shows and conduct private signings. They feel collectors shouldn't have to incur a fee for their autograph. They will sign only at the ballpark which makes it more difficult to obtain their signature on your items. It may be a good idea to purchase signed items only from an established dealer with a good reputation and reasonable prices. The reputable dealers must offer you a money-back guarantee on any autographed item you purchase.
- **Hall of Fame collecting is more desirable.** A single-signed Hall of Fame baseball collection has become very popular. From the 1980s to the present time the price has increased for these signatures on baseballs and other items. Age, health factors, and untimely death has significantly affected the value of Hall of Famer signatures. Hobbyists are encouraged to invest in this type of collecting.
- **Proceed with caution when you purchase at an auction.** Many auction companies have established a successful marketing plan and comprehensive color baseball catalog with many appealing items. Understand all of the terms and conditions prior to making a

bid. Many auction houses add on a 10 to 15 percent buyer surcharge on the winning bids. An overzealous buyer can easily get caught up in the excitement of bidding and end up with an overpriced acquisition. Collectors should purchase these informative catalogs with quality photographs and a detailed description of the items available. The information provided is good research material and should make one more knowledgeable about this type of acquisition. It is imperative that one understands all of the conditions before participating in an auction. Remember, proceed with caution here. It is possible that some items will become more valuable in the future.

- **Trade with other collectors seeking a historical or theme approach.** Find a trading partner who collects the same items that you collect. Before you make a trade be certain that all of the items are properly represented. Both traders need to establish acceptable terms and conditions for each trade. It is important to determine the condition, the type of writing tools used on items — use of a Sharpie on a single-signed baseball is inappropriate and unacceptable. You need to agree that should the signed item not be acceptable to your standards, you will immediately return it (and receive restitution). Sometimes collectors with good intentions will provide an incorrect interpretation. Many collectors have established a good collection by trading. Trading is another great way to network with other collectors.

- **Avoid purchasing unreasonable and overpriced memorabilia from dealers.** It is very easy to be enticed by the autograph craze. Collectors should be careful about purchasing the 1998 New York Yankees team baseballs and other items from some dealers. A New York company conducted a limited signing of 500 Yankees team baseballs with an excessive unit price of $1,200. Collectors realize the Yankees have a rich tradition and history; however, the hefty price was determined prior to the outcome of the 1998 World Series. Collectors can estimate fair market value, and unfortunately this New York company wasn't even close. As the Yankees became the 1998 World Champs, some collectors were consumed with the autograph craze, attempting to share in their historic season and impulsively purchasing overpriced merchandise. Some knowledgeable baseball sources feel the 1998 New York Yankees will be considered the greatest baseball team in history. They recorded 114 wins during the season, a record accomplishment. After winning the 1998 World Series, a Yankees team baseball was valued between $600–$800. Some unethical dealers were charging close to $2,000 for a 1998 New York Yankees "World Champions" signed team baseball (immediately after the World Series). In 2008, this "World Champions" signed team baseball is valued between $1,200–$1,400. Collectors should be prudent about getting caught up in this autograph craze.

- **Use the in-person approach to acquire autographs.** This is probably the best way to deal with the autograph craze and most cost-effective. Refer to the suggestions that have been provided in the previous chapters. It is worthwhile to mention again a formula that will make you a successful collector. Follow the outline on the next page.

- **Be organized**—have your items ready and use correct writing tools. Use a digital camera to authenticate the items that were signed.
- **Be unobtrusive**—blend in with others, and act like you belong.
- **Be discreet**—make a polite request, and then reveal your items.
- **Shake hands with the player**—forces a player to stop, so you can receive a good signature without the player moving.
- **Be sincere and polite with phone requests**—call players at their hotel at an appropriate time, and explain what you want in a sincere manner. It is more practical to meet the players in the hotel lobby.
- **Keep flat items on a hard surface**—use a clipboard or other hard surface. It enables the players to have better support and a good signature.
- **Learn to speak another language**—many more Spanish-speaking popular players have become fan favorites. You will have more of an advantage when you converse in Spanish, and the players understand your request.
- **Be different**—use an approach others would never think of. For example, you could type a letter and fax it to the player at the stadium. The player will probably receive this letter quicker than regular fan mail. And when you drive out to the stadium, you can give team personnel a mail request package. Your items will be placed in the player's dressing area that day. You could get lucky and receive your signed items in a short period of time.

The collector should become more cognizant of acceptable hobby standards. From time-to-time they need to examine their reasons for acquiring autographs on their memorabilia. Hobbyists collect for many reasons, but mostly to have fun and build a unique collection. The autograph craze is a temporary condition which can be attributed to unethical dealers and promoters driving the prices up on their memorabilia. The hobbyist can find other ways to acquire autographed memorabilia and should not become impulsive buyers. The dealers who charge unreasonable prices and take unfair advantage of buyers will quickly learn who controls the marketplace. Remember, the value or worth for an item is only what one is willing to pay.

Collectors must continue to reassess their reasons for continuing to accumulate autographs. Most new collectors, as well as the established ones, simply collect for their love of the game of baseball. It reinforces special memories of historic events and childhood experiences with families and friends. These serious collectors refuse to get caught up in the autograph craze and find other unusual items to have the players autograph.

The hobby will continue to grow and improve. As families continue to interact, a new crop of parents and children will emerge in the hobby. It is the company sponsors, promoters, and dealers who must find an acceptable approach to reach out to the new breed of collectors. Above all, Major League Baseball should reach out to the collectors and fans and become more involved in the hobby. In the long run, the escalating costs for player signings at baseball shows could have a negative effect on the hobby in the future. The major concern for hobby professionals is to find new ways to attract new collectors, children and parents and to make collecting memorabilia exciting and inexpensive.

7. The Hat Collection: Single-Signed and Hall of Fame Hats

Baseball memorabilia has become the most sought-after of all sports collectibles. Collecting baseball relics is a hands-on experience for the hobbyist who desires the addition of other different game items in their collection. Hats are typically most representative of the game of baseball. Collecting game-used items and replica equipment is another excellent option. The purpose of this chapter is to furnish the novice, as well as the established collector, with a cost-effective approach and to explore an inexpensive way to acquire other equipment. While jerseys, signed and numbered limited edition lithographs, game-used baseballs and bats are very attractive for collectors, these items are more costly for the average collector. A practical and economical approach can be the acquisition of authentic baseball hats that have been worn by the players.

Major league baseball hats can be purchased at the stadium, sporting goods stores which carry licensed baseball products, memorabilia shops, at baseball shows and through advertisements in sports periodicals. These hats are full-fitted, sized numerically with increments in fractions (7, 7⅛, etc.). They have New Era 5950 labels and should have Authentic Diamond Collection labels inside, with the major league logo at the back of the hat. Official hats are designed exactly as those worn by the players. Unsigned team baseball hats cost $20 to $36. The New Era official team hats with the major league logo costs $32. The New Era performance on-field game hats are fitted hats for many teams and the cost is $20 to $36. You can purchase these official and licensed baseball hats from the New Era Cap Company by going online to **www.neweracap.com**

Hats are a logical choice for collectors because the fans seem to always be wearing them, they require little storage space, and collectors can acquire game-used hats from the players, at the stadium, from online auctions or purchase them at hobby stores. Game-used hats that can be documented in some manner, by the players or dealers, will have the greatest value. Some of the players have been receptive to giving away their hats. Hats have become more appealing as a collectible and blend in well with other baseball memorabilia. The hobbyist is encouraged to use a hat collection in his design of a memorabilia room.

Major league baseball includes special event hats — All-Star Game and World Series team hats which can be easily purchased by the collectors. Usually, at the conclusion of the World Series, you will see the players on the winning team wearing the clubhouse World Championship hat. Within a day or two, these hats will be available for everybody to purchase at shopping malls and hobby stores. At some baseball shows, the promoter will have a player from the winning World Series team sign the brim of the World Championship hat as a special event item. Many teams furnish team hats as giveaways in a promotional manner.

On July 15, 2008, the 2008 All-Star game was held at Yankee Stadium, "The House That Ruth Built," during Yankee Stadium's final year, as the Yankees will move into a new stadium in 2009. The New Era Cap Company designed three different special event All-Star game hats for collectors and fans to purchase to commemorate the 2008 All-Star game. The 5950 fitted hats can be purchased online for $36 and are described below:

1. Yankees 2008 All-Star on-field game cap with side patch. The side patch is inscribed with MLB (Major League Baseball), All-Star Game, NYC (New York City) and 2008 is written on the patch. The front of the hat has the Yankees' logo and this is the same hat the Yankee players are wearing on the field.

2. Yankees 2008 All-Star game Pinstripe cap. The memories of this All-Star game at Yankee Stadium are designed on this special hat. The fitted 5950 hat is in a striking navy pinstripe. The Yankee's logo is located on both the right and left front of the hat. Major League Baseball All-Star Game is embroidered on the back. The New Era flag flies on the left side.

3. Yankees 2008 All-Star game Fanquest hat. This 5950 fitted hat has the 2008 All-Star Game and the Yankees' logo is inscribed on the front. A map locating the stadium is on the visor and an outline of the stadium is embroidered on the back. The New Era flag flies on the left side.

To initiate a hat collection, collectors could use a silver paint pen or a blue or black Sharpie permanent marker. Although both are used on hats, the silver paint pen seems to show up better on the brim of the hat. Many players will sign on top of the brim, while some sign under the brim. Most often you should use the paint pen for signing; however, a black Sharpie will be acceptable on lighter color hats.

Collectors learn from acquiring single-signed baseballs that it is their responsibility to instruct the players where they want their items signed. As you hand your hat to a player, in a polite manner "Please sign my hat on top of the brim. Thanks, I appreciate it." Similar to a baseball collection, one should request from the players additional writing on a single-signed hat collection. Always ask the players to add historical data — personal information, statistical data and records, significant events (the highs and lows of the game), and career accomplishments. A team media guide is an excellent source that will help collectors ascertain player information. As you begin to conduct your own research, you are becoming a new type of baseball historian with relevant information on the memorabilia you collect. A hat collection is another avenue for collectors to pursue.

Suggestions for Beginning a Hat Collection

- **Planning and preparation is essential for a successful collector.** You need to purchase team hats and writing tools well in advance of the events you can attend. When you wait for the last moment to purchase items, they are usually unavailable. Team hats are not as readily available in stores as are baseballs.

- **Establish a collecting goal.** How do you plan to develop a hat collection? Will you utilize an in-person approach, mail requests, trade with other collectors, and purchase signed hats from hobby stores or at auctions? Whatever approach you use, you should set practical goals that are reachable. As you prepare to meet your goals, you should have plenty of fun learning more about the hobby.

- **Prior to establishing a hat collection, you need to research and know the correct team the players appeared on.** *The Baseball Encyclopedia* is a great resource for this information. Purchase the current edition at your local bookstore. Look for other books with statistical data from the 1940s to the current season. Keep records of career accomplishments of players you may meet. Many of the older players participate on the baseball show circuit.

- **Use the mail request approach to acquire free signatures on hats.** The older retired players continue to be responsive to mail requests. You should be very careful packing a hat because you want to avoid damaging it. Compose a letter with your request and include a paint pen for signing the hat. Instruct the players on how to properly handle your collectible when they return it. It is always a good idea to include special types of pens and protective materials that you want to be used.

- **Be organized when you approach the players.** You should have your hat and signing tools ready when the ballplayers appear. Good organization is an essential skill that will help you succeed with your autograph requests. Hats take more time to sign than other collectibles. Prior to signing, shake the paint pen vigorously up and down for twenty seconds. Press the tip of the pen on a piece of paper to initiate the paint flow. You don't want the players to have to do this. You should take the cap off the pen before handing it to a player.

- **Be courteous and firm with your requests.** Assert yourself in a polite, friendly manner. Practice the following approach in a firm voice. You could say, "I would be honored to have you sign these items." "May I please have your autograph on these items?" "Thank you, I really appreciate it." Should you have an extra item, ask the player if he would like to have it. Being sincere, polite, and assertive in a positive way will make it easier to receive a positive response from the players.

- **Initiate a hat collection.** On a piece of paper, you can make a list of possible baseball themes to pursue. A theme hat collection is an innovative approach and offers a variety of opportunities to collect hats. You can begin with a favorite team collection, popular players, retired player collection using the old-style hats of the 1950s — include players from the Brooklyn Dodgers, New York Giants, Boston (1946–1952) and Milwaukee Braves (1953–1965), and other teams from that era. The Major League Baseball Cooperstown Collection designs the hats of the teams from yesteryear. These hats can be found in hobby stores and sporting goods shops that sell officially licensed Major League Baseball products. The New Era Baseball Cap Company may have some of the old-style vintage hats from the 1950s and 1960s. You can make it an historic theme hat by adding the signatures of a combination of teammates or other players who were involved in memorable events. Would you think about adding Josh Beckett and Mike Lowell on a Boston Red Sox or Florida Marlins hat? They appeared together in the 2007 and 2003 World Series. A good approach for the novice collector is to pursue a single-signed hat collection of the current and future stars of the game. Be creative as you develop unique ideas, and have fun collecting.
- **Design a category for special achievement hats.** Some of the themes in this category include Rookie of the Year, Manager of the Year, Most Valuable Player, 500 Home Run Club, 300 Win Club, 3,000 Hit Club, Cy Young Award, batting leaders, no-hitters, save leaders, and others categories. On a San Diego Padres hat, you could request Tony Gwynn to sign and add "**8 Time Batting Champ.**" The more data collected on a hat, the greater the historical significance for your collection. More and more hobbyists are initiating a theme collection with other memorabilia they collect.
- **Create a Commemorative All-Star hat collection.** A limited amount of specially designed All-Star caps are produced each year prior to the All-Star game. The hats are used as promotional items and given away to sponsors. Baseball fans and collectors can purchase these fitted hats from hobby stores and online from the New Era Cap Company. You can develop a single-signed hat collection of the All-Star players who appear at signings and use a silver paint pen when they sign.
- **Initiate a team hat collection.** This is more of a challenge and will take more time to complete. With this type of collection, you should use a ballpoint pen and request the player signatures under the brim of the hat. The signatures are more legible in this area. Using paint pen for a team hat collection is not the desired method. A single-signed hat collection has more value than a team signed one. With team hats you should acquire 20 to 25 players and include the manager and coaches. A pen enables more players to sign; paint pens and Sharpies take up more space with less room for player signatures.
- **Be discreet at hotels, restaurants, and other places where memorabilia is discouraged.** Larger items like hats should be concealed in a plastic bag until you have permission

from the players to remove it. Always blend in with the other guests and act like you belong there. When you meet the ballplayers, initiate conversation in a polite and courteous manner. At the appropriate time, ask for permission to have your item signed. Only when they approve, hand the hat and pen to be autographed.

- **Collectors can request the player's game-used equipment.** When you develop a relationship with a player who is receptive to signing your items, you should indicate that you collect game-used hats. Offer the player a unique item you would trade for their hat. Some of the players will be receptive to your request and may furnish you their game hat or provide a new signed one. Always be enthusiastic when you approach the players.

Single-Signed Hats

A single-signed hat collection has become more common at baseball shows today and in hobby publications. In addition to selling unsigned baseballs and photographs, the promoters have included the players' hats from the teams they represented, and for the older players — the old-style hats of yesteryear. Also, some promoters at baseball shows have established a limited edition number of signed hats, with in-person and mail-order requests. A

A single-signed hat collection is popular and cost-efficient, and looks great on the wall of a memorabilia room.

single-signed hat will cost a little more than a single-signed baseball, but is affordable for collecting. For the baseball collector, a single-signed hat collection is another wonderful choice for initiating a great collection.

A single-signed hat collection is more desirable for collectors than a multi-signed (two or more signatures) or a team-signed collection (entire team). The hobbyist can develop a theme of interest, such as a single-signed player collection. It is much easier to approach the players in your local area where you can meet them at the stadium, signing events, and baseball shows. This is a good way to begin this type of collection. Whenever possible, you should always use the in-person approach for autograph acquisition.

When you use the mail request approach for autograph acquisition, begin with the less popular players and the older, retired stars. The success rate for these players is much greater. As you gain more experience, you begin to learn more about the hobby and develop more confidence in your ability as a collector. Soon you will make new contacts and find interesting ways to acquire the signatures of the more difficult players.

The previous list of suggestions for beginning a hat collection are applicable for establishing a single-signed hat collection. Additionally, collectors could devise their own commemorative theme hat. From the previous discussions on historic events and individual player accomplishments, you can now create a fascinating commemorative single-signed hat collection. For player accomplishments, for example, you would request a player who received the 2006 National League Rookie of the Year Award, to inscribe this achievement on your hat as follows: Below the player name, he would add, 2006 NL ROY.

Hall of Fame Hats

A single-signed Hall of Fame hat collection could be the pinnacle for the collector. Although this type of collection hasn't received the same attention as a baseball collection, it is becoming more popular. Imagine what a unique experience it would be to collect one autographed baseball hat from each living member of the Hall of Fame. Initiating a Hall of Fame hat collection is a very realistic goal. Collectors are encouraged to pursue a single-signed hat collection using a creative approach in a similar manner to acquiring an autographed baseball collection.

Prior to beginning the collection, the hobbyist should match the player with the appropriate team. The astute collector should first inquire as to which team the players were inducted with. You can obtain this information by contacting the Baseball Hall of Fame Museum. This information is also available by purchasing the Hall of Fame Plaque Card set from the Baseball Hall of Fame Museum in Cooperstown, New York. These Hall of Fame Plaque Cards are commonly autographed by the players and make a great addition to your collection.

To begin a single-signed hat collection, you should purchase the team hat that was worn by the players during the period they played. Many of the hobby stores in Cooperstown, New York, carry the old-style baseball hats from the 1940s through the present day. Refer to hobby publications and inquire at the Baseball Hall of Fame Museum about locating some of the more difficult to find hats. You can also find some specialty stores at shopping malls that sell only the official baseball hats for each major league team.

Single-signed Hall of Fame player baseball hats have more value than multi-signed ones. Actual game-used player hats have the greatest value. A Cal Ripken, Jr., signed, game-used hat from the 1993 season was auctioned for $395. When a player gives you his hat, it is a good practice to write down the date it was given and the circumstances surrounding the gift — teams playing, any historic events that day, and so on.

Another choice for collectors is to purchase single-signed Hall of Fame player hats from reputable dealers. Below is a sampling of the cost — with the lower and higher prices given for an autographed official major league hat. This information has been reported in the *Sports Collectors Digest* hobby publication. Some of the Hall of Famers are listed below.

	Signed Hats — Store Bought
Yogi Berra	$ 95 to $ 110
Joe DiMaggio	$350 to $450
Bob Feller	$ 45 to $ 59
Al Kaline	$ 55 to $ 69
Willie Mays	$ 150 to $ 169
Stan Musial	$ 100 to $ 115
Mike Schmidt	$ 89 to $ 99
Duke Snider	$ 65 to $ 75
Warren Spahn	$ 85 to $ 99

Recommendations for Beginning a Hall of Fame Hat Collection

- **Acquiring the signature of every living member of the Baseball Hall of Fame on an official hat is a practical goal.** Although not as popular as a single-signed baseball collection, collecting single-signed hats is an exciting venture. These autographed hats will make an attractive display in a memorabilia room and blend in with other items.
- **Investigate which players will accommodate your mail requests.** You should utilize the *Baseball Autograph Collector's Handbook*, other reference sources and the Internet address directory. Also, the Internet address directory will include phone number listings. You can call the players and use the skills you have learned about in-person requests. In a sincere, polite manner introduce yourself as a collector and request permission to mail your items to be signed. Remember, nothing ventured, nothing gained.
- **Utilize the services of reputable dealers.** The resourceful dealers could be a real asset in helping you develop your collection. At baseball shows and private signings the players

are paid a negotiated fee based either on an hourly rate or a maximum number of items signed. The dealers will have the players sign all types of collectibles in large quantities. When they have a greater supply than the demand, they will most often lower the price to increase their sales. As a collector you should learn to negotiate on these items. As you become more cognizant of the value of signed hats, don't be afraid to make a reasonable offer prior to purchasing the items.

- **Purchase vintage game-used hats either at an in-person, online or telephone auction.** This is a great way to obtain the game-used baseball hats that were worn by the Hall of Famers. By now you have become a discerning collector, one who requires documentation for any item you may consider purchasing. The vintage game hats will be more expensive. You must require in written form the origin and pertinent information about your purchase.

- **Acquire the old style baseball hats the retirees had worn.** You can purchase the popular older hats of teams like the Brooklyn Dodgers, New York Giants, Milwaukee and Boston Braves, and other style team hats in many stores. At baseball shows you could've purchased the Boston Braves hat and garnered the signature of Warren Spahn with "363 Wins" added on the top of the brim. On the Milwaukee Braves hat you could include Hank Aaron with "755" and Eddie Mathews added "512," representing their career home run totals.

- **Purchase extra paint pens like the Pen-Touch permanent opaque pen.** These quick-drying metallic ink pens need to be replaced periodically. Prior to attending a signing event, you should check the condition of the pen ink. You might consider including an extra new one when you appear at in-person events. Also, include a new one when you make a mail request.

- **Contact the major league baseball teams to acquire game-used hats.** At the completion of the baseball season call your favorite teams to see if you could purchase game-worn player hats. Many teams will donate these hats for charitable events or sell at Fanfest events during the season. It doesn't hurt to make an effort to purchase these game-used hats. The team sales department may indeed be receptive to your requests. In the "Directory of References" the major league baseball team address and telephone numbers are provided.

- **It may be more cost effective to purchase official baseball hats in bulk.** Collectors should contact hobby stores and examine publication advertisements to see whether buying hats in quantities of a dozen or more will provide better prices. Having a large supply of hats will not only make you more prepared for other collecting opportunities, but will enable collectors to be creative in developing distinct Hall of Fame themes. Many of the Hall of Famers participate on the baseball show circuit throughout the year, as collectors are always looking for a challenging approach in autograph acquisition.

A team hat collection is an example of a theme display.

Hats are beginning to generate a newfound interest for the hobbyist who wants to acquire other game equipment that identifies the game of baseball. They offer the collector an inexpensive choice and make a great addition on the walls of a memorabilia room. It blends in well with other memorabilia, as well as providing an opportunity to display game-used equipment furnished by the players. The most appealing type of hat collection is a single-signed player collection. This offers collectors an interesting approach to obtain the signatures of the current players, retired players, and the older players from yesteryear — from the 1940s through the 1950s. As with other types of collections it is important to use the official major league hats, commemorative hats, and the Cooperstown Collection old-style hats.

Initiating a team hat collection of the entire roster of players is more of a challenge, but is time-consuming and can be very difficult to accomplish. It may not be desirable and practical for many collectors. A more practical approach might be the addition of a few players from the same team signing a team hat (multi-signed hat collection).

As the hobby continues to mature, collectors can find other creative and unique methods to design a hat collection. Another interesting approach can be a single-signed

A baseball hat blends in with other collectibles and makes an outstanding display.

accomplishment hat collection with the players adding their significant contributions to the game of baseball (their achievements and records). Many baseball show promoters will provide a special show item, such as single-signed official major league hats with the autograph guest adding their significant accomplishment on the hat.

As the collectors become more aware of interesting ways to design a collection, they can share their information with others. The ultimate goal is to collect baseball memorabilia for fun.

8. The Bat Collection

The pitcher looks in for the sign from the catcher, the batter stares back in defiance, the pitcher unleashes a fastball towards the plate, and the batter decides in an instant to swing. It is the crack of the bat against the ball that epitomizes the game of baseball. The words "stick" and "club" refer to a player's most valuable tool, his bat. In the movie *The Natural*, Roy Hobbs electrifies the crowd with his bat, hitting monumental home runs that destroy the stadium lights. The bat has provided significant appeal for collectors and baseball.

Since 1990 there has been an increased interest by collectors in acquiring autographed bats. Game-used bats are most preferable and more costly. Collectors can find bats from the great players of the 1970s in hobby stores for bargain prices. You can find a game-used bat that was used by George Brett and Robin Yount between $1,500 and $1,700.

From 1997 up to the present time, a new interest in the hobby is collecting commemorative bats and obtaining the signatures of the Hall of Fame members on single-signed professional model bats. The hobbyist can purchase a professional game model bat online for $50 to $75. Some collectors will purchase a store bat (pro stock model) and add 25 to 30 Hall of Fame player signatures on the bat. Although not as easily procured as other game-used equipment, bats can be obtained from the players. Team personnel and many players will often give away bats to collectors. Some baseball teams will sell cracked, game-used bats at the stadium souvenir store. You can also find game-used bats at hobby stores and from online auctions, and from time-to-time these bats will appear at team charity events.

Game-used bats provide a historical perspective of the game of baseball. Imagine having a game-used Hank Aaron bat in your collection. You may wonder if this bat could have been used when Hank hit one or more of his 755 record home runs. How about acquiring Sammy Sosa's stick? For the collector, the addition of a bat collection will embellish the physical appearance of their memorabilia room, as it blends in with the other different collectibles they have obtained. A bat collection is another innovative approach employed by the hobbyists.

Author Mark Allen Baker reported in his book *Baseball Autograph Handbook* that the greatest obstacles for the novice collectors have been the lack of accurate information to

Opposite: **Game-used bats mixed in with a baseball collection makes an interesting display.**

identify particular bats and the sources to purchase them from. The dealers lack the proper terminology to describe a bat, which adds to the problem. The dealers and collectors need to investigate the classification of bats they acquire, otherwise it will be a poor investment by the beginning collectors.

Because there has been more of an interest in collecting bats, collectors should only deal with knowledgeable dealers who comprehend the system of classifying bats. Before you make a purchase you should ask many questions, no matter how trivial they may seem — a knowledgeable dealer will exhibit patience and answer all of your questions. This is how you attain more knowledge to become a good consumer. When you want to purchase an autographed game-used bat, you may want a letter of authenticity from a major authenticating company certifying that it is real.

In this chapter you will learn about four classes of bats. A bat collection of game-used bats is an expensive venture. Suggestions will be provided so collectors can initiate a bat collection inexpensively.

Classes of Bats

There are many styles of bats, but only four classes of bats:

1. Authentic cracked or uncracked game-used bats
2. Commemorative bats
3. Mint condition (new bats)
4. Model or store-bought bats (pro stock model)

Authentic cracked or uncracked game-used bats

These bats were owned and used by the player whose signature is stamped on the bat or printed in block letters. They are made to the player's specifications as to weight, length, and other personal characteristics. Collectors should be informed that some popular players from time to time will experiment with other players' and team bats during the season. Besides ordering player-designed models, the ball clubs purchase team bats as extras, in case the players use up their allotment of bats.

Team bats vary in size and weight, and are available for all players. These bats have the team's name on the barrel of the bat as a substitute for the player's signature. Under the team name will be a model number as such, Louisville Slugger C271. On the Rawlings Big Stick bats, the player's name appears on the barrel of the bat, but the model number is on the knob. Popular player bats include the Louisville Slugger T141, M110, S318 or the P72.

Opposite: **Autographed game-used bats make valuable and awe-inspiring additions to any collection.**

Cal Ripken used a black P72 bat at times during the season. Some of the popular players who commonly had given their sticks to fans include Brett Butler, Eric Karros, Don Mattingly, Juan Pierre, Cliff Floyd and many others.

Hobby publications will include the bat company and model number the players used. This will make it easier to correctly identify a particular player bat. For example, knowing that Brett Butler commonly used a Louisville Slugger T141 two-tone brown bat will make you more aware that the bat is authentic when you see one in a hobby store.

Assessing game use is important, and chips, scuffs, dents, and the amount of pine tar used give you clues to the degree of game use. Cracked bats are more readily available because they usually end up with the clubhouse attendant. Some teams have been selling these bats at the stadium or during Fanfest sessions at the beginning of a new season. Generally, the more severe the crack, the less the bat is worth. A bat shattered in half is worthless unless it can be completely repaired without the repair being noticeable; however, the buyer must be informed that the bat was completely shattered during a game.

Collectors should consult with knowledgeable contacts who can provide an objective opinion on the authenticity of a player bat. Additionally, you should do some research on bats before you make a purchase. The most accurate way to determine game use is to have witnessed a player using the bat and obtaining it from the player. Having a player or reputable dealer provide in writing the provenance of the item you have received or purchased will make it a more unique experience.

Authentic, uncracked, game-used bats are less accessible for collectors because most players become attached to and comfortable with their bats. They add tape, file the handles, rub them with sandpaper, add pine tar and find other ways to care for their most prized possession. You can't expect players to want to part with their bat, but from time to time they have given collectors their uncracked or cracked bat as a pleasant gesture when you have requested it. That is why while establishing a relationship with a player, you should try to be honest and sincere, letting him know you collect novel memorabilia he may have more than one of, and may be willing to give away.

A game-used uncracked baseball bat has greater value than a cracked one. The more severe the crack, the more the price should be negotiable. Collectors must scrutinize the appearance of bats to determine whether or not the condition may indicate a hairline crack. When you cannot determine whether the bat is cracked or uncracked and the dealer cannot guarantee the exact condition, you should avoid purchasing that particular bat. Below are some characteristics of authentic cracked or uncracked game-used bats.

Characteristics of authentic game-used and store-bought bats

- **You can detect ball marks, scuffs, dents, and chips which are indications of game use.** Examine a few game-used bats and you will observe the same characteristics. Always ask plenty of questions prior to making a purchase.

- **The bat handle is sticky from the use of pine tar, and the bat may be wrapped with tape to satisfy the needs of the player.** These observations indicate game use.
- **Many players write their number on the knob and barrel end of the bat.** They have used either a Sharpie marker or a paint pen so they can quickly recognize their bat in the rack during the game.
- **On the Louisville Slugger model bat look for the words "Louisville Slugger 125," "Powerized" with the word "GENUINE" followed by the model number.** Under the model number you will find the signature of the player and below it the team name. For example, should you find an Eric Karros model bat at a baseball show, you should observe the aforementioned characteristics on the Louisville Slugger and look for D113 which is the model number of his bat. The model number is adjacent to the word "GENUINE." Karros usually had given away cracked bats during spring training. It was previously mentioned that the Rawlings Big Stick player bats have the player's name stamped on it with the team name below it; however, the model number is on the bat knob.
- **The Rawlings bats are easy to identify with a single colored ring inscribed around the trademark label of the bat.** The Rawlings Big Stick is the companion bat to the Louisville Slugger in the major league bat market.
- **The Adirondack bats continue to appear at hobby shows.** Collectors can detect the style numbers "302" and "302F" on the bats. The 302 style has been a popular selling bat, a personal player model for professional use, while the 302F style is a store-bought bat. The Adirondack Bats, Inc., was purchased by Rawlings.
- **The player bats made from 1943 to 1975 had the model number appear on the knob end of the bat.** These were the Hillerich & Bradsby, Co. bats. The Hillerich & Bradsby Co. logo in the center of the bat was replaced by the current name "Louisville Slugger" in 1980.
- **All Louisville Slugger game bats have the word "Powerized" to the right of the label.** Should you see the word "Flame Tempered" or other writing on a bat, then it can be classified as a store model bat.
- **On the Louisville Slugger bat the player's signature will appear in script if he has a contract with the company, in block letters if he doesn't have one.** Above his signature you will find the word "GENUINE" with the model number alongside it. Under the signature, the team name will appear.
- **Bats represented with numbers and letters and "34 inch" written on the barrel is indicative of a store model bat.** You should carefully check every bat to determine which one is an authentic game-used bat. Ask plenty of questions when you are not certain whether a bat is game-used or a store model.
- **In addition to the Louisville Slugger and Rawlings bats, collectors should become familiar with other game-used bats from companies such as Mizuno, Worth, Cooper and new companies endorsed by Major League Baseball.**

- **Many collectors will acquire from a player or team representative a new bat or one in mint condition.** Since this bat has no game use it cannot be classified as an authentic game-used uncracked bat. It will fall into another type of classification.

Clearly the in-person approach to obtaining a player's bat is undoubtedly the best way to establish a bat collection. All of the characteristics of game use will appear on the player's bat. As a collector, whenever you obtain the player's bats, you should notate either on your computer or on an index file system the date you received the bat, whether it is an authentic uncracked or cracked bat, when it was last used during the season and whether you requested the player's signature on the bat. When you meet the players you can ask some of these questions.

Commemorative Bats

The commemorative bat is a historical piece that honors players, teams, stadiums and special events, including induction into the Hall of Fame and participation in events like the World Series and All-Star games. These bats are appropriately called commemorative because they are dedicated to the memory of certain players, places and historic events.

Commemorative bats make for a great display in a memorabilia room. The bats are most distinguishable by their quality design and decorative style. They allow the collector to design a single-signed as well as a team signed bat collection. Some of the more popular commemorative bats are the ones that honor the Hall of Fame inductees and the stadium bats. A blue or black Sharpie should be used to autograph the bat. For darker color bats a silver or gold paint pen can be used.

The commemorative bat is more affordable than authentic cracked or uncracked game-used bats, more fashionable than the store model (pro stock), and designed for display purposes — all reasons why commemorative bats have been the favorite choice for many collectors. New products that are produced in a limited edition commemorative series have become available for collectors.

The Cooperstown Bat Company, located in Cooperstown, New York, has been licensed by Major League Baseball to create and produce many different limited edition bats —1,000 in a series. These bats are designed in their factory to commemorate the great players, places and events of baseball. They use traditional colors: vibrant ones suitable for current teams, and vintage shades for the old style baseball bats. When you visit the Baseball Hall of Fame Museum in Cooperstown you should stop at the Cooperstown Bat Company at 66 Main Street. Call their toll-free number, (888) 547-2415, to obtain a free catalog.

Opposite: **The bat at left is a game-used, uncracked Brett Butler model, and the other is a cracked, game-used Eric Karros model.**

The Cooperstown Bat Company produced the Limited Edition World Champs Bats (1,000 bats per issue) from 1996 to 2005. Because of the popularity of commemorative bats, these bats were sold to collectors and can only be purchased at hobby stores, through hobby publications, trading with other collectors and from online auctions. The Cooperstown Bat Company has sold the entire collection of the Limited Edition World Champs Bats. From 1995 to 1999 the bats cost $65 unsigned. From 2000 to 2002 the bats were purchased for $75. And from 2003 to 2005 the cost was $85.

The bats featured the team logos with colorful graphics and the World Series notation with the year painted on the bat. Since the bats are a light color, you could request the players who appeared on these teams to autograph the bat with a blue Sharpie. The following limited edition World Champs Bats are listed below and are available in the hobby stores, hobby publications and from online auctions.

- **2005 World Champs White Sox Bat**
- **2004 World Champs Red Sox Bat**
- **2003 World Champs Marlins Bat**
- **2002 World Champs Angels Bat**
- **2001 World Champs Diamondbacks Bat**
- **2000 World Champs Yankees Bat**
- **1999 World Champs Yankees Bat**
- **1998 World Champs Yankees Bat**
- **1997 World Champs Marlins Bat**
- **1996 World Champs Yankees Bat**
- **1995 World Champs Braves Bat**

Famous Player Series

This is the most popular autographed Hall of Fame player series, with a limited edition of 1,000 bats per player. Each bat has a photograph of the player painted on the bat with their name and statistics in colorful graphics. The first Famous Player, the "Pee Wee Reese" bat, initiated this series in 1988. Other Hall of Famers signing 1,000 bats in the Series are George Brett, Yogi Berra, Ernie Banks, Carl Yastrzemski, Stan Musial, Duke Snider, Frank Robinson, Mike Schmidt, and Johnny Bench. In addition to a player photo shot, the bats provide the home stadium in the background. Because of the great demand for these bats, only Brett is currently available for $250. The Hall of Fame player series bats can be purchased in hobby stores today for $275 to $300. This is an excellent price considering the bats are signed by the players.

In 2007 Cal Ripken Jr. was inducted into the National Baseball Hall of Fame, and The Cooperstown Bat Company produced a limited edition (1,000 bats) Cal Ripken Jr.

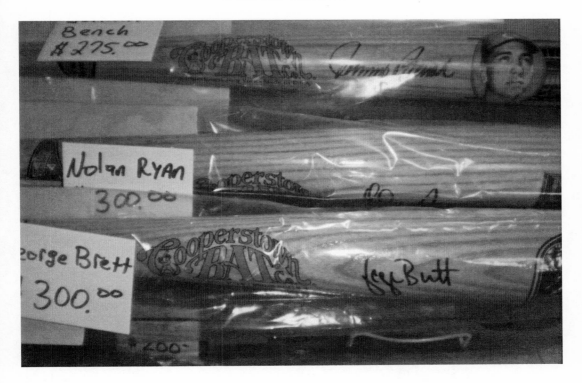

The player series Hall of Fame commemorative bats are a historical addition for a bat collection and can be purchased at hobby stores.

bat. The bats feature a photo of Ripken with colorful graphics, the Hall of Fame logo and inscribed with Cal Ripken Jr. Class of 2007. The cost for each unsigned bat is $105. Ripken autographed 150 bats, which are being sold for $350 for each.

Goose Gossage will be inducted into the National Baseball Hall of Fame on July 27, 2008. To commemorate his induction, The Cooperstown Bat Company designed a Gossage Hall of Fame bat that features a photo of him with 2008 National Baseball Hall of Fame Inductee, his number 54 and his career achievements inscribed on the bat. Gossage signed 554 bats, which are being sold for $300 for each.

During the 1998 season a Famous Pitcher Series Bat was initiated with Nolan Ryan becoming the first pitcher in this series. Tom Seaver was added in this series and he is currently available for $250. The Nolan Ryan Bat was a limited edition of 1,000 autographed bats; the price was $250. All of the autographed bats from the Famous Player Series come with a certificate of authenticity from the Cooperstown Bat Company. The Cooperstown Bat Company sold all of the Ryan commemorative bats and his bat can be found in hobby stores and from online auctions.

Each year since 1993 the Cooperstown Bat Company has produced a 1,000-bat limited edition commemorating the All-Star Game. This bat bears the official All-Star logo and game date. The bat is unique for the collector of special event memorabilia. These bats commemorate the greatest players of the Mid-Summer Classic. Some collectors will acquire the signatures of the American and National League players.

The Stadium Series Bats commemorated the classic ballparks built from 1900 to 1925. The greatest players had memorable games at these wonderful parks. The stadiums that are featured in this series include Forbes Field, Comiskey Park, Sportsman's Park, Briggs/Tiger Stadium, and Jacobs Field.

The Vintage Club Series honor the historic teams from the "good old days" of baseball. The nostalgia of eight teams are featured with colorful graphics, and the team history is painted on the bats. The teams represented in this collection include the Brooklyn Dodgers, Boston Braves, Milwaukee Braves, New York Giants, St. Louis Browns, Washington Senators, Kansas City Athletics and Philadelphia Athletics. Many collectors have pursued the more popular Brooklyn Dodgers and New York Giants players and acquired the

Commemorative team bats are designed for either single or team player signatures. They are affordable and have a decorative appeal.

signatures of many team players on these historic bats. Many teams schedule a theme reunion of the older players from historic teams each season.

The Team Series Bats are designed for the team collector. The commemorative bats recently sold out and were designed with a full-color official team logo, franchise history, and pennant and series wins. Most of the teams are represented in this series in a beautiful 34" white ash bat with a hand-rubbed finish. The player signatures will show up well on these commemorative bats and look great in your memorabilia room. These bats can be purchased in hobby stores and hobby publications.

The Club Series Bats allow autograph collectors to establish a theme collection. The bats have the theme logos in outstanding color decals or can be engraved for Baseball's 300 Win, 3,000 Hit, and 500 Home Run Clubs. You will find many styles of the Cooperstown Bat Company commemorative bats at baseball shows and in hobby stores. The novice bat collectors should investigate these limited edition bats, as they are reasonably priced and make a great addition in a hobby collection. Also, since these bats are limited edition in production, a signed bat will be more valuable in your collection.

Louisville Slugger has joined in with the Baseball Hall of Fame to issue limited edition bats commemorating the induction of players and other personnel into the Hall of Fame. The name of the inductee is engraved with gold letters on the barrel of the bat. Some bats are sold at the Hall of Fame during the induction ceremonies to collectors and members. Since 1988, for each annual ceremony 1,000 bats have been produced.

Mint Condition (New Bats)

The bats classified as mint condition or new bats are authentic bats that lack game use and have no indication that they even touched the hands of the player whose signature is stamped on the bat. Upon examining the bats, there are no physical characteristics like chips or ball marks, which would indicate game use. These bats are often used as promotions for a charitable fundraiser (auction) or as a team giveaway. Some of the players will provide the hobbyist with a new bat during spring training. The bats are considered authentic, as they are made to meet the precise player specifications. The grade of lumber and treatment may vary with mint bats. Some of the player models, which are great for autographs, lack a finishing stain on the bat. Additional tape and pine tar hasn't been added on these new bats.

From the previous discussions of authentic cracked and uncracked game-used bats and commemorative bats, readers should understand that the value varies considerably with mint bats. A game-used uncracked bat has the greatest value — it has a history of actually being used by a particular player and remains in good condition. Player accomplishments were obtained with these game-used uncracked bats. A game-used cracked bat had player usage, with some value, which can only be determined by how bad the crack appears on the bat. The mint condition bat has the least value when being compared to authentic cracked and uncracked game-used bats. It may have the same value as the commemorative bats, which most collectors often use for acquiring player signatures. When Don Mattingly appeared at spring training while playing for the New York Yankees, many of the bats he signed and donated to charities were mint condition bats. These bats were Louisville Slugger T141 model.

As a knowledgeable collector, you should avoid dealers who grade mint bats as authentic cracked and uncracked game-used bats with higher prices. As with other types of memorabilia described herein, collectors should require a written statement authenticating the bats they want to purchase.

Model or Store Bat (Pro Stock)

Bats that can be purchased in any sporting goods store and from hobby publications are referred to as model or store-bought bats. Some players have a contract with a bat company to display their name on these bats as a marketing tool. Many model bats have notations that indicate them as such. These models have notations on the knobs with a single digit number or both initials of the player whose name appears on the barrel of the bat.

Other bats might have the words "PRO STOCK" stamped on the model with MODEL C271 as an example. Both the model number and PRO STOCK are printed in block lettering. Should you find bats with a number, letter and size specification on the barrel, it is likely a store-bought model. These bats can be the Louisville Slugger model that looks like major league versions with a stain finish; however, they weigh less than an authentic game-used bat and do not meet the player's specifications.

Many store bats are designed to appeal to a particular market. The bats may vary in dimensions from a little league type of bat to a semi-pro style. These model bats are not as popular as the previously mentioned bats, but some collectors have initiated a Hall of Fame Bat Collection using the PRO STOCK model bats. These bats can be purchased at sporting goods stores from $20 to $35 for an unsigned bat. It enables the collector to establish a unique bat collection that looks impressive and is inexpensive. The bats are worth much less than an authentic cracked or uncracked game-used bat, commemorative or a mint condition bat.

The older vintage model bats of the great players from the 1940s, found at auctions, are very popular for the established bat collectors. Many baseball teams today sponsor Bat Day as a promotional event and furnish player model bats to the children. Understanding the classification of bats will make you a well informed collector and a better consumer.

Suggestions for beginning a bat collection

- **The beginning collector could pursue a single-signed bat collection.** Both the commemorative and store model bats are more practical to purchase than authentic, game-used bats. It is less costly and less time consuming to acquire the signature of one player than purchasing the signatures of an entire team (team bat collection). Remember, a team bat collection becomes valuable when a team becomes World Champs. Each single-signed player bat from the same team will collectively have more value than one single-signed team bat.
- **You should initiate a bat collection for the thrill of participating in a fun hobby.** You collect autographed bats because you love the game of baseball. A bat collection is a good investment, but for most hobbyists it is far less important than the pure enjoyment of acquiring a unique collection. Most collectors haven't entered the hobby for economic gain, but rather to create valuable collections. Establish a collector-to-collector network for trading and building a unique collection.
- **Become familiar with team sources.** Attend team events and volunteer to assist at team sponsored activities. Interact with the members of the team staff—team executives, business office staff, equipment manager, clubhouse attendants, secretaries—all staff concerned with the day-to-day operations. These contacts can help you acquire authentic game-used bats or mint condition bats and other memorabilia. Reveal to your contacts that you are a collector seeking player bats. With perseverance and patience you will establish an interesting bat collection.
- **Attend team charitable events.** Make a donation for the event, which includes bidding on memorabilia and this is a good opportunity to purchase a collection of either single-signed and team bats. Team players make appearances at these events and this is another excellent opportunity to interact with the players.
- **Approach the players in a positive and sincere manner.** Interact in a favorable way with the players. Make a strong statement that will get their attention so they will want to relinquish their bat. It is easier to make a good impression when no one is around. Some of the best settings to accomplish this are at the stadium when the players arrive, after batting practice or meeting the players early in the morning at their spring training camp. When you meet the players in other places, at restaurants or at the shopping mall, you should approach them in a friendly and positive manner. Come across as a serious collector, and make a good case why you would be interested in having one of their bats in your collection. Should they respond in a favorable manner, make arrangements to obtain their stick. Since many players are superstitious, they will probably give you a new bat.
- **Acquire product knowledge.** Lack of good information and reliable sources to depend on make it essential for collectors to research particular bats that they consider purchasing.

Properly classifying bats will make you a better collector. Consult with other collectors who are extremely knowledgeable about this area of collecting. Get good advice from the collectors you network with prior to making a purchase.

- **Purchase commemorative bats.** Besides being cost effective, the bats signify memories of great players, stadiums, and historical events. They have quality graphics and each bat is hand-finished. The Cooperstown Bat Company has a magnificent arrangement of commemorative bats in a limited edition series. Call the Baseball Hall of Fame Museum to inquire about purchasing the commemorative Hall of Fame Induction Bats. These bats are produced for each induction class, each year.

- **Collect game-used bats from dealers who are specialists in this area.** Some hobby professionals have a relationship with the teams and players, who furnish their game-used cracked and uncracked model bats. These dealers will stand behind their product with a guarantee of authenticity. As a hobbyist beginning a bat collection, you should ask many questions to acquire knowledge prior to making a major purchase. A reputable dealer will share that knowledge because they know an educated collector is good for the hobby and becomes a good customer. It is important to be loyal to reputable dealers who help you accomplish your collecting goals.

- **Purchase store model player bats at hobby shows.** Sometimes at baseball shows you will find a handful of unsigned bats at reasonable prices, with the name of the autograph guest appearing on the bat. When you purchase this replica player model bat and acquire the signature of the player, your item will likely be worth more than what you paid for the items. As an investment, a bat collection will appreciate over time.

- **Establish a Hall of Fame bat collection.** It could be a challenging pursuit to obtain the signatures of all of the living members of the Hall of Fame on a single-signed bat. You can purchase a professional game model bat, use a store-bought player model or commemorative bat, which are inexpensive to purchase. At baseball shows you will pay more for the signatures on a bat than for baseballs or other flat items (photographs or posters). Like other collections, a Hall of Fame single-signed bat collection is the pinnacle. Some collectors will use the PRO STOCK model bat to complete a multi-signed bat collection with 40 to 50 Hall of Famers on a single bat.

- **Develop your own theme bat collection.** From the previous chapters, some of the more popular themes include a single-signed player collection, multi-signatures of two or more players from the same team, an all-time team collection on a stadium or other commemorative bat, historic collecting of the World Series events, and an achievement collection — 500 home runs, 300 wins, 3,000 or more strikeouts, 3,000 or more hits, etc. A good imagination will make your bat collection outstanding.

- **Collectors should use appropriate writing tools.** You should use the popular Sharpie permanent marker for autographing bats. Either the blue or black color is acceptable. You can use opaque inks (paint pen) for autographing darker colored (black) bats. A silver or gold paint pen is acceptable for signing. Most collectors request the signature near the name of the player on the barrel of the bat.

The bat collection offers collectors another avenue to pursue their hobby. Fans interested in the history of baseball, special events like the World Series or All-Star games, and the 500 Home Run Club or 300 Win Club will enjoy collecting commemorative bats, which are great for autographs and display. The black or blue Sharpie is most commonly used and shows up well on the surface of a bat.

Authentic, game-used bats are more expensive to purchase and can be acquired from reputable dealers or through in-person or telephone auctions. Some teams sell cracked bats from the previous season at their Fanfest events each new season. Each bat signed by a player represents a memory that can be stored on the walls of a memorabilia room.

Team bats offer a more challenging pursuit and are worthwhile for team collectors. A World Championship team bat collection has the greatest value. The older vintage autographed team bats may appear at auctions and are more costly to purchase.

More and more collectors are beginning a single-signature bat collection of the more popular players, as well as a Hall of Fame collection of single signatures on commemorative bats. Collectors are searching for interesting ways to document their memories of the great events of the game of baseball. A bat collection is another unique opportunity to collect appealing baseball memorabilia.

9. The Photograph Collection

Baseball is a game that evokes images that are very important to fans but even more meaningful to serious collectors. A photograph collection is another fascinating way to acquire the signatures of the players who educe such visual memories. You can have a signed baseball, hat or bat, but a signed photograph "is worth a thousand words." As you look at a photograph you begin reminiscing about the player or the significant event. The moment captured by a camera is a reflection of an era and a replay of historical events. It freezes that moment of time forever. Most fans can recall their whereabouts when they look at the most historical photographs. In the most storied photographs — the celebration scene of Bobby Thomson's "Shot Heard Round the World," Willie Mays' amazing catch in the 1954 World Series, the Yankee players carrying David Wells on their shoulder after his perfect game in 1998, and who could forget Mark McGwire pumping his arms high above as he rounded the bases during his record-breaking 62nd home run — the action says it all. These spectacular images have seized the moment in such a way as to make a photograph collection a truly special experience.

Mark McGwire's accomplishment of 70 home runs, Sammy Sosa's 66 home runs, and Cal Ripken's 2,632 consecutive games played were great endings to the storybook 1998 season. It was a magical season, a historical one which heightened our love for collecting memorabilia and our passion for baseball. As new records were accomplished by many players, collecting baseball memorabilia became more of a craze. The fans came back to the game as major league baseball experienced increased attendance. The demand for both signed and unsigned items became steadily stronger as new products emerged into the hobby.

The 1998 baseball season will be remembered as a season of historic numbers. For the baseball fans and occasional followers it was an unbelievable visual experience. Thousands of fans and media came to the ballpark very early to watch the players in the home run-chase participate in batting practice. When the game started, as McGwire and Sosa waited patiently for each pitch to reach the plate, the fans took a ready position, waiting for the players to swing, as they simultaneously pressed their cameras. In an instant, the flashing cameras created a beautiful light show, as this routine took place every game, in each new city the players appeared, from August 1998 through the end of the season. The same was true in 2007 when Bonds had belted 755 home runs to stand alongside Aaron. The media and the fans waited for each pitch to reach the plate as they flashed their cameras to capture the historical record-breaking 756th home run. Many baseball fans and professional photographers flashed their camera to capture history in the making. An amazing visual experience, pictures featured daily in the newspapers, and photographs that will be produced by companies like Photo File, licensed by Major League Baseball, will appear at baseball shows and hobby stores for years to come.

Photo File, a New York sports company which sells the official photographs, has the world's largest library of player photographs from Babe Ruth to Stan Musial to Larry Walker. Their photographs include current and retired players, as well as team composite photos and composites of the past and present stars. The photographs that appear at baseball shows are usually purchased from Photo File, which features both an action photo and a portrait shot. Each new season these photographs become available for most players. The collectors have a choice to purchase either photo or both, which can be signed by the players at a baseball show. Most collectors prefer using a blue Sharpie, although some will use a black one on some photographs.

The hobbyist can select a player photograph in the following sizes: 8" × 10", 11" × 14", and 16" × 20". The most common size photograph that can be purchased by collectors is the 8" × 10". Collectors are encouraged to use the smaller photograph for the following reasons: First, at many shows you will be charged a higher autograph fee for larger photographs. Second, since you are encouraged to design your own memorabilia room and display (designing your memorabilia room will be discussed in Chapter 11), you may consider including a photograph collection. When you use an 8" × 10" photograph, you will be able to display more pictures on your hobby room walls than with either the 11" × 14" or 16" × 20" photograph. Therefore, the smaller photograph is probably more practical if your goal is to maximize the amount of photographs displayed.

Photo File includes some other interesting products. Photoramics is a new type of photograph, which is a multiple photograph put into a collage and has a glossy finish. It is a 12" × 36" photograph that includes the 2007 Red Sox World Champions, Mets players Jose Reyes and David Wright in multiple photographs together and a four-team photo display of Nolan Ryan. In 2009 the New York Yankees will move into a new stadium. A multiple photograph was designed into a collage displaying the history of the old Yankees Stadium. A Photoramics display looks awesome in restaurants and memorabilia rooms. The popular Hall of Fame Induction Day Card and the Supercards were discontinued by Photo File.

Another type of photograph collection is a combination photo with two or more players appearing in the same picture. Some are team combinations with the players appearing together. In past years a popular Yankee combination included Joe DiMaggio, Mickey Mantle, Whitey Ford and Billy Martin. New combinations include the current players. Another combination photograph that appears at baseball shows is an unsigned photograph that includes Derek Jeter and Alex Rodriguez. Other combinations include the following:

Brooks Robinson and Frank Robinson
George Brett and Wade Boggs
Will Clark and Tony Gwynn
Willie Mays and Hank Aaron
Rickey Henderson and Lou Brock
Pete Rose, Joe Morgan, Johnny Bench and Tony Perez

You should contact Photo File at (800) 346-1678 to request a catalog of their baseball photographs or visit the Photo File Website (at www.photofile.com). They have a great selection of 8" × 10" individual player photographs (each team), combination photos, a team composite, retired players, and a World Championship team photograph collection. Playoffs and World Series highlight photos become available as soon as they happen.

You can purchase double matted photos, vintage photos, studio portraits, posters, photo keychains, plaques, and Mark McGwire's record-breaking 62nd home run in an 8" × 10", 11" × 14" or 16" × 20" photograph. His photograph was sold for awhile, however McGwire had requested the action photo be discontinued. The company has produced a Sammy Sosa photograph collection which is available for baseball fans. Collectors should find acquiring unsigned photographs easy to accomplish and very affordable.

On the back of each photograph you will read the following disclosure: "The major league club insignias depicted on this product are trademarks which are the exclusive property of the respective major league clubs and may not be reproduced without their written consent. You should never make copies of photographs that you might want to trade or sell. It is illegal and all photo processing companies will look for this disclosure to avoid any problems. You should only purchase signed or unsigned photographs from reputable dealers, or those companies licensed by Major League Baseball."

Photograph Themes

As a collector you may consider pursuing one or more of the following photograph themes:

1. A single player collection of current players from your favorite team.
2. An all-time individual player collection of your favorite team.
3. A photograph collection of the stars of the game.
4. An individual Hall of Fame player collection.
5. A photograph collection of retired and common players (it is easier to obtain their signatures in person or through mail requests).
6. A personal photograph collection where you appear with the players. Some collectors like the players to personalize their signature with the addition of the collector's name.

7. A photograph collection which includes lithographs, posters, paintings and prints of the 500 Home Run Club, 300 Win Club, 3,000 Hit Club or other award categories.

8. A photo collection of stadiums, including stadium prints and drawings. An 8" × 10" photo of the old stadiums like Ebbets Field, the Polo Grounds, Crosley Field, Forbes Field, Comiskey Park and others, looks great in black and white. A 16" × 20" stadium print is recommended for acquiring the signatures of the players who appeared in games at these stadiums. Because you want to add plenty of signatures on a stadium print, the larger-sized ones are more desirable. You should use a blue Sharpie for all player autographs on the prints.

9. A photograph collection of a combination of two or more players. Many collectors will acquire the signatures under each player. You can find team composites with three or four players appearing together at baseball shows and at hobby stores.

10. A team photograph collection of the entire roster. It takes more time to acquire the signatures of the 25 player roster with the manager and coaches.

11. A World Series team photograph collection with the eight position players, starting pitchers, closer, manager and designated hitter for American League teams. It would take less time to collect the signatures on this photograph as these players will become available at different team signing events and during spring training.

12. A photograph collection of World Series game-winning hits, home runs (walk-off) and players scoring the winning run. At baseball shows you can find action photographs of the players with these accomplishments and the special event photographs become available when the players appear at a baseball signing event.

Personal Photograph Collection

Collectors will find many photo opportunities where the players are usually cooperative and delighted to pose for polite people. This is a good time to request their signature on other photographs or items you may be carrying. You should have your camera setting and flash ready when you press the shutter release button. When you hurry to take pictures, most often the photos will look blurry or distorted. It is important to hold the camera securely with both hands. Keep your camera as still as possible, and gently press the shutter release button.

Most collectors today use a digital camera, which is a camera that takes still photographs and video digitally by recording the images on a light-sensitive sensor. These compact cameras can record sound and moving video as well as still photographs. They are easy to use, can be stored in your pocket and have a build-in flash with zoom lens capability. Unlike a regular camera, a digital camera can display an image on the camera's screen immediately after it is recorded and has the capacity to take thousands of images on a single memory card. Digital cameras have the ability to record video with sound, the ability to edit images and the deletion of images allowing re-use of the memory card that is provided. Digital cameras outsell the 35-millimeter type camera, and the more sophisticated digital cameras take the quick action image shots that you get with the 35-millimeter type.

The high-end Nikon D300 camera is suited for the more serious camera buff and has the ability to record images with dimly lit light and can take action shots, six frames per second. It has outstanding photograph quality and can be purchased for under $1,800. The mid-range Olympus FE-230 digital camera is a more practical compact camera which is small enough to be kept in your pocket, it has good picture quality, a built-in flash of low power, sufficient for nearby subjects, a good zoom range and can take many images which can be stored on a memory card. This camera can be purchased for under $200. Digital cameras today will have improved features and you should check in Consumers Reports for newer models that are suitable for a photograph collection.

Some hobbyists use inexpensive throwaway cameras, while a small number of collectors continue to use the 35-millimeter type with a zoom lens. This type of camera gives you the freedom to frame everything, including player portraits and detailed close-up shots. A built-in auto flash helps you capture a subject on a dimly lit night or on a hazy day. Since most of the operations, including film-loading, film speed settings, winding/rewinding, focus and exposure control, are automatic, you can take great pictures with little effort. Also, this will enable you to concentrate on the players, which will help you take consistently superior pictures. Another good feature of a zoom lens camera is a consecutive shooting mode, which enables you to take action shots of the players in succession frame by frame. You should definitely purchase a good camera that you can use for many years when you consider a personal photograph collection. The 35-millimeter camera today is not as popular as the compact digital cameras.

For the novice collector, some practical points are indicated below.

Photograph Process

- **Use a good digital camera with a zoom lens.** The price will vary according to the features you are seeking. Check out newspaper ads and look for sales, especially when newer models become available. You can research cameras on the Internet or look in magazines like *Consumer Reports* at your local library.
- **When the players sign your items use a digital camera to make a video clip with sound.** This is another good way to guarantee that the signatures are authentic. The video clip is stored on the memory device.
- **Check the image on the camera's screen immediately after it is recorded.** Since your focus is photographing individual players, you should take many pictures of each player. You can edit images that you want to have enlarged. Be aware that some pictures will be of poor quality, appearing blurred or distorted and can be deleted. When you photograph your subjects outdoors, it is advisable to avoid shooting into sunlight, as it will

affect your pictures. Always include extra batteries when you attend baseball shows or other events.

- **Purchase the correct film speed for a 35-millimeter camera.** Depending upon whether you will take pictures outdoors or indoors, you should purchase the appropriate film for the setting. Look for DX coded films with ISO ratings (film speed) from 50 to 1600. Use high-speed film such as 400 ISO for shooting indoors, and low speed such as 100 ISO for outdoors. You should consult with the photo processing professionals who can assist when you are unsure what to use.

- **Construct your own photograph collection.** Learn to properly take good pictures and use the zoom mode for close-up player portrait shots. A good way to improve your skills is through practice. Read the manual for your camera which may provide tips on the proper use. You can attend classes on photography which should help you improve your skills.

- **Print your pictures with the use of a personal computer and a printer.** You can print your pictures at home from your digital camera with the USB cable attached to your personal computer and use photo paper to print. You can bring your memory card to a store that has photo processing equipment and select the pictures you want to keep.

- **Upload the images you want to purchase online.** Email the images you've uploaded to the website of the photo processing store and complete the online order form. The images you've selected will be printed online and you should receive them in a couple of days.

- **After developing your pictures, you should enlarge the best photographs.** It is more cost-effective to make an 8" × 10" arrangement which is a desirable size for acquiring autographs. At the photo store you should match your best pictures with the correct negatives (35-millimeter camera), and complete the order form which will be sent to the photo laboratory with your negatives. Your enlarged photographs should be ready in about an hour after it has been digitally scanned at the photo laboratory.

- **Protect your photographs in order to avoid deterioration.** Your enlarged 8" × 10" photographs should be protected from wear and tear and excessive touching, and can be stored in a plastic photograph insert (toploader). You can purchase a soft or hard plastic insert at hobby stores. Preservation techniques will be provided in Chapter 11.

You will find more material written today about a photograph collection in hobby publications, online at team websites, from newspapers and books. Like other types of collections, this is an exciting way to acquire the autographs of active and retired players, as well as historical photographs. Many of the historical photographs enable you to add the signatures of two or more players who played a key role in the outcome of the event. When you meet the players at other events ask questions about the photograph you want signed. You should inquire as to the year and where the photograph was taken. You could ask the players what they remember about the particular picture. Many of the retired players will share a story or experience pertaining to the photograph you handed them. You will listen to some interesting stories.

In 2008 the *New York Daily News* designed photo collection books commemorating the New York Yankees final season at Yankees Stadium. It covers the period of time from the 1920s through 2007. It includes the great teams of the late 1920s, 1950s, 1960s and from 1996–2000. Collectors can go online and purchase this interesting photograph collection from the *New York Daily News*.

For players whose signature is more difficult to obtain in person or through the mail request route, you can purchase cut signatures and canceled checks from dealers and through hobby publications. A cut signature is generally a player's signature on a piece of paper or other type of writing material, which is less expensive to purchase than signed items like a baseball, hat, and bat. You cut around the signature of the player which you can mat on an unsigned photograph.

Canceled checks are the personal checks of the players with their name and address at the top, and their pen signature at the bottom. You can take an unsigned photograph of a deceased player and mat their canceled check with the photograph. While the price for canceled checks has increased, more of these have emerged into the hobby from family members and from the estate of friends of the players. Some of the harder to find autographs of players like Babe Ruth, Ty Cobb, Hank Greenberg, Cy Young and Jackie Robinson are more readily available on canceled checks (you can purchase these at auctions and from reputable dealers).

You should employ the services of a professional framer who will mat your photographs in an attractive manner. This process involves the placement of an autograph between two pieces of cardboard-like material so the signature and photograph are both framed. It is well worth the expense you will incur for a qualified framer's expertise.

Framers possess the skills, tools, and knowledge to use acid-free matting board material (museum quality), which provides the appropriate thickness to prevent the autograph from touching the glass of the frame. Your framed photographs with cut signatures or canceled checks will be well preserved and become more valuable over the years. You should consider that what you have to pay for professional care is a small price for an appreciable investment. The suggestions below are provided to make you more aware of different collecting options. You may utilize some of these ideas to help you design a superior photograph collection.

Suggestions for Beginning a Photograph Collection

- **Initiating a Hall of Fame photograph collection is a realistic goal.** Similar to a single-signed baseball collection, single-signed photographs of the elite players are a more desirable type of collection. It is very easy to acquire player photographs and their signatures at baseball shows. Player photographs can be purchased inexpensively. Many of the Hall of Famers will sign photographs through mail requests. Some request a nominal signing fee for their favorite charity. You should first question the players with a letter to see if they will sign for free, or what they will charge for autographing your photograph. Some of the current players will sign a photograph at the stadium address.

- **Preparation is paramount for a quality photo collection.** You should purchase the necessary materials prior to traveling to events. Keep extra batteries for a digital camera on hand for convenience when shooting outdoors or indoors. Read your camera operation manual to learn the correct method for taking good pictures.
- **Always approach the players in a polite and friendly way.** First request their signature on your items, then obtain permission to have the players pose for a picture. You can begin by saying, "I would be honored to take your picture to include in my photograph collection." You should have your camera ready as the player responds to your request. When you receive their approval you should take a few extra shots, just in case some of the photographs appear blurry or come out over- or underexposed. Don't forget to thank the players for taking the time to interact with you. You might ask other people to assist you by taking a picture of both you and the player standing together.
- **Initiate an individual player photograph collection at the stadium.** Begin taking pictures when you arrive during batting practice. Stand by the dugout area to take great close-up shots of the players in their pre-game practice. You can purchase tickets close to the field on either the first or third base side to take good portrait shots. Prior to game time, some of the players will pose for pictures when you get their attention.
- **It is a good idea to check the team schedule for team Photo Day.** This is an excellent way to go on the field and take pictures of many players. You can enlarge your photograph to an 8" × 10" photo (most common in the hobby and a good size to display), which you can mail to the player at the team stadium with a written request for his signature. Don't forget to include a self-addressed stamped envelope. Many players will honor your request, but due to the volume of mail they receive, it could take a couple of months to receive your signed material.
- **For a personal collection of player photographs, you should develop a good record-keeping system.** Over time it is easy for your items to get lost or damaged, or you may not be able to identify them. Collectors should include the following information: player name on the photograph, brief description of the picture, date when it was taken, and comments about the item. If you still use a 35-millimeter camera you should label your negatives for future use. Keep your individual player photographs in an expandable file alphabetically. You can also store the written information on your computer by using the word processor.
- **Design a theme photograph collection.** The number of baseball themes is endless. Like the baseball, bat, or hat collection, the themes you can create are very similar. Beginning

collectors will find it easier to acquire a single-signed collection of the current players and many Hall of Famers who attend baseball shows. You should look for photographs on items such as the cover of the game day programs, and periodically the Sunday newspaper magazine section will feature a baseball photograph on the cover page.

- **Look for original art, lithographs, prints, and other interesting baseball items related to a player's accomplishment.** Famous artists (Leroy Neiman) create originals and prints in a limited edition, numbered series with the artist signing the piece. You can find these items in art stores, at online auctions, hobby stores and at local art fairs. Some of the more exceptional baseball artwork can be found in museums, which may sell copies (prints) of the artwork. Collectors can purchase these unsigned prints and have the players sign them.

- **Begin a collection of current and older magazines which feature a baseball player on the cover.** The older magazines are not as readily available as player photographs; however, these periodicals have become very popular. You can find unsigned magazines, like *Look, Life, Time, Sport, Sports Illustrated* and others, with a baseball player appearing on the cover at hobby shows and at flea markets. Collectors should acquire the player signatures on a magazine cover using a blue Sharpie. An autographed magazine collection is a unique collectible and is more valuable than a single-signed photo collection. Based on current hobby guide values, you can pay $50 to $75 for an unsigned older magazine (ones with Hall of Famers on the cover may be more costly).

- **Develop basic preservation techniques with a photograph collection.** You want to keep the photograph and the autograph in the best condition possible. New collectors should demonstrate extreme care in properly handling their photographic material. Always hold the edge of the photographs to prevent tears or smudging. When you purchase signed or unsigned photographs, you can also request the hard plastic inserts to protect the photos. The ultimate goal for the photograph collector is to display their signed items. You want your photographs framed by experts who use only use acid-free archival materials.

- **Network with team personnel who have access to player photographs.** When you attend team functions, you can interact with familiar faces from the administrative office. Many of the staff enjoy collecting memorabilia, and this is a good opportunity to trade extra unique items you may have for professional photographs they may possess. It is a good idea to become friendly with the team photographer, who can help you obtain player photographs.

- **Request companies that sell licensed major league photographs to include you on their mailing list.** Photo File, which has the largest collection of baseball photographs, will send you periodic product updates. You can purchase the latest historical and individual player photographs on the telephone. This is an easy way to be prepared for upcoming signing events. In addition, join the National Baseball Hall of Fame, which will send you periodic product updates as well.

- **Purchase unique photographs using your personal computer.** A collector-to-collector shopping service that you can access on the Internet will enable you to purchase photographs, prints, posters, player photo cards, and other interesting items. Some of the more hard to find magazines you may be interested in might be found on the Internet. You can make inquiries when you e-mail other collectors.
- **Store your photograph collection on your personal computer.** Keep your photographs in a folder in your documents and provide a name for the folder. This is an easy way to email photographs and share the pictures with other collectors.
- **Shutterfly.com is a website that deals with a photograph collection.** This website offers photograph books, posters, prints and more. You need to set up an account, upload your photographs from your camera, and either purchase prints from your favorite images or select one of their many pre-designed templates to create your own photograph album and personalized poster. This website will keep your photographs backed up on their server so you will always have access to them.

A photograph collection is another opportunity to collect the signatures of the past, present, and future stars of the game of baseball. Properly framing your photographs with the team colors is recommended. Every collector is encouraged to display their photographs on the walls of a hobby room. Education is the key to becoming a better collector. Collectors can investigate hobby related research materials and share their information with each other. Collectors should read books about the hobby and share the information with other collectors. Like the baseball, bat, and hat collection, a photograph collection is a fun way to collect baseball memorabilia.

10. In Their Own Words

Baseball is a game of skill, strategy, and an accumulation of statistics. It is a team game where the players come together for a common goal — winning games and playing baseball in October at the World Series. Each player aspires for greatness, to accomplish individual and team goals, and one day to be inducted into the Hall of Fame.

For the collector, baseball is a game of fond memories of past and present events, which are preserved by the memorabilia they collect. The hobbyist is searching for unique items from their childhood heroes to the present day. Collectors are a diverse group of individuals who vary in their educational and occupational backgrounds; however, they have a common interest in collecting baseball memorabilia. Each has their own area of expertise, focusing on a theme for their collection.

Many concentrate on a single player collection of baseballs, photographs and other single player items. Some purchase game-used equipment like bats, hats, jerseys, and unusual game items. Others seek an approach to collect individual players, teams and special event pieces in a creative and inexpensive manner. Although they use different approaches, all collectors are searching for the most appealing items for their collection.

The hobbyists are classified by organization of their collections. Some have collections based on themes and others have general collections. Theme collections include baseballs, hats, photographs, bats, letters and surveys relating to individual players, and personal letters obtained from correspondence with the players or others connected with baseball. Theme collections focusing on a multitude of memorabilia signed by one player are usually very interesting. This collection commemorates a player's career and accomplishments; it includes Hall of Fame plaque cards, single-signed Hall of Fame player baseballs, game-used equipment, team produced commemorative items in a limited edition, newspaper accounts, magazine covers, historic prints and other unusual items.

Team executives and family members have direct access to the players, which has afforded them a greater opportunity to plan the best theme collections. Most collectors are unable to obtain such an extensive collection in person; therefore they might find other ways to develop a similar collection. The appeal is usually greater for theme collections, and collectors should expect to pay a higher premium for this memorabilia.

A general collection has no established goals or characteristics, and lacks good organization. It can include many signatures on different items, but it lacks a connection to a baseball theme. The collector is usually inexperienced and doesn't consider grouping the items they collect. They usually purchase inexpensive items, with little concern for authenticity. A general collection is more haphazard with the collector's memorabilia being unrelated to baseball events or milestones. This type of collection lacks cohesiveness due to the collector's inexperience and their random purchases. It can include a baseball signed by a Hall of Fame player, many bench players and coaches from different teams with no team connection or theme.

As you gain more experience, you will obtain a better understanding about collecting baseball memorabilia. Through your associations with other hobbyists, you will begin to establish theme collections, which have become the choice for many collectors.

Some collections have an abundance of unusual autographed memorabilia on a particular player. Some items have been acquired from the player's estate, from family members and friends; other items have appeared at auctions or through hobby publications. The really serious collector will go to extremes to acquire unusual items related to a player's career and accomplishments. They often collect letters from friends, signed contracts, canceled checks, school yearbooks, personal photographs, every baseball card produced for that particular player, and even the player's driver's license (personal possessions).

Collections based on unusual items are becoming more popular in the hobby. In addition to collecting autographed balls and bats, other novel items that you can consider in your collection are team pennants, Hall of Fame postcards, individual player plates, stadium plates, player statues, player bobbing-head dolls (bobbleheads), mini-helmets, player Beanie Bears, books, yearbooks, programs, team-issued collectibles — commemorative pins, commemorative prints, patches, player photo cards, and other unusual memorabilia.

The collector of pins or patches is more interested in acquiring the entire collection rather than individual players' items. It is more meaningful for collectors taking this approach to look for material, rather than the autograph itself. Acquiring an entire set of team pins each season is important to this type of collector. The entire set of pins is related to team events or significant players on the team. Due to their popularity, theme collections have been featured as exhibits in museums and educational centers.

In order to design a significant theme collection of autographed baseball memorabilia, the collector should focus on a creative approach that makes his collection more distinguishable. An innovative hobbyist will search to find an interesting procedure for acquiring autographed items. An interesting and creative approach that most hobbyists haven't explored is a written survey collection prepared for the current and retired baseball players, managers, umpires and others connected with the game. For the more outgoing collector, this is a challenging approach to obtain historical recollections in their own words. This survey collection is called "In Their Own Words."

Survey Collection

This is a self-directed approach, a collector-fashioned written survey collection which can easily be prepared on the word processor of your personal computer with the use of a printer. Collectors can compose their own survey items which provide an insightful perspective on the players, biographical data, individual and team accomplishments, memorable events and historical information. It is an exciting and informative way to document the memories of their performance, in their own handwriting. Through their written words the players are recreating important historical events they've experienced. This is a rare and unique type of collection.

You can design colorful graphics to make the survey more appealing. This is a rare opportunity to acquire the player's response to your survey items in their own words. How many times have you wished you had posed some questions to the players you've met in person? This is a clever approach to use when you meet the players in person and with mail requests.

The Baseball Hall of Fame Museum depends upon donations from individuals with interesting and unusual collections. A well-designed survey collection could be added to the museum for public viewing. A hobbyist choosing to display their collection is providing a wonderful opportunity for the baseball community to share and experience. An example is provided below.

In Their Own Words

Please complete the items below with your signature on item #7. Thanks for taking time from your busy schedule to complete this survey.

1. Name (Nickname)
2. Date of birth
3. Favorite baseball player
4. Occupation after retiring from baseball
5. Provide two highlights from your career
6. Most memorable event from your career
7. Signature

Carl Erskine, a popular Brooklyn Dodgers pitcher, appeared in five World Series, all against the New York Yankees, and was a member of the Brooklyn Dodgers 1955 World Championship team. He was the only pitcher in baseball history to throw two no-hitters at Ebbets Field and in the 1953 World Series, he struck-out a record 14 Yankees batters. He completed the survey collection (In Their Own Words) as follows:

Name (Nickname): Carl "Oisk" Erskine
Date of birth: December 13, 1926

Favorite baseball player: Babe Ruth

Occupation after retiring from baseball: Insurance and Banking

Provide two highlights from your career: I was honored by the New York baseball writers for being the only pitcher to ever pitch two no hit, no run games at Ebbets Field — Cubs — June 19, 1952 and Giants — May 12, 1956

Most memorable event while playing with the Dodgers: As a team the 55 World Series. As a player, setting the World Series strike-out record of 14 against the Yankees — October 2, 1953 — 3rd game.

Signature: Carl Erskine

A written survey collection is a theme collection which concentrates on individual retired and current players. It is a fascinating player collection filled with information about their career, and the uniqueness is having it completed in their own handwriting. The collection is particularly appealing because the information you obtain is firsthand source material in the original form, which can include historical data. Also, this collection can be used for research purposes, and the demand is usually greater for material containing historical content. For example, a set of twenty or more completed player surveys focusing on the Brooklyn Dodgers of the 1950s (Brooklyn Dodgers theme) would be more worthwhile to a serious Brooklyn Dodgers collector who has fond memories of this team and era.

A written survey collection is a thought-provoking experience that you could adapt to your own collecting needs. The aforementioned illustrated "In Their Own Words" survey sheet is a recommendation that will help you begin developing your own interesting survey items. Prepare well thought-out ideas that can attract the players to complete your written survey letter.

In your written mail request or in-person meeting with players, you can demonstrate a genuine interest in, and knowledge of, the players' accomplishments. You might conduct your own research on their career as a way of being well prepared. You want to make a good impression with your presentation, which should be directed in a sincere and friendly manner.

Another creative and interesting approach is to design an "In Their Own Words" collection through the utilization of video and audio equipment. When you meet the players in person you can request their permission for a short interview with a digital camcorder which can record sound. You can ask about six well-planned questions which you can transcribe into a written report on your word processor. After your written report has been completed, you should mail two copies to the players you've interviewed, requesting their signature on one of the copies and providing one for the players to keep. The players likely will value your gesture and enjoy reading the typewritten interview. Don't forget to include a self-addressed stamped envelope (SASE) so your item will be returned in a timely manner.

Please answer the questions and sign below. Some of your answers will appear in a baseball memorabilia book.

1. Name(Nickname) _CARL "OISK" Erskine_

2. Date of Birth _DEC 13, 1926_

3. Favorite Baseball Player As A Child _BABE RUTH_

4. Occupation After Retiring From Baseball _INSURANCE & BANKING_

5. Provide Two Highlights From Your Career _I WAS HONORED BY THE N.Y. BASEBALL WRITERS FOR BEING THE ONLY PITCHER TO EVER PITCH TWO NO HIT NO RUN GAMES AT EBBETS FIELD. CUBS 6/19/52 GIANTS 5/12/56_

6. Most Memorable Event While Playing with the Dodgers _AS A TEAM THE 55 W.S. AS A PLAYER SETTING THE WORLD SERIES STRIKE OUT RECORD OF 14 AGAINST THE YANKEES - OCT 2, 1953 - 3RD GAME._

7. Signature (I will include some of your comments in a story)

Carl Erskine

Another interesting feature of a written survey collection is the educational value of a writing experience that teachers bring into the classroom. Many schools invite baseball players into the classroom to help the students improve their education and become good students. Children are encouraged to be creative and can elicit their own responses to the In Their Own Words survey which can be modified as follows:

Please complete the items below with your signature on item #7.

1. Name
2. Date of birth
3. Favorite teacher, family member and/or baseball player
4. Occupation after graduating from school
5. Provide two interesting experiences you can recall
6. Most memorable event in you life
7. Signature

This is a great opportunity for children to improve their writing skills and develop their own written survey collection.

A written survey collection is important for the hobby as it documents the player responses in a collectible form. Much of this material will be passed on to family members and a future generation of new collectors. Some of the material will be offered through hobby publications and at auctions. Some players understand the importance of the survey process and enjoy sharing their rich baseball experiences. This is an ideal collection for the novice and others who are motivated to collect for their innate love of baseball—a simple game rich in memories and history.

For those who would like to pose questions to the players, you can develop a questionnaire approach with pertinent questions about their career, accomplishments, teammates, memorable individual and team events, as well as what type of memorabilia they have collected during their lifetime. You can design a written letter in a question-answer format, but you should prepare brief and thoughtful questions. When you obtain the written response from the players from a particular team with great history (Yankees, Dodgers, Giants, Indians, etc.), you have acquired a quality historical collection which is a valuable one. Additionally, you have no concerns about authenticity when you document your collection with video and audio equipment, which you use while questioning the players in person.

A written survey collection is time consuming yet very inexpensive to carry out. The opportunity to conduct this approach in person and through the mail is a unique experience for the collector. In a way, you have become sort of a baseball historian as you accumulate a wealth of information "in their own words."

You have been presented with many ideas throughout this book for beginning different types of collections. You are encouraged to collect for the intrinsic value of having fun.

Although some collectors always ask what their items are worth, the real collectors look at their collection with appreciation and dedication, not as a great investment.

Suggestions for a Written Survey Collection

- **Prepare a written survey in typewritten form.** Use your word processor on your personal computer or a laptop to design an easy to read and neat survey. You may want to increase your font size on your computer for the older players. You can include attractive graphics to make your survey more appealing.
- **Provide simple and easy to read instructions to complete the written survey.** Before you provide directions for the survey items, you can add a sentence thanking the players for taking time from their busy schedule to assist you. Use one precise sentence that provides clear directions to complete the items. You don't want to use too many words. You want this to be a positive experience for the players, so they won't mind helping you by completing the survey items.
- **Design a brief, written survey letter.** Be reasonable with your request. You might prepare a one page letter with a maximum of six items and a line for the player's signature. Each item that you consider using shouldn't exceed one typewritten sentence. You want to keep it simple so the players will want to respond. Your goal is to plan interesting and thoughtful items.
- **Prepare a personal cover letter.** Devise a brief and sincere cover letter to include with your survey. You can include a typewritten letter with no more than two paragraphs that will explain your request. Indicate in the second paragraph that you are most appreciative for their taking time from their busy work schedule to assist you. You could be personable by including a positive response as to why you are interested in a survey collection. Remember to include a self-addressed stamped envelope (SASE) for a timely response.
- **Make a request using the telephone.** From your personal computer you can obtain the player's phone number on the Internet. For the more outgoing collector, you can approach the players in a courteous manner, explaining the type of collection you've designed, and you would be honored to have them complete your survey. Many players would be very receptive to an honest and sincere telephone request. You should be confident and friendly when you speak on the telephone.
- **Be creative with your request.** Be aware that the players receive autograph requests on a daily basis. It may be a while before they even have a chance to read your letter. Prior to mailing your cover letter and survey, you should consider an approach that will make your request stand out among the hundreds of letters they receive each week.
- **Conduct research on your subjects.** A well-designed subject collection, such as a written

survey, requires accurate and detailed research application. Prior to preparing a written survey request or a questionnaire, you should authenticate the information you plan to use by consulting verifiable sources for research materials. You can obtain current information that may not be readily available in *The Baseball Encyclopedia* by contacting the Baseball Hall of Fame Museum Library in Cooperstown, New York. Go online to *www.baseball-almanac.com* to obtain current player information.

- **A written survey collection is a valuable educational experience.** When the students formulate questions for player responses (in written form), this is the beginning for students to conduct research. This is a self-directed approach and the students collect biographical and historical information on the players they survey.
- **Purchase a facsimile machine for home use.** When you conduct research for a survey or questionnaire collection, some of the sources you can contact include the sports department of local and national newspapers, the Baseball Hall of Fame Museum, local libraries, hobby publications, the office of Major League Baseball, baseball teams etc. The reference staff from these institutions can fax the material that you need in a timely manner. These machines are inexpensive to purchase and can save you plenty of time in conducting your own research.
- **Collectors might consider sharing their survey collection with others.** The written information that the players have provided is a desirable contribution to the hobby. Collectors could share their interesting material with other hobbyists, send copies of the written surveys to hobby publications, sports journals and other print media services. The publishing community can benefit from this original material which is sought for research purposes. A well-designed survey collection can be displayed as an exhibit for others to experience and enjoy.

Collectors considering constructing their own written survey collection can include the following themes:

1. A team collection of single players from a particular era.
2. Current players from your favorite team.
3. A Hall of Fame individual player collection.
4. A collection of interviews of baseball managers and coaches.
5. A survey of team executives — the owner, general manager, and team president.
6. An all-time collection of single players from teams with great history.
7. Individual players involved in historic events. The highs and lows of baseball.
8. A collection of interviews of retired players from all teams.
9. A collection of interviews of new players (rookies) beginning their career.
10. A collection of surveys of baseball commissioners and former league presidents.

As a collector you will find creating your own survey collection a rewarding experience. You should establish realistic personal goals and good planning techniques. Like other collections, this is another challenge for the hobbyist to find an interesting method to acquire autographs.

The personally handwritten surveys that you receive will be full of interesting stories, humorous anecdotes, fond memories of the game and good lessons about life. Each day you will look forward to your mail to see if the players responded and included their autograph. Many baseball purists and collectors would love to examine the players' thoughts about baseball events that shaped their lives and the lives of the baseball fans. This is exactly the direction for a survey or questionnaire collection — to provide the players' stories in their own words and handwriting. Have fun designing your own collection.

11. Designing a Memorabilia Room and Display

One of the greatest accomplishments for a collector of autographed baseball memorabilia is designing a memorabilia room and display. The ability to design a quality theme collection with different types of items is a realistic goal and a satisfying experience. Throughout this book collectors have been provided with many suggestions to collect autographed baseballs, photographs, magazines, hats, bats, Hall of Fame Plaque Cards, plates, figurines, game tickets, pins, patches, newspaper clippings and other unusual memorabilia. For those who paid strict attention to the suggestions for beginning various types of collections, you probably have acquired a vast amount of memorabilia and knowledge.

In addition to the satisfaction of collecting, an important goal for the collectors of baseball memorabilia is to properly display their collection. This chapter will focus on the organization, planning, storage and design of a memorabilia room in your home or office in an attractive and informative manner. The effort, time and money you spend designing a spectacular collection is well worth it.

In this chapter you will learn how to design and display an autographed memorabilia collection and other unusual items using a theme approach. You will be familiarized with storage devices that have minimal contact with the autographed material and provide protection from environmental deterioration. Information on archival framing techniques for fine works of art will be provided for collectors with a unique photograph collection. Appropriate practices for storing autographed memorabilia will discourage improper handling of the signed items. Planning is an essential element in the process of designing a memorabilia room and display.

Storing your collection can be accomplished fairly inexpensively in a way that preserves the signatures for many years. Many of the materials that you will need to protect and preserve your collection can be readily purchased in hobby stores, at baseball shows and through the advertisers in hobby publications.

Different types of protective cases for your baseballs, bats, and other collectibles, which may be suitable to your particular needs, will be presented in the design phase of your memorabilia room. The names of the suppliers and a telephone listing where you can call to purchase the essential materials will be furnished in the "Directory of Resources." As the hobbyist initiates a collection, it is in his best interest to follow a plan to properly organize, plan, design, use a storage approach, and display his collection. A careless approach to any of these factors can cause your collection to deteriorate and become worthless. Good organization becomes more important as you acquire more memorabilia.

Many serious collectors have traditionally kept their accumulated memorabilia in a closet, in storage boxes, and some have even stored valuable items in a safety deposit box, while others have used nothing more than flat wooden shelving for displaying their collection. Memorabilia that you have no intention of displaying should be properly stored. Proper handling and storage of your items should be maintained with the same degree of care when as you started acquiring the items. A photograph collection that you may wish to display later on should be stored in plastic sleeves in a three-ring binder (loose leaf). It is a good practice to develop written information about each photograph in your collection. In the planning phase of this chapter, you will learn what written information to include with the storage filing system for your photograph collection.

Proper storage of your items is an essential element of preservation. When you visit hobby stores, you can find some autographed baseballs that have become discolored with the signatures fading. Direct sunlight or store lighting too close to the items, over a period of time, can be contributing factors that cause deterioration and diminish the value of the items.

Collectors should initiate a plan of action as a starting point. You can begin to develop your own ideas to avoid problems that may occur from improper handling or storing of the items of your collection. You might want to address the following concerns — how to deal with the concern of direct sunlight, maintaining the proper room temperature, what you plan to do to prevent environmental contaminants, where do you find acid-free materials that you plan to use for storage, the location where you plan to design your memorabilia room, and what materials you plan to purchase based upon the budget you have in mind. These are some of the factors that you should begin to think about. Practical suggestions will be furnished to help you overcome some of your concerns and become motivated to design an interesting memorabilia room and display.

Planning Phase

This is an excellent opportunity to compose a written outline of all the baseball memorabilia that you plan to display. The planning phase is the appropriate time to begin organizing your collection by developing a filing system that is best suited for your needs, as it enables you to document information about each item you've acquired. It is very easy to

Opposite: **An informative display includes baseballs, hats, bats, postcards, photographs, and other items.**

forget the details about each of your acquisitions and very unpleasant when you cannot identify how you obtained the material.

Collectors are urged to initiate a filing system that is specific to their needs. You can develop your own approach that will provide the essential reference information about each item obtained. It really is a good idea to have a filing system so you can always explain the details of every item when questioned. For those collectors who have access to a personal computer with a printer, this is an easy way to record and store your data on each item in your collection. Store the information in your documents and keep it in a labeled folder. The fact that you can find good deals for a computer system with printer and monitor makes this a good choice for collectors to consider.

Establishing a filing system on your computer can be a fun experience, as it eliminates much boring paperwork with written bookkeeping for each item you describe. The benefits for a collector are the easy application of word processing, it allows you to speed up correspondence with others and provides neatly formatted descriptions with automatic spelling-check operations. Additionally, you can network collector-to-collector in the convenience of your own home, you can purchase the newest products for your collection online and investigate other hobby sources through the Internet. You can print out collectible material — a product catalog from the advertiser's webpage — and have the material in your home in a matter of a minute or less. Information on where you can purchase products that preserve your collection will be included in the "Directory of Resources." The use of the computer is the greatest technological contribution that has enhanced the hobby.

Another storage approach utilized by some collectors is a vertical or horizontal file cabinet system. An adapted version of this system, which is recommended for new collectors, is a simple index card and file box system. This index card file system is a cost-effective approach where collectors can construct their own reference information about each item they've obtained. It is easy to record the information about each acquisition on index cards and store each card alphabetically by a theme area or player (team) name in a file box.

You can use larger files for photographs and store them in a file cabinet. Reference material, like brochures, catalogs, periodicals about collecting, and purchase receipts, should be stored in a separate reference file. When you purchase memorabilia from dealers always request a receipt which documents the item, providing the price and date of the acquisition. You will want to include this receipt in your reference file, and don't forget to request a guarantee of authenticity (reputable dealers will provide one).

For valuable documents, lithographs, prints, historic photographs or important letters, you should make copies or photograph the larger items to avoid handling the material. These collectibles that you want displayed should be matted with museum-grade, 100 percent acid-free, cotton rag board material and framed with 97 percent ultraviolet-protected glass. It is recommended that collectors utilize the services of professional framers to preserve and display their valuable artwork, photographs, prints, letters and documents.

According to Mark Allen Baker, in his book *Team Baseballs*, the importance of a filing approach is essential for developing a good display. Whether you use a computer, cabinet file, index card and box storage, or other storage system, you should include the following information (the approach was modified and suggested by Mark Allen Baker):

> Player (team) name, brief description of the item, how item was obtained — acquired in person or purchased, date of acquisition, selling price, seller information (name, address, phone number), condition of item, and for team baseballs include every name inscribed on the baseball and indicate whether the baseball is the official American or National League ball.

Developing the aforementioned approach to help you identify the background of each of your acquisitions will make your collecting experience more meaningful. As you group your collection into baseballs, photographs, hats, and so forth, it will help you in the long run to include a filing storage system approach for each item you've obtained. Whenever you need to document an element in your collection, you know you have this information readily available. Proper cataloging is beneficial for all collectors.

You can use the illustration below as an example and modify it to suit your own needs. Store the information in your personal computer or file cabinet (box). As you initiate the planning phase, you will begin to formulate a design plan for an appealing memorabilia room and display.

Acquisition Profile: List the type of item you've acquired. Provide player name or team name.

Description of Item: Type or write a sentence that best describes the item.

Condition of Item: Indicate whether it is in excellent, good, fair, or poor condition.

Acquired Item (In-Person or Purchase): Indicate how you acquired the autographed item.

Selling Price: The amount you paid for the item.

Seller Information: List the name, address, and phone number of the source.

Date of Acquisition: Record the date and year you obtained the signed item.

Team Baseball: List the names of all players whose signature appears on ball.

Type of Baseball: Official American or National League baseball, fotoball, commemorative or unofficial baseball.

Example of Storage Filing System or Computer Approach

Acquisition Profile: Old-time Milwaukee Braves hat

Description: Replica Cooperstown Collection Hat used from 1953 to 1965

Condition: New hat

Acquired: Purchased at baseball show and signed by the autograph guest, Eddie Mathews

Selling Price: Milwaukee Braves hat $25, Eddie Mathews autograph $20

Seller Information: Hollywood Collectibles, Sterling Road, Hollywood, Florida
Date of Acquisition: December 7, 1997
Type of Hat: Officially licensed by Major League Baseball

Collectors should save any brochures or written material they've obtained about the baseball shows or other collecting opportunities. Newspaper articles promoting the shows where you can purchase player signatures are worth saving. This is good reference information that can be kept in a cabinet file or can be scanned and saved in your personal computer. Should you forget to save this information on your computer, you can always refer to the brochures you've saved from the baseball shows, which will help you update your filing approach.

A good approach to categorizing your baseball collection is by arranging your items into common themes. A theme collection is a good example of a specific interest collection which beginning collectors have been encouraged to pursue. A theme collection can be a single player collection of a special classification of players, like the members of the Hall of Fame; it can be an all-time player collection of all players who played at one time or another for the Detroit Tigers. The information below is provided to assist collectors in planning to organize their collection into a theme grouping. This approach is most effective when you clearly indicate the significance of the items that you group together. You can design your own collection around baseball events that you feel are significant for your personal collecting goals. Use the themes below as a guide for you to follow or to help you develop your own unique themes.

Another interesting approach for experienced collectors can be planning an exhibit of an individual player or a team exhibit demonstrating the rich history of the team through your collection. In either exhibit you can initiate your planning by organizing your collection in chronological order by designing your items around events or accomplishments that occurred at different periods in a player's career or in the team history. For an individual player exhibit, you can arrange signed photographs taken earlier in their career, newspaper clippings, a single-signed baseball and other collectibles that you received later in their career. Presenting a single player collection in sequential order will make your exhibit more interesting for others to experience.

Theme Planning

Some of the themes that can be planned include the following:

- Single-signed Hall of Fame baseball, photograph, hat or bat collection.
- Multi-signed Hall of Fame baseball and bat collection.
- Single-signed Hall of Fame commemorative baseball collection.
- Single-signed Hall of Fame Plaque Card collection.

- Single-signed Hall of Fame Induction Day Cards.
- Single-signed plates, figurines, magazine covers, programs and posters.
- Team-signed stadium artwork — photographs, prints, posters and plates.
- Team-signed baseballs, yearbooks, helmets, bats — yearly collection.
- Single-signed All-Star baseball for the American or National League stars.
- Team-signed All-Star baseball with the players from either or both leagues on the baseball.
- Single-signed commemorative bat collection — Cooperstown Bat Company.
- Team-signed commemorative bat collection — Cooperstown Bat Company.
- Single-signed World Series baseball — players from either league.
- Team-signed World Series baseball — American or National League.
- All-time team signed baseball, bat, print or stadium photograph collection.
- Single-signed old-time hat collection.
- Commemorative accomplishment baseball, bat or photograph — achievement theme includes 500 Home Run Club, 3,000 Hit Club, 300 Win Club, 3,000 Strikeout Club, Most Valuable Player Awards and Rookie of the Year Winners.
- Pins, buttons, patches, pennants, team bobbing-head dolls, player bobbleheads, Beanie Bears, and other unusual items.
- Historic events collection of signed baseballs or photographs of two or more players. Photographs where two or more players appear (combination signatures).
- Single-signed whole game tickets (World Series), ticket stubs, pocket schedules, baseball cards.
- Single-signed canceled check and cut signature collection.
- Historical figures baseball collection — single-signed baseballs of presidents, baseball commissioners, league presidents, retired managers, actors appearing in baseball movies and the great radio and television baseball personalities.
- Signed books, newspaper clippings, special commemorative edition issues (*Sports Illustrated* and other magazines) and media guides.
- Single-signed inaugural team baseball or photograph collection. These collectors will include a display of all unusual inaugural items, team giveaways or purchased items.
- Combination signatures of historical figures who experienced the highs or lows of significant events (World Series, All-Star Games) with their signatures on baseballs, photographs, commemorative items, and other collectibles.

Design Phase

The hobbyist has learned organizational procedures essential for designing their baseball collection. Good planning, cataloging each acquisition in your own collection and developing a theme approach are important characteristics that should encourage you to properly display your collection. Collectors should be aware of storage application procedures, using the appropriate materials to display a creative collection. Collectors are urged to remove their memorabilia from the boxes in their closets and properly store their collection in a memorabilia room where others can view and share their memories.

Natural elements, especially ultraviolet radiation, can have devastating effects on a baseball collection. Collectors need to avoid excessive handling of items that haven't been placed in a storage device. It is during the design phase that you should plan to prevent deterioration, which should be of paramount importance. An explanation of the appropriate materials that can be used for storing and protecting your memorabilia is provided below. These products can be purchased locally at hobby stores or through hobby publications and are essential in the design phase of your memorabilia room.

Storage Application

Some of the storage devices indicated below can be purchased inexpensively. Collectors will be given options to use either the less costly plastic storage devices or the more elegant customized acrylic cases (Lucite cases), which are more expensive but will make your memorabilia room more beautiful. Ultimately, collectors can decide the most practical approach based upon their needs and budget.

Ball Holder

Most collectors store baseballs in round, cubical, or wooden baseball holders. Each one is designed to prevent handling of the baseball, and the selection of the type of ball holder used is based primarily upon your own preference and needs. Some collectors prefer the cube holder for its unique look, and it provides easy stacking. You can request an engravable nameplate for a cube, which should adhere to the plastic. The wood-base ball holder is a round holder attached to an attractive wood base and designed for the placement of an engravable nameplate. Others like the round ball holder (known as a gold base holder) because the baseball has limited movement with an appealing gold base.

When purchased in bulk these materials are very inexpensive. A case of ball holders contains either 36 round- or cube-shaped holders. A case will cost you $52. It will cost about $1.45 for each ball holder when you purchase by the case. This is a good opportunity to share the expense with a friend or other collectors. You can purchase baseball holders at hobby stores or online from hobby publications.

Ball and Card Holder

This attractive display includes a plastic round ball holder and plastic baseball card holder mounted on a wood base with an engraved nameplate. Collectors can include a single-signed

A cube baseball holder has a unique look and is easy for stacking.

baseball in the round holder with the player's baseball card protected in the plastic case. The baseball card could either be signed or unsigned.

Photograph Plaque with Engravable Nameplate

An autographed 8" × 10" photograph can be mounted on the 10" × 13" marble finish plaque with an engravable nameplate. The plaque comes in the following colors: blue, black, teal, burgundy, white, and cherrywood. It is less expensive for collectors to purchase separately the plaque and engraved nameplate, and it is very easy to mount your own photograph with the nameplate.

If you prefer a customized mounted piece from the dealer you will pay more. Some companies that specialize in customized plaques and acrylic displays (see "Directory of References") can provide customized plaques for different sized photographs, yearbooks, commemorative programs, All-Star and World Series game programs, magazines, newspaper clippings, and other types of periodicals.

Baseball Display Case; Three Ball Display Case; 500 Home Run Baseball Display Case; 300 Win Club Display Case

These are common customized hobby storage devices that can be purchased in person or through hobby publications. The aforementioned display cases are elegant storage cases that hold one, three, and all of the single-signed baseballs of each member of the 500 Home Run Club (300 Win Club). Each baseball is stored on a golden display holder with an acrylic cover that slides easily on and off. The acrylic cover sits on an exquisite black acrylic base supported by gold risers. An engraved nameplate can be added on the case, and this is considered the ultimate baseball display.

Baseball Hat Display

An interesting, common, customized storage piece found in many hobby stores and at baseball shows, a hat display is designed with a clear acrylic cover that rests on an attractive black base. Collectors can display a single-signed baseball hat on the black base with the autograph appearing on the brim of the hat and the signature facing the display. You can also find a beautiful clear acrylic batting helmet display case with a black base and a gold glove baseball next to the helmet. Both the batting helmet and the baseball are usually signed by the same player (theme collection).

Photograph and Baseball Display

Collectors can store a single-signed baseball and an 8" × 10" player photograph on a ⅓" thick acrylic black base. A round, clear plastic ball holder is attached on the black acrylic base with an engravable nameplate. Most collectors will include a single-signed baseball in the baseball holder and a signed photograph in the display. In this manner you display different items of a particular player (autographed baseball and photograph). This is a good beginning for developing an interesting theme collection of the more popular players.

Cereal Box Display

Another common hobby storage device is a cereal box display. Collectors can acquire a commemorative limited edition cereal box honoring the accomplishment of a player or a world championship team. Different cereal companies have produced this commemorative series collector's item which can be signed, preferably with a Sharpie. The cereal box can be stored in a clear acrylic display case (looks like a cereal box), attached to a black acrylic base, and includes an engravable nameplate.

The New York Yankees' 1998 World Championship has been showcased on the front of Wheaties boxes in New York. Other commemorative cereal displays have featured individual players such as Cal Ripken, Jr., Ken Griffey, Jr., and Mark McGwire.

Baseball Bat Case

Collectors have a couple of choices available for themselves when they consider a protective storage device that discourages improper handling of an autographed baseball bat. The hobbyist can purchase inexpensive bat tubes to store and protect their signed bats. Another option is a customized deluxe baseball bat case with a clear acrylic cover attached to a black base. The customized case is more expensive and is appropriate for wall mounting. Collectors can purchase a customized bat case suitable to store up to five bats.

Card Plaque; Double Card Plaque; Photograph and Two Card Plaque; Photograph, Card and Ball Plaque

These customized plaques are readily available at hobby stores, baseball shows, and can be found in hobby publications. Each of the aforementioned plaques comes with a cherrywood finish and engravable nameplate. Collectors can display a signed or unsigned baseball card in the 4" × 6" card plaque. A double card plaque, which is 6" × 8", is supported with two baseball cards on the plaque. The photograph and Two Card display is a 12" × 15" storage case which houses an 8" × 10" player photograph and two baseball cards. The photograph, card and ball plaque is an elegant exhibit displaying a signed 8" × 10" photograph, a player baseball card, and includes an autographed baseball in a round ball holder. The ball holder has a gold base attached to the cherrywood finish. In this exhibit, collectors will feature the identical player photograph, baseball card, and a signed baseball. Some collectors will display an autographed photograph, baseball card, and baseball from the particular player being exhibited.

Baseball Storage Case

Hobby companies have developed a 15, 30, 36, and 60 ball holder display case (see "Directory of References"). These customized cases have become common hobby displays desirable for wall mounting and can be designed with natural oak or Lucite material. Storage cases vary in size, style, and by the construction materials used.

Collectors should determine the appropriate size storage case to accommodate the size of their baseball collection and dimensions of the room where the case will be displayed. Storage cases have become more accessible to collectors. A hobbyist who obtained a single-signed baseball collection of all living players inducted into the Hall of Fame could use either two 60 ball holder storage displays or three 30 ball holder displays. Individual preference, as it pertains to the size and style of the display case to accommodate the size of the memorabilia room, is an important factor that collectors should consider when selecting storage displays.

Toploaders (Plastic Inserts)

These products are inexpensive plastic material that protect and store baseball cards, photographs, magazines, programs, pennants, newspaper clippings, and other flat items which vary in size. Collectors can purchase the plastic insert material at office supply and hobby stores, and at baseball shows. Toploaders are used to store items that have been autographed, as well as items that will be signed in person and through mail requests.

This storage device prevents improper handling, accidental folds, tears, creases, and smudges of items that have been signed. Creative collectors can mount their own flat items using a toploader with two-sided adhesive tape, and by purchasing the correct size plaque. The two-sided tape adheres to the back of the toploader, which is mounted onto the plaque.

Shadowbox Photograph Display

This protective storage display includes the plastic frames used to feature the photographs taken with the players and the store-bought player photographs. These box-like frames are an inexpensive way to dress up your autographed pictures. They come in a variety of sizes: 3" × 5", 4" × 6", 8" × 10", 8" × 11", 11" × 14", and 16" × 20". They can be purchased at home improvement-type stores in the shopping malls in your community. This box-like frame has a clear plastic cover that fits into the box portion of the frame. It is easy to assemble and it protects and preserves the autographed photograph.

Custom Framing (Museum Quality)

Large print, lithograph, and poster display for 16" × 20" or larger photographs should be professionally framed by knowledgeable sources who use museum-grade, 100 percent acid-free, cotton rag board matting material and other archival quality material. This process will cost a little more, but it is well worth it in the long run. For a 16" × 20" print, the frame should be 20" × 24", so always allow more space on your wall than the size of the photograph. Let the experts handle your valuable photographs; they know the correct materials to use to prevent any problems.

In planning and designing your own memorabilia room and display, you might plan to utilize many of the aforementioned storage materials in your specific design. Below is a checklist of storage displays that may be suitable for your collection and easy to purchase. You can use the information as a reference tool for your own collection.

Listing of Storage Displays in Designing a Memorabilia Room

Wall-mountable 15, 30, 36, and 60 baseball display cases
Wood, Lucite, and mica shelving

Opposite: **A clear acrylic bat case protects a single-signed bat and makes a great display on a wall of the memorabilia room.**

Baseball storage cases are the ultimate device for a museum-quality display room.

Wood-base baseball holder
Round, gold-base baseball holder
Cube- or square-shaped baseball holder
Wood-base baseball and card holder
Acrylic hat display case
Baseball, photograph, and card holder storage display
Batting helmet with gold glove baseball holder
Major League Baseball jersey display case
Gold Glove single baseball display case
Golden classic deluxe single baseball for a team-signed or single-signed player baseball
Golden classic deluxe three baseball display case
Photograph and baseball display
500 Home Run and/or 300 Win Club display cases
Photograph plaque with engravable nameplate
Customized acrylic bat case
Customized three and five bat storage cases

Store-bought plastic storage bat tube
Custom framing and matting, museum quality for large prints
Magazine, yearbook, program, newspaper custom storage case
Shadowbox photograph storage display
Cereal box storage case
Baseball card plaque display
Double card plaque
Photograph and two-card plaque
Toploaders (plastic inserts — protective covers for small and large items)
Shadow box frames — postcard size for Hall of Fame Plaque Cards

Preservation

Preservation is an important process to carefully protect your collection from harm. You want to deter aging and prevent deterioration due to various conditions that would adversely affect the life expectancy of an object of appreciation. Collector awareness about the care and maintenance of their collection is a major concern.

Preservation issues, such as the prevention of deterioration, the elimination of environmental contaminants caused by lighting, temperature, humidity and the collector himself, as well as the use of museum-grade, acid-free, archival quality materials are important elements that prolong a memorabilia collection. Some concerns that collectors can manage include protecting their collection from the elements of deterioration; avoiding excessive handling of unprotected autographed items; storing paper products such as cards, photographs, magazines and prints in acid-free, museum-grade products; and preventing material from coming in contact with other materials. When paper products come in contact with each other the high acidity will cause the paper to discolor, and the autograph can gradually disappear.

Collectors should become aware of preservation issues prior to the design phase of their memorabilia room. It is very important to understand the correct approach to maintain and care for your collection before you invest a significant amount of time and money to display your collection. Collectors who ignore preservation issues and design their collection in a haphazard manner will assume the risk of making a good collection worthless.

Appropriate preservation practices should be addressed to make the hobbyist cognizant of problems that may arise during the display phase of their collection. Factors that one doesn't consider can contribute to deterioration. Deterioration is a slow process that takes place over a long period of time. Collectors need to use the appropriate writing tools on their items, use the recommended storage devices to protect their collection and frequently inspect their collection to see if there is any deterioration.

The collector's primary concern is to learn how to store and care for his most cherished acquisitions. Preservation knowledge should become the primary responsibility for all collectors. Unusual and historical items that collectors have acquired may be donated to the Baseball Hall of Fame Museum. Ultimately, collectors can care for and maintain good conditions for their collection by acquiring the proper preservation materials to eliminate deterioration. Practical suggestions to help collectors avoid deterioration problems are provided below.

Preservation Suggestions

- **Only use a good quality ballpoint pen to autograph baseballs.** A poor quality ink can fade or discolor over a period of time. Use a Sharpie on photographs, plates, light colored bats, or hats. Some collectors prefer using a good grade blue ink on baseballs. You can use a paint pen on uniforms, baseball shoes, and a black bat. The silver color is outstanding. When a baseball is signed, immediately place it into a plastic baggie to prevent smudging.
- **Avoid displaying your collection in direct sunlight.** Use shades and blinds to block out peak sunlight. Ultraviolet radiation found in sunlight and fluorescent light can have devastating effects on your baseball collection. Collectors can protect their autograph collection from ultraviolet radiation by using Plexiglas framing or other nonreflective glass materials to help shield sunlight in their memorabilia room.
- **Use indirect lighting for display purposes.** Design a lighting system three to five feet away from the signed memorabilia. Heat from light fixtures in a wall unit can cause fading and deterioration. A good lighting system is an incandescent 100-watt bulb, indirectly focused from a distance at least three feet away. Place a fan and light fixture in the center of your theme room a good distance away from storage displays. Avoid high-intensity lighting fixtures that can produce damaging temperatures above 70 degrees.
- **Recommended room temperature for storage and display is 65 to 70 degrees.** The storage area humidity conditions should be 40 to 50 percent. A ceiling fan can supply adequate ventilation with the addition of either central air conditioning or a wall unit. Purchase other shielding materials that will help to keep the room cool and protect your collection from ultraviolet radiation.
- **Humidity can present problems to an autograph collection.** Avoid storing papers in a basement, garage, or closet unless it is properly ventilated. Excessive humidity can cause mold and ruin your autographed materials. One way to deal with this problem is to purchase a dehumidifier for the room where autographed items are stored.
- **Keep the memorabilia room free from environmental contaminants.** Avoid smoking, eating and drinking in the memorabilia room. Always wash your hands before you handle an item. Avoid touching unprotected autographed items. Keep your autographed

baseballs in plastic baggies until you store them in a protective ball holder. When you transfer a signed ball into a protective display, you should grasp the seam portion of the baseball with a couple of fingers and fit it in the display.

- **Dust can be harmful to your collection.** Periodically remove dust and dirt from display cases, plaque displays, baseball holders, storage filing cabinets, fan blades and other storage cases that attract it. Dust carries chemical particles that can cause deterioration. Use the appropriate cleaning materials recommended by the manufacturers.
- **Avoid handling memorabilia.** Keep your memorabilia in display cases. Hold the cases and the baseball holders to examine the signatures. Periodically check all of your signed items for any signs of deterioration. Should some of your autographed baseballs begin to fade or discolor, which are signs of deterioration, you should request professional assistance.
- **Always develop an appropriate plan of action prior to acting.** Design a sketch of your memorabilia room with the display items that you intend to use. Take measurements of your room and purchase the storage display cases that will accommodate the specific size of your room, and address your ventilation needs. Plan to maintain a stable environment for room temperature and humidity.
- **Purchase acid-free, museum-grade materials to preserve your collection.** Use acid-free products for paper materials and baseball clothes (jersey, pants, and jackets). Purchase acid-free envelopes for photographs, postcards, and small prints. Because photograph paper is highly acidic, you should store each autographed picture in a separate envelope. Purchase an inexpensive three-ring binder (loose leaf) to store your photograph collection.
- **Use acetate folders to protect autographed letters and documents.** Acetate folders are available at office supply and photograph supply stores. You can also purchase acetate folders designed for a three-ring binder to make your storage a lot easier.
- **Use professional framers to display valuable photographs.** Let the experts assist you. They utilize 100 percent museum-grade, acid-free cotton rag board matting material and other archival quality materials. A 97 percent ultraviolet-protective glass will prevent the autograph from fading due to lighting conditions. Although the framing process is more costly with professional assistance, it will make the photograph more valuable over a period of time and achieve museum quality. Request the framer to utilize double matting material for historical and significant photographs.
- **Ask the framer to display your magazines or newspapers without using adhesives — staples, glue, or any permanent material that would affect its value or your ability to remove it from the frame if you desire.** Also request that the whole magazine or newspaper be displayed in such a manner as to avoid covering its facing edge by the matting. This will allow the viewer to fully appreciate the effect of the framed item by keeping the item in full view. If the framer doesn't know how to do this treatment, then seek another more qualified framer.

- **When you display framed pictures, you should plan to increase the length and width of the display by a minimum of four inches.** Use the following information as a guide: 8" × 10" photo — frame 12" × 14"; an 11" × 14" photo — frame 15" × 18"; a 16" × 20" photo — frame 20" × 24"; and an 18" × 24" poster — frame 22" × 28". Remember to always allow more space on your display wall than the actual size of the photograph.
- **Consult knowledgeable hobby sources for helpful preservation techniques.** Confer with manufacturers of storage supplies, companies who sell acrylic storage display cases and other reputable dealers for valuable information pertaining to preservation management.
- **Conduct your own research on preservation techniques.** You can consult your local library and museum for reference materials that will help you care for and maintain your collection. Confer with conservators who will furnish helpful preservation ideas.
- **Avoid storing any signed memorabilia with other items.** You should keep the surface of the autographed item free from contact with other materials. Always plan to isolate autographed newspaper articles or photographs in separate acid-free plastic folders.
- **Only use the official American and National League baseballs.** If you cannot purchase the official American and National League baseballs, use the Official Major League baseballs with Selig inscribed on it. Collectors can check a baseball's surface prior to autographing for signs of defective construction and a discoloration on the baseball. You can exchange a defective baseball for one in good condition at your local hobby store. Keep baseballs in plastic bags after being signed to avoid smudging and to prevent improper handling.

Every serious collector of autographed baseball memorabilia has an obligation to preserve their collection. This will require a commitment by collectors to use the proper materials to protect and maintain their prized collection. Neglect on the part of collectors must be avoided because the Baseball Hall of Fame Museum depends upon donations of significant and historical items from collectors to enhance the museum. It is the very unique, most unusual, and appealing items that should be shared with the baseball fans who visit the Hall of Fame Museum each year. The appropriate care and maintenance of a baseball collection rests in the hands of the collector. The responsibility to preserve the past will enable the hobbyist to become more prepared for the future.

Archival Framing Techniques for Fine Works of Art

Museum quality framing: All materials used in museum quality framing should be 100 percent acid-free. Art should be mounted in such a way as to maintain the art in as close to the original condition as possible with no deterioration or damage to the artwork. Acid is one of the most destructive chemicals in framing. Usually the acid found in framing is from wood and wood pulp products such as paper mats, non acid-free paper and tapes.

Light is another destructive property in framing. Ultraviolet lighting is the most damaging given off by natural outside light, fluorescent and halogen lighting. Remember that ultraviolet is non-directional so the art does not have to be in direct light to be damaged. A window in the same room or a fluorescent bulb nearby can still fade art. Cutting any artwork to adjust size or for any other reason is forbidden as it will depreciate the value of the artwork greatly. The goal of conservation framing is to keep the artwork in as close to the original as possible.

Mounting Methods: Mounting methods will vary depending on the type of art being mounted. Standard mounting usually has an acid-free mounting board, usually an archival mounting mat material which is then supported by a stronger material, such as acid-free foamcore or acid-free corrugated board. The art should not be hinged to the foamcore or corrugated board.

The standard method of mounting works of art on paper is using a T hinge with archival tapes or rice paper. Rice paper will require either a rice starch or a methyl cellulose type paste. The hinge should always be fastened to the back of the artwork so there is no chance of damaging the face of the artwork. Also, some pre-pasted tapes are acceptable. A professional framer should test all pre-pasted tapes to make sure they are reversible with distilled water and will not leave any residue behind. The art should only be hinged on the top edge so it will hang freely between the front window mat and the mounting board. If the art is taped on more than one edge it will not allow for expansion and contraction which will cause buckling of the art. The hinge paper should be a lighter weight than the art, in the event it becomes stressed, the hinge will tear before the paper of the art.

Methods for mounting archival photographs differ from that of paper art. If at all possible, no adhesives should be used on photographs. Acid-free photograph corners are available, and framers will make their own corners by folding acid-free papers and then taping the folded corners down so no tape will appear on the photograph.

Cotton rag mats are made of pure cotton fiber which is acid-free and an excellent product. Cotton rag mats are classified as being museum quality. Some acid-free mats are made of wood pulp, which have been totally acid neutralized and buffered with alkali. All matting should be 100 percent acid-free.

Glazing or glass that is used in framing should have good ultraviolet (UV) filtering properties to prevent fading. All glass filters some UV, but only the glasses that have been coated to filter up to 97 percent of UV are considered conservation quality. Acrylic is also another option for glazing and is also available with UV filtering properties. No photograph should be touching any glazing surface.

The frame should be substantial enough to support the art package and glazing according to size. There are methods of support to allow smaller frames to be used on larger pieces. A dust cover is then adhered to the back of the frame to prevent elements from intruding from the rear of the frame. There is an acid-free paper that is available for dust covers. Most framers will do a complete acid-free package and then place a cheaper paper with acid on the back of the dust cover.

Archival Elements of Standardized Framing

Matting: 100 percent rag core, museum-grade mat board provides an acid-free barrier in front of the artwork.

Backing: 100 percent rag core, museum-grade backing board provides an acid-free barrier in the back of the artwork, as well as support for the artwork.

Glazing: 97 percent ultraviolet-protective glass protects artwork against fading due to various lighting conditions. Not to be confused with nonglare glass.

Mounting: Museum-mounting, hinge-mounting, or tab-mounting are some of the most common methods for securing artwork in place. Acid-free tapes or securing devices should be used.

Fillets: When fillets are used they should be lined with acid-free tape or barrier paper to prevent acid from transferring to the artwork. Fillets are decorative wooden mat liners which often come in contact with the artwork.

Frame: Quality frame should be used, matched to the size of the artwork to provide the proper support.

Special Needs: Magazines, newspapers, programs, posters, fliers, and brochures usually require special handling to be displayed properly. These paper products are highly acidic. Magazines and newspapers are printed on paper made of wood pulp. You should research the current market value for your item, then determine if it is worth a minimum or maximum investment to preserve it.

Do's and Don'ts

- Buy the best material you can afford.
- Establish priority in terms of cost for the materials that are essential for the artwork, such as matting and backing.
- Ask if the core is 100 percent rag. Many framers sell an acid-free mat which is only acid-free on the surface paper. They are usually labeled on the sample mat as having an acid-free buffer or 100 percent rag. Avoid using acid-free buffer material.
- Avoid cardboard or chipboard.
- Avoid Formica or plastic frames.
- Avoid permanent mounting adhesives.
- Request information on how your artwork will be handled.
- Ask specifically what materials are used during the construction of the total piece.
- Have a dustcover placed over the back of the completed framed art.
- Avoid taping the rear of the framed art, which is commonly done in place of a dustcover.
- Beware of framing advertising promises. Be a knowledgeable consumer.

- Your most valuable artwork should have the best materials for display. Use good framers for storage and preservation of your artwork.
- Attend art shows and museum exhibits.
- Consult with experts who have a huge investment in artwork. Request their recommendations for the quality framers to utilize.

Display Phase

To properly display a collection, the hobbyist should be aware of good organizational procedures — good planning, designing, storage application, and preservation methods. These essential elements have been discussed in this chapter with suggestions to properly care for and maintain a valuable collection. Frequently refer to the preservation suggestions as you begin to display your own unique collection. You want to avoid any problems that you have the ability to control.

This display phase is the appropriate time to share your collection, through appealing and informative presentation, which provides a feeling of great accomplishment for the collector. It is a remarkable experience to finally be able to properly display your collection after many months of planning themes and exhibits. The good organizational approach has also enabled you to design the best materials to store and protect your collection, and understand proper preservation suggestions that can prevent deterioration problems. The collector should derive as much pleasure in displaying his collection as he did in obtaining it.

The most innovative and inspiring displays can be seen at the Baseball Hall of Fame Museum. Every collector should plan to visit the museum in Cooperstown, New York. The staff at the museum has spent an inordinate amount of time and research to create magnificent displays and exhibits. The displays and exhibits have recreated the memories and nostalgia surrounding the game of baseball. A visit to the museum can motivate you enough to design your own spectacular display. Local museums, baseball memorabilia stores and sports restaurants can provide the collector with good ideas to plan exciting displays.

As you begin creating your own display, you want to develop a common theme which clearly identifies each item and its significance. Sharing your display with other collectors (hobby community) demonstrates the importance and value you have for your collection. A good display with interesting themes will be informative to an observer.

When displaying a single-signed baseball collection of all living members of the Hall of Fame (popular theme), you can install an inexpensive display of wooden shelves on a wall in your memorabilia room. You can store each single-signed baseball in a cube baseball holder and display the baseballs in a stackable manner on the shelves. You should position the baseballs in each cube so the autograph can be viewed by an observer. Every year collectors update their collection by adding new members who are inducted into the Hall of Fame.

A player exhibit in a memorabilia room can include unusual items — team soda-pop bottles, pocket schedules, player team-produced photograph cards, and special whole game tickets from an All-Star or World Series game.

A more creative approach for the hobbyist searching for an appealing way to display their collection has been accomplished by companies designing a variety of wall-mounted display cases. These plastic (acrylic) or natural oak cases, made in several sizes and styles, are becoming more readily available to collectors through advertising in hobby publications and at baseball shows.

A well-designed collection presented in an informative manner, with attractive displays, will have museum appeal. You might select collectible items for your display that clearly represent the message you are trying to convey over the space you have available in your memorabilia room. Attention can be directed on the arrangement of a collection — the size, style and the details of the display. Many of the acrylic display cases have an aesthetically pleasing black background that enables the autographed baseballs to look very impressive on the display walls. The collector is presented with ideas below to utilize the storage materials they've purchased to design their own interesting and decorative display.

Suggestions for Displaying Your Own Collection

- **Use wooden shelves or plastic (acrylic) display cases for a baseball collection.** You can use the cubes and or round ball holders on wooden shelves. On the acrylic display cases each baseball fits into the custom-made case. There is no need for a baseball holder on an acrylic display case. Check the "Directory of Resources" and hobby publications to find these appealing displays.
- **Use the appropriate display case for your collection.** Companies have designed a 15, 30, 36 and 60 baseball case (common custom-made pieces) suitable for your collection. The display cases have either removable tops that slide up and down or a door that opens and closes. You should select a display case that is most suitable for the size of your memorabilia room and for the quantity of autographed baseballs that you've acquired.
- **Design a bat display.** Display companies construct acrylic and natural oak bat cases for a wall-mountable single bat display, two bat, three bat and five bat display. You can purchase these bat cases with telephone orders and you should ask for written instructions for proper wall mounting. Determine the size of the area you plan to use prior to purchasing a particular display. Ask the display company for the measurements of the bat storage case to see if it will accommodate the display area.
- **Plan a hat display.** An easy and inexpensive approach is to display autographed hats on the wall(s) of a memorabilia room. Purchase a box of plastic or aluminum push pins at office supply or school supply stores. Place the push pins at a 45 degree angle to display hats a few inches below the ceiling. This display can wrap around the walls and be used as a border covering. It makes an attractive arrangement with the signature on the brim of the hat very visible. A more costly approach is a customized acrylic hat display case that can be purchased from display companies and hobby stores. These storage cases can be displayed on the shelves in your hobby room.
- **Display a theme photograph collection.** Use one wall to display your autographed 8" × 10" photographs. You can display single-signed player photos using an inexpensive 8" × 10" shadowbox display and or photograph plaques, which come in a variety of sizes. The hobbyist can mount the shadowbox display using a push pin and placing it at a 45 degree angle on the wall. Memorabilia stores supply the plaques and can custom order them for different size photographs. Collectors display All-Star Game programs, World Series Game programs, magazines and commemorative programs on a wall-mounted plaque display. The plaques are very easy to mount on the walls of the hobby room. You can purchase framed photographs that are matted with team colors from hobby stores.
- **Use mica or Lucite shelves to display your collection.** You can purchase the materials and supplies at home improvement stores and mount them on your walls. The shelves are easy to hang on drywall and you could do this yourself. These shelves store wood-base ball and card holder displays, plates, bobbleheads, books, small picture frames,

postcards, tickets, pins, buttons, and other unusual small items. Use the shelves to design an exhibit of a particular player or theme.

- **Create a single-signed exhibit display.** Use a wall-mounted plaque display that is designed to store a baseball in the ball holder, a photograph and whole game ticket, or a baseball card. Display other items of significance relating to a player's career and accomplishments next to the wall-mounted plaque. Display game-used items in a storage case. Be creative in your approach and let your imagination take over.
- **Display interesting artwork.** It is a good investment to use the services of professional framers to handle valuable lithographs, prints, photographs, paintings and other one-of-a-kind items. The appropriate materials will preserve and enhance the artwork, and will also make it more valuable in the future.
- **Plan to secure your collection.** It is advisable to install a home security system. Many security companies have developed a cost-efficient wireless alarm system. Collectors should photograph their collection or make a video of the displays in their hobby room as this is a requirement of a majority of homeowners' insurance policies. Some insurance companies offer coverage for a collection and require an appraisal at the owner's expense. Also, most collectors should have documented their collection using a file cabinet system or storage approach on their personal computer.

The ultimate experience for every collector who has spent years accumulating baseball memorabilia is being able to design a memorabilia room and display. The personal gratification in completing the task and sharing your collection with the public is a wonderful feeling. As the hobbyist has spent time and effort in re-creating the memories and nostalgia of their collection, they should budget some of their funds to protect and preserve their entire investment. The goal for every serious collector should be designing a memorabilia room and display, and having fun in the process of collecting baseball memorabilia.

12. Spring Training and Collecting Autographs

For baseball fans and players spring training is a winter phenomenon, a new season, a new beginning, with expectations of hope, initiation and renewal. It is an exciting time when every team has high hopes and everybody thinks about their team playing baseball in October. For some players spring training brings despair, rejection, and for the old veteran, the injured and the unlucky player, the either comforting or terrifying prospect of closure. Some unknown prospect may step forward to claim his place in our affections. But for six weeks the players hone their skills and practice daily drills that we like to call the rituals of spring training.

Spring training is a happy time after a long, dreary winter without baseball. The winter chill sends baseball fans, families, college students and retirees packing for Florida or Arizona. About the middle of February, the pitchers and catchers and some veteran players report to their spring training camps. The position players usually report to camp during the third week of February, but they are contractually obligated to report around March 2.

Spring training is a time of optimism during the practice days and for about thirty exhibition games. At each camp, the players are relaxed and have pleasant dispositions. For those next six weeks, they will autograph memorabilia for over thousands of fans. The average player signs an enormous amount of autographs each day during spring training.

These fans, collectors, and dealers will begin the annual rites of autograph acquisition by forming long lines, sending a message to the players to sign only one item at a time. A player like Jeff Kent, a 5-time All-Star and baseball's all-time leading home run hitter among second basemen is not one of the more outgoing types. He rarely provides autographs each day during spring training, but in passing he may quickly sign some items. During the Dodgers final spring training in Florida in 2008, he was observed signing for about 200 fans, requesting they act in a polite manner, engaging in good-natured conversation and posing for pictures with everyone who requested his picture. Kent may be inducted into the Hall of Fame one day.

At many spring training camps it is a ritual to wait in long lines for the star players to complete their workout, and hope they will autograph one of your items. Some of the more popular players will autograph one item at the completion of their afternoon workout or after their work is completed during an exhibition game. Usually at many camps you can find lines of 50 or more autograph seekers waiting for their moment to obtain a signature. Some of the players are very accommodating, as they sign for about an hour for the fans. It can become frustrating when you wait in line without acquiring a player signature on your memorabilia. The hobbyist might find it easier to seek out other players they may need in their collection when the players are heading to the clubhouse from the stadium.

Sometimes the players are focusing on their daily preparation during spring training. The general public should realize that what might look like leisure time to the players is actually preparation time. The majority of players are willing to provide autographs for the fans at convenient times. Some may sign at the completion of the morning workout, prior to having lunch. Others might sign when they move to different practice fields or prior to a game. To be a successful autograph collector, it is imperative to approach the players with lots of patience, in a sincere and polite manner.

Most players enjoy signing autographs for children and collectors, but they are turned off by the dealers, who are abusing the opportunity. These offensive dealers attempt to accumulate many autographs by sneaking back into line to get signatures to sell for a profit. The players often agree to a private signing for the dealers — for a fee. Unfortunately, some dealers make it bad for the real collectors by using children to get many autographs.

When the crowd becomes larger during the spring training games, only request one signature on a piece of memorabilia. During the exhibition games, when the players are replaced after a few innings, they appear on the sidelines, signing for the masses of collectors. Once the season begins, acquiring autographs becomes more difficult in person. The players are less accessible during the season, and the teams may schedule occasional 30-minute autograph sessions prior to the game, with a few players appearing. At these events there is a limit of only one signature per person, with a maximum of 300 people placed on three lines.

Spring training is the best time to collect autographs. It is a more intimate time, with many stadiums seating 6,000 to 7,500 and the dugout and bullpen areas close to the fans. Patience and politeness, more that anything else, have enabled collectors and fans to collect an abundance of autographs during spring training.

In this chapter, general suggestions on how to collect autographs during spring training will be provided. Autograph acquisition can be a fun and successful experience at the training sites. Practical suggestions will be given to those individuals who may consider visiting each of the following camps: the spring training site of the Baltimore Orioles, New York Mets, and Los Angeles Dodgers. Each camp is different in its design, but certain similarities exist as far as collecting autographs is concerned. The majority of the major league baseball teams conduct spring training in Florida.

In Florida you can visit the spring training camps of the Grapefruit League on the east and west coast. The Orioles, Mets, Cardinals, Nationals, and Marlins camps are located on the east coast, off Interstate Highway 95. Beginning from the Orioles camp in Fort Lauderdale, the drive on I-95 North at Commercial Boulevard to the Cardinals and Marlins camp in Jupiter takes about an hour. The Cardinals and Marlins share Roger Dean Stadium, which is the newest as well as a state-of-the-art facility. From the Cardinals and Marlins training site, continue north on I-95 for thirty minutes to the Mets training camp at Port St. Lucie. Proceed north from Port St. Lucie approximately 30 minutes to Dodgertown, the home of the Dodgers and which is located in Vero Beach. The Dodgers completed their final spring training in Vero Beach in 2008. In 2009 they will move to Glendale, Arizona and share a new stadium with the Chicago White Sox. And from Vero Beach, head north on I-95 for a 40 minute drive to Viera, where the Nationals conduct their spring training. Collectors will need about three days to visit the spring training camps on the east coast of Florida.

On the west coast of Florida you can visit the camps of the Twins, Red Sox, Reds, Yankees, Pirates, and other teams by driving west on Interstate Highway 75. State Road 60 runs east and west and intersects with U.S. 27, which is close to the camps of the Braves, Astros, Royals, Indians, and Tigers. Many of the spring training sites are nearby, so it is possible to visit two or three camps each day during your stay on the west coast.

Initiating a spring training experience in Arizona might be best accomplished by beginning in Phoenix. From Phoenix the spring training camps of the Cactus League are readily accessible in all directions. The main highway heading north is Interstate 17, while the main approach from the south and southeast is Interstate 10. Driving from the east, U.S. 60 joins with Interstate 10. Fans and collectors vacationing in the Phoenix area can visit the spring training sites of the Angels in Tempe, the Cubs in Mesa, the Athletics and Brewers in Phoenix, the Padres and Mariners in Peoria, the Rangers in Surprise and the Giants in Scottsdale. These camps are all nearby, a 30 to 45 minute drive. From Phoenix proceed south on Interstate 10, a two hour drive to Tucson, to the camps of the Rockies, Diamondbacks, and White Sox. Depending upon the amount of time spent at each site, a collector can possibly visit the three camps in the Tucson area in one or two days. The White Sox will be in Glendale in 2009.

At many spring training camps you will find former players and Hall of Famers serving as spring training instructors for the teams they may have played on. Baseball executives, former baseball commissioners, celebrities from the movies and television, and politicians appear daily with the players during spring training. Collectors have many opportunities to meet appealing personalities.

The retired players and Hall of Famers are very approachable and will sign many of your items during your visit. Many collectors enjoy spring training more than the regular season because of the great potential to build an autograph collection.

Collectors and fans need to realize that the players are not obligated to provide autographs. Their preparation time is for improving their skills and focusing on the game. The hobbyist needs to establish an "autograph etiquette" to make spring training a successful experience. Use the following information as a guideline.

1. Try to be reasonable: hand the player one or two items to sign.
2. Practice good manners and always say "please" and "thank you."
3. Never throw items at players without requesting their permission.
4. Avoid asking for autographs when the players are on the field practicing. It's not an appropriate time to be asked to sign during preparation.
5. Understand that a player doesn't always have time to stop and sign. Sometimes they are focusing on their preparation and shouldn't be disturbed.
6. Interact with the players near the clubhouse after practice.
7. After getting a player to sign an item, collectors need to vacate the area (spot) where they have been standing and allow others to have an opportunity to collect an autograph. Collectors need to be more polite and courteous to each other.

A spring training directory of Florida's Grapefruit League and Arizona's Cactus League has been provided at the end of this chapter to be used as a planning tool by baseball fans and collectors. The directory includes the addresses and phone numbers of the teams, where to write or call for ticket information and call for general information.

Use the phone directory after February 1, when the ticket office is operational. The exhibition games begin at the end of February, so make written inquiries about tickets and request a spring training schedule to be sent to your home. Include a self-addressed stamped envelope with your written request. The stadium telephone operators can be helpful and will provide information about nearby hotels or motels and local restaurants. Prepare your questions prior to calling for information. Purchase individual game tickets using a credit card when you plan to arrive two or three weeks prior to the exhibition games. When the stadium personnel cannot mail out tickets in a timely manner, inquire about picking up the tickets at the "will call" window (separate ticket area with a WILL CALL sign).

Suggestions for Collecting Autographs During Spring Training

- **Make the appropriate preparations for a visit to a spring training camp.** Dress comfortably, wear a hat and good walking shoes. Apply plenty of sunblock and expect the weather to be sunny and hot. Protect your eyes with good ultraviolet-rated sunglasses. Drink plenty of fluids to avoid dehydration and prepare a bag lunch should you plan to stay a few hours or more.
- **Develop a plan of action.** Before arriving at a spring training site, organize your materials, pens, Sharpies, baseballs and other items you may need. Decide which players, spring training instructors and managers you would like to add to your collection. Collectors can plan a single-signed baseball collection which is more practical to initiate. Acquiring a team-autographed baseball collection is a unique experience, but very time

consuming to complete. Use a digital compact camera to document player signings which will guarantee the authenticity of the items they signed. Store this information on your computer.

- **Utilize a waterproof carrying bag large enough to store memorabilia.** It makes it easier to transport and hand different collectibles to the players. Keep baseball cards, photographs, programs and magazines in protective storage holders (toploaders) to prevent stains and the edges from tearing or bending. Keep signed baseballs in plastic baggies or ball holders, and be more careful when it begins raining. The ink can smear and spread when water comes in contact with it.

- **Baseball cards have become popular for autographs.** Purchase inexpensive common baseball cards for autograph purposes. Use an extra fine Sharpie felt-tip pen on baseball cards. Rookie cards and other valuable older cards should never be autographed, since their value is directly related to their condition; that is, collectors prefer such prized items pristine, or nearly so. (The typical signing calls for the card to change hands at least twice and the player, facing what may be hours of hand-cramps and forced smiles, isn't likely to treat your souvenir as gently as you.) Always have your cards and writing tools available when the players approach to sign. Remove the cap from the Sharpie as you hand the players your materials.

- **Acquire a team media guide.** You can either purchase a media guide at the souvenir shop or request one from the team officials who are very accommodating. This informational guide contains the 40-player roster and information on each player, including a profile of statistics from the previous season and over the player's entire career. Also, it makes it very easy to identify players, especially the ones without a name tag on their uniform.

- **Visit one of the spring training camps when the pitchers and catchers report.** Arrive early in the morning, around 8:00 A.M., when not many fans are present and autographs are easy to obtain. For a team baseball collection, start with the manager on the sweet spot, and include the coaches, pitchers and catchers you feel will make the team. Try to be objective with your assessment of which players will make the opening day roster. On autograph requests, ask the players to sign no more than two or three items, depending upon the size of the crowd.

- **Inquire as to which veteran players will be in camp.** Although the focus of this camp is on pitchers and catchers, some veterans arrive early at spring training. They will be working with instructors and move from one area to another. When they complete a drill and move to a different station, this is a good time to approach for an autograph. Have your memorabilia readily available so the players won't have to wait. They may be more receptive to signing a few items when the collectors are prepared. Look for the team executive office and request written materials about the team. At many camps the office staff is very accommodating. Some veterans report early to get in extra batting practice in the cages and on the field. They report with the pitchers and catchers, and you're less likely to find long lines and crowds at this time.

- **Look for familiar faces in the crowd.** Celebrities from other fields, retired players, Hall of Famers, actors, authors, astronauts, and others make appearances at the spring training camps. The celebrities interact with the players and usually spend more time in conversation with the team manager and other team officials. You may find it very easy to acquire autographs from these celebrities.
- **Purchase the local area newspaper.** Collectors can find good information about the players, daily reports on spring training, and which personalities may be appearing at the training site that day. Call the newspaper office and request a spring training issue, a special edition that many newspapers produce. Check the team website online; you can find good information about daily events at spring training.
- **Establish an autograph goal at each spring training site.** Plan to accomplish your goal in a couple of hours and move on. Visit another spring training camp nearby on the same day. Purchase another team media guide and begin the process over again.
- **Plan to return to the camps when the position players report.** Arrive early in the morning, when very few fans are present. The baseball glove manufacturers have a trailer on the complex at many camps where the players go to be fitted for new gloves. This is a perfect opportunity to snag players for their signature. At the beginning of spring training they will definitely be more receptive to signing your memorabilia. Although players may be close to you, never ask for autographs while they are working on drills. When they are finished and walking to a different area, you should volunteer to hold some of their equipment, like a bag or a bat, so that their hands are free to sign for you.
- **Ask a player for their game-used equipment.** If the opportunity presents itself, request a cracked bat, hat or batting glove. You could possibly leave camp with a game-used piece of equipment. During spring training many players have provided children with their jerseys, baseball shoes, cracked and uncracked game-used bats, hats, glove, wristbands and other items. Be sincere and outgoing when you make a request. You can offer a new item as a trade — such as a collectible the player has never seen — for one of their game-used items.
- **A good way to obtain a legible autograph is to approach a player standing still.** When meeting players on the move, greet the player with a hand-shake, which will slow him down. Be personable and request an autograph on your item. In this manner, most players might provide a neat autograph.
- **It's more ideal to wait at the players' clubhouse at the completion of practice or exhibition games.** Most often the players will pass by when leaving, so it is a good opportunity to acquire autographs. Many players sign for 15 to 30 minutes after practice. Some may refuse to sign, but promise to return after showering and changing their

clothes. Be polite and never make a derogatory remark or act annoyed when a player refuses to sign.

- **Approach the players at the stadium prior to the exhibition games.** The players usually interact with the fans and are more receptive to being photographed standing next to you. Request their permission and have your camera ready. This is also a good time to request an autograph on one item.
- **Enlarge photographs that you would like autographed.** Have the local photo processing store convert some of the best photographs into an 8" × 10" size. Collectors can either have their enlarged photographs signed in person during another visit or mail the photos to the player's home stadium during the season. Provide a typewritten request to have the photograph autographed or personalized for you.
- **The players' parking area is another good location to collect autographs.** At some spring training camps, the players' parking area is the same as the public parking. Many of the veteran players carpool with teammates during the exhibition games. The majority of the fans wait by the team bus and are not aware of this. The player parking lot is rarely crowded. The players are receptive to signing a couple of items for the polite and prepared fans when the crowds are smaller after the completion of the game.
- **Purchase the bleacher seats, which are inexpensive and a great location to acquire autographs during an exhibition game.** The bleacher areas at most spring training stadiums are adjacent to the bullpen and outfield area. Collectors can stand by the fence, next to the players, who might sign prior to, during, and at the completion of an exhibition game. During spring training, the players are replaced after a few innings. Most of the players run in the outfield area for about 20 minutes. After the players complete their workout, many might sign in the bleacher area for 15 minutes.
- **Approach the players by the dugout area, which is an easy place to collect many autographs.** Collectors might attend the intra-squad games when the players arrive during the first and second week of camp. Usually, the attendance is sparse at these practice games, which are free for the public to attend. This is a perfect opportunity to collect many player autographs. When the players begin to leave the stadium engage in friendly conversation and request one of their game-used bats. Many players give away their game-used equipment.
- **Many teams schedule a fan appreciation promotional event during spring training.** The teams may arrange for 20 players to provide autographs a half hour prior to the game. The fans are allowed on the field for the signing session with one autograph request per player.
- **Enter the bleacher area, free of charge after the fifth inning.** At many spring training sites, this is a good time to attend an exhibition game. Many of the regular players are replaced and continue to workout near this area. At the completion of their workout many autographs can be obtained.

- **Network with other collectors you meet at spring training.** Collectors should interact with others who have similar collecting interests. This is the perfect time to exchange e-mail addresses, home addresses, and telephone numbers for future correspondence.

Spring Training Camps

Fort Lauderdale

Fort Lauderdale, the Gold Coast of South Florida, is a resort town with miles of quality beach that attracts vacationers to return each year. In 1961 the city fathers enticed the New York Yankees to make Fort Lauderdale Stadium their winter home for the next 34 years. It started with the arrival of Roger Maris and Mickey Mantle, and over the years, when the players reported to camp, you could meet Catfish Hunter, Reggie Jackson, Thurman Munson, Ralph Houk, Yogi Berra, Bob Lemon, Billy Martin, Whitey Ford, Moose Skowron, Hank Bauer, Derek Jeter and the highly publicized owner, George Steinbrenner.

The Yankees had three owners and 13 managers, and won seven pennants and three World Championships during their 34-year stay. In 1994, Steinbrenner decided he could negotiate a better deal in the city of Tampa and move his team into a larger spring training complex. The Yankees remained in Fort Lauderdale in 1995, until their lease agreement with the city expired.

The city fathers quickly negotiated with the Baltimore Orioles who signed a two-year lease for 1996 and 1997 to play at Fort Lauderdale Stadium. The Orioles have continued to sign a one-year agreement each year and are guaranteed to remain in Fort Lauderdale through the 2009 exhibition season. The collectors will be looking forward to garnering autographs from the likes of Cal Ripken, Jr., new players such as Nick Markakis and Melvin Mora, as well as Jim Palmer, an Oriole television analyst and Hall of Famer.

COLLECTING AUTOGRAPHS AT FORT LAUDERDALE STADIUM

Practice Sessions — daily practice for seven to ten days for the Orioles players.

- **Plan to attend the practice sessions.** The stadium is open to the public at no cost. Arrive early in the morning and stand in line by the locked gate. When the stadium gate opens at 10:00 A.M., sit in the first row by the Orioles dugout. This is the best location for acquiring autographs and becomes quickly occupied by 10:30 A.M. From time-to-time retired Orioles players and celebrities appear on the field adjacent to the dugout area.
- **Assume a ready position, with your items, when the players leave the dugout.** Some of the players might provide a few autographs prior to their stretching and working out. The most appropriate time for the acquisition of autographs is after the players complete their workout.

- **Establish friendships with the people sitting next to you.** You and your buddies can assist each other when you need to use the restroom facilities or purchase food and beverages. Vacant seats are quickly taken by incoming collectors. Always have your friends save your seat when you need to leave for a short time.
- **Plan to be prepared for the hot weather.** The practice session usually lasts three hours before the players return to the dugout area. On some days the temperature and humidity may be very uncomfortable. Wear a short sleeve cotton shirt, hat and comfortable sneakers. Don't forget to apply the appropriate sunblock, wear sunglasses and drink plenty of fluids. You should apply the sunblock at least thirty minutes prior to being outdoors. The proper measures taken can help prevent heatstroke. It is a good idea to include a cellular phone in case of emergencies.
- **After completing their workout, the players return to the dugout.** Many will sign along the first-base side and some near home plate. Cal Ripken, Jr., will visit from time-to-time, and is considered the best at providing autographs. When he played he would usually sign daily, providing one autograph for polite collectors. Most of the time he would use his own pen and Sharpie, and sign for about an hour. You could've requested a photograph taken with him, which he was most receptive to.
- **Some players will head for the clubhouse and offer to sign in the player parking lot.** At Fort Lauderdale Stadium this area is fenced in, but along the fence are designated openings for autograph opportunities. You can hand the players items like baseballs, small photographs and bats which fit through the opening. Many players usually accommodate the fans and sign one item.

   Signing habits during the exhibition games —10 to 15 home games.

- **Purchase ticket(s) in the bleacher section.** The visiting team is situated on the third-base side, while the Orioles' bleacher section is on the first-base side. On either side, stand by the fence adjacent to the clubhouse. There is an opening in the fence to hand memorabilia to the players. The players use the clubhouse entrance throughout the game, since there are no restroom facilities in the dugout. When the players return some may sign an item.
- **Stand by the bullpen fence during the game.** After the pitchers complete their pre-game drills, some will come over by the fence and sign for the fans and collectors. Arrive early, when it is less crowded. Although the players are not encouraged to sign during the game, some will provide autographs by the bullpen fence. The entire group of the pitchers sit by the fence.
- **Congregate by the outfield section of the bleacher area when the players are replaced.** During the exhibition games, frequent player substituting is common. When the players are replaced, they run in the outfield for a short time. Many players are responsive to autograph requests when they complete their workout. Most of the visiting team

players sign on the left-field side, while many of the Orioles players sign on the right-field side. Leave one side in the bleacher section and head over to the other side.

- **Cal Ripken, Jr., would sign on either side of the outfield.** When he was replaced during a game, he used the adjacent field to continue working out. He returned to the bleacher section with his own writing implements. He would sign for about an hour and interact with his admirers. Parents would ask him to hold their small infants and pose for a picture, which he was most responsive to. He usually repeated this daily, but was unpredictable as to which side of the bleacher section he would autograph items. Ripken may appear at 2009 spring training as a special instructor.
- **Wait at the bullpen fence or stand by the fence opening by the visitors' clubhouse at the completion of the exhibition game.** Some of the visiting team players might remain and provide autographs. Many fans wait in this area for the players to return from the clubhouse. Some of the players may sign before boarding the team bus.
- **Some of the veterans carpool and congregate in the public parking area, where there are hardly any collectors.** Some visiting team players travel to the camps in their own vehicles. The player parking area is located outside the bleacher section at Fort Lauderdale Stadium. The players may be more accessible to providing autographs here. Always act in a polite and courteous manner, and request only one or two autographs. This is one of those best-kept secrets.
- **Leave the bleacher section and return to the main stadium entrance.** Look for the Orioles executive office and a door leading into the Orioles clubhouse on the right side. Most fans are unaware of this area, which could be a good opportunity to meet some of the players when the stadium has emptied. Collectors will discover the clubhouse when they notice an employee wearing a black Orioles shirt and shorts outside, cleaning the players' baseball shoes. Next to the clubhouse is the Orioles weightlifting room. Some players stay after the game and continue to workout. With patience and time, this could be another way to collect more autographs. The players are approachable and might sign at the completion of their conditioning. This area is usually less crowded after the games.
- **Patronize the more popular restaurants.** Ask the Fort Lauderdale residents where the more popular eateries and entertainment facilities are located. Beach Place in Fort Lauderdale has become a favorite spot for many vacationers. This facility is similar to a mall setting with many stores and restaurants and is located across from the beach. Some players may appear here; however, collectors should never request autographs while they are dining.
- **Autographs can be obtained at the Orioles' hotel.** Spend one evening at the team hotel and keep a low profile. This is a good occasion to meet the current and retired players. Many baseball officials and celebrities appear in the lobby area. Sit in the hotel lobby and act like a hotel guest. Strike up a friendly conversation with the players prior

to making an autograph request. At the appropriate time and in a discreet manner, make your request. Use a plastic type of gift bag to store writing tools, baseballs, photographs, cards, and other small memorabilia that might be signed. Remember to keep your memorabilia in a bag and never expose it for the hotel security to see. They frown upon collectors and will ask you to leave the hotel. Hotel information is provided in the team media guide.

• **Always keep a bag with your materials in your car when traveling.** Collectors may observe the players at local restaurants, malls, and the clubs on the beach. Be polite when you approach the players. Approach the players when they have finished eating or are planning to leave. Request permission to obtain an autograph before you take the memorabilia from your car.

Spring training and collecting autographs at the Baltimore Orioles camp in Fort Lauderdale can be a challenging and positive experience. The close proximity of the stadium, hotel, local eateries, malls, and other areas of interest provide a great opportunity to meet many of the players. This is a time when the players are more relaxed and, in a way, on vacation, too. When you meet players in a setting other than the ballpark, strike up pleasant conversation and let them know you are a collector. Keep the items in a bag, so they aren't visible, and let the player's disposition decide whether he will or will not sign.

Port St. Lucie: The New York Mets' Winter Home

After completing your visit to Fort Lauderdale with a wonderful experience at the Baltimore Orioles spring training complex, you are ready to head over to the New York Mets complex in Port St. Lucie. The collector will drive a short distance east on Commercial Boulevard to Interstate Highway 95, approximately a five minute drive from Fort Lauderdale Stadium. Continue north on I-95 for an hour-and-a-half drive to Port St. Lucie. Exit on 121C, St. Lucie West Boulevard, bear right and make first left onto Northwestern Peacock Blvd. There will be signs along the way to direct you to the Mets spring training camp.

March 5, 1988, marked a new era in Port St. Lucie, Florida. That rainy afternoon, the New York Mets hosted the Los Angeles Dodgers in the first exhibition game at their new spring training headquarters. The fans attending the dedication ceremonies for the new stadium received the first collectible—a game-ticket key holder. The outcome of the game that day wasn't significant, but later in the season the Mets and Dodgers would meet in the playoffs. The Dodgers defeated the Mets and went on to beat the Oakland Athletics in the 1988 World Series.

The St. Lucie County Sports Complex has five-and-a-half fields, as well as covered pitching and hitting areas. The stadium seats 7,367 and the field dimensions are similar to Shea Stadium. The area surrounding the complex is one of the fastest growing regions in the state.

St. Lucie West has become a self-contained multi-dimensional community with residential, commercial, educational, and recreational areas. The area has attracted tourists to its beautiful beaches, new condominiums, restaurants and exceptional fishing and boating. Like Fort Lauderdale, families, college students, and retirees leave the winter behind to spend a week or more at spring training. Some vacationers, known as "snowbirds," spend two to three months here. Some even purchase season tickets to all of the home spring training games at Tradition Field, the home of the New York Mets.

COLLECTING AUTOGRAPHS AT TRADITION FIELD

Practice sessions — daily practice for seven to ten days for the Mets players.

- **Establish a plan of action for autograph acquisition at this complex.** Arrive early in the morning and check out the stadium. Scan the field around the dugout area to detect any players. Look for other areas, where the players might be more accessible, to acquire autographs. To quote Carl Sandburg, "Nothing happens unless first a dream" — an appropriate thought for collectors to develop a vision to accomplish their mission. In his first spring training with the Mets in 2008, Johan Santana attracted huge crowds to the complex. He was the most difficult autograph to obtain and he signed from time-to-time.

- **Plan to attend the practice sessions.** The stadium is open to the public and the Mets began charging $2 admission in 2008, with the money donated to a charity. The players practice daily, seven to ten days. During the week the crowds are much smaller, which affords the collector more opportunities to obtain many autographs. The field level is in close proximity to the stadium seating, which makes it easy for the fans to interact with the players and acquire autographs. Request information at the executive offices — ask for or purchase a media guide and any free publications about the Mets.

- **At spring training collectibles are for sale.** The Mets feature a mobile souvenir truck selling official major league baseballs for $15, every type of Met item including shirts, jerseys, hats and bats with "Spring Training 2008" embroidered on the items.

- **Walk or drive over to the back fields, which are close by.** The pitchers, catchers, infielders, and outfielders work in groups on different fields. The players work on seven smaller diamonds which are fenced off, and rotate with the blast of an air horn every fifteen minutes. The players work on fundamental skills for about a fifteen-minute session. They are approachable and will sign prior to and after the sessions.

- **Observe the players' daily routine.** When the pitchers and position players complete their drills they move to other fields. As they pass by the collectors, they will usually sign for a few minutes.

- **Stay inside the stadium close to the dugout area.** Many players sign inside the stadium after completing their workout. The players walk from the dugout area and sign along the third-base side. Some will sign along the first-base side.

- **After the practice sessions wait outside by the parking lot.** Some of the players will sign outside the stadium, after showering. The players approach the collectors along the closed-in fence of the parking lot, which is on the third-base side of the stadium. The collectors may have a better chance of acquiring many autographs here, since there are only a handful of waiting fans.

   Signing habits during the exhibition games — 10 to 15 games.

- **The best location to obtain autographs is in the bleacher section.** Purchase ticket(s) here and stand along the outfield fence before the game. After the players complete their pre-game drills, some will come over to the fence and sign your memorabilia. Arrive early when there are smaller crowds and a better chance to collect autographs.
- **Stand by the visitors' side of the bleachers, by the fenced-in pitching mound.** Before and during the game, some pitchers might congregate in this area. It is easy to approach the players in this section.
- **Wait along the outfield fence in the bleacher section, either on the first- or third-base side.** During the exhibition games, frequent player substituting is common. When the players are replaced, they run in the outfield for a short time, and many are responsive to autograph requests. Let the players complete their workout before you make a request.
- **Leave the visitors' section of the bleachers after the fifth inning and enter on the Mets' side.** Usually, no employee is collecting tickets at this late juncture in the game. After the sixth or seventh inning you will generally find a group of players congregating in the outfield area. This is also a good opportunity to approach them. At the completion of the game, some players might sign in the stadium along the dugout area to the outfield fence.
- **The players are more receptive to signing after day games instead of night games.** When the players leave the stadium at night, expect the players to be tired after a long day at the ballpark. The fans need to understand that the players are not obligated to sign all the time. Some players may sign in the parking lot for a few minutes. Avoid requesting autographs at the completion of night games.
- **Hall of Famers, broadcasters, and other celebrities are present in the press box area during spring training.** Collectors can approach this area as these individuals leave the booth and exit with the fans. Some collectors wait in the parking lot area. The Hall of Famers and other retired players have been very approachable outside the stadium.
- **Leave the bleachers section on the visitors' side (first-base side) after the fifth inning.** Walk around the stadium to the right field side. As you pass the parking area, you will notice a fenced-in area, which is the bullpen. The bullpen bench is up against the fence with many players congregating. This area is one of those best-kept secrets and is usually unoccupied. It is the best place to obtain many autographs from the pitchers.

Between innings, collectors can approach the players and request their autograph on items.

- **Take a quick drive over to Jupiter, to Roger Dean Stadium.** Head south on Interstate 95 to Donald Ross Road. Go east about a mile to the stadium. The drive from Port St. Lucie to Jupiter, spring training home of the Cardinals, should take approximately 30 minutes. At this site it is possible for collectors to acquire the autograph of Albert Pujols on a single item. Establish a plan of action and be extremely patient with the huge amount of fans who want his autograph.

- **Visit the Cardinals' and Mets' team hotel.** Plan to have dinner at the hotel restaurant and later relax in the hotel lobby. Appear unobtrusive as you observe many players passing by. Some player interviews for the nightly news are conducted here. Approach the players, baseball officials and retired players in a discreet manner. Collectors have been advised throughout this book to always keep a low profile and not to attract any attention. That will encourage a successful experience for acquiring autographs. Purchase the team media guides to provide hotel and player information.

- **Take advantage of the Port St. Lucie area.** It is a great resort town with exceptional recreational activities, entertainment, fishing and dining for all budgets. It is in a good location, close to the spring training camps of the Marlins, Cardinals, Nationals and Orioles.

Dodgertown: Vero Beach, Florida

When you leave Port St. Lucie, travel north on Interstate 95 to Vero Beach, Florida. After a 30-minute drive to Exit 147, continue east on State Road 60 for about seven miles. Turn left on 43rd Avenue. As you enter the city of Vero Beach, there will be signs indicating that Dodgertown is about a half-mile on your left. The Dodgers executives decided that the 2008 spring training would be the final year at Dodgertown.

After 61 years at Vero Beach, Florida, the Dodgers made an economic decision to build a larger stadium with more seating capacity in Glendale, Arizona. The team officials wanted to be close to their fan base in California, which would be a six hour drive from Los Angeles to Glendale. The baseball fans in Florida were saddened by the news of the Dodgers departing the longest held spring training site of any major league team in Florida and Arizona. It has been rumored that the Reds or Orioles would be interested in moving to Vero Beach.

In 1948 the Dodgers came to Florida's Treasure Coast through the efforts of local businessman Bud Holman, for whom the stadium is named after. Before 1948, this location was a United States government naval station. After World War II, the government turned it over to the city of Vero Beach who needed a tenant for this huge piece of real estate. The Dodgers were looking for a spring training home, and Mr. Holman convinced them to come to this sleepy little community for spring training. The Dodgers had signed Jackie Robinson in

1947 and had the vision to bring integration into baseball. At Dodgertown, a self-contained community was developed where white and black players were integrated together — to train, play games, eat in the Dodgertown facilities and sleep in the army style barracks, away from a society that frowned upon integration. And for 61 years the Dodgers had their own spring training camp. A visit to the hallowed grounds of Dodgertown for those baseball fans who have never had the opportunity of experiencing a place known as "baseball heaven" must be included when you plan to visit the Mets, Cardinals and Marlins spring training camps.

The Dodgers play their exhibition games at Holman Stadium, which has a 6,500 seating capacity. The Dodgertown complex, which is a privately owned spring training facility, has six practice fields, ten batting cages with pitching machines, four indoor batting and pitching tunnels, pitching and bunting instructional areas, a state-of-the-art workout room, a 90-unit housing facility, meeting rooms, large swimming pool, four tennis courts, jogging trail, recreation room, and a movie theater. The Dodgertown complex is baseball's most comprehensive spring training camp. It is a baseball hotel and haven for the players, and twice yearly the Dodgers conduct a Fantasy Camp here. A residential community, a public restaurant and lounge, and a golf course at Dodger Pines Country Club encompass the facility.

Visiting the Dodgertown complex is a unique experience where ordinary people walk and interact with the greatest Dodgers players. The enormous facility enables collectors to accumulate autographs everywhere. Dodgertown is considered one of the best spring training sites to obtain autographs because of the facility's wide-open layout. Walking from the practice fields to Holman Stadium, where the exhibition games are played, affords the hobbyist a chance to collect autographs from the likes of Sandy Koufax, Tom Lasorda, Steve Garvey (the 1974 Most Valuable Player), and other Brooklyn and LA Dodger greats. Dodgertown is a fan's delight for its easy accessibility to the players, who enjoy providing autographs.

COLLECTING AUTOGRAPHS AT DODGERTOWN (A TEAM FROM
THE GRAPEFRUIT LEAGUE WILL MOVE INTO THIS UNIQUE COMPLEX)

Practice sessions — daily practice for seven to ten days for the Dodgers players.

- **Plan to attend a practice session.** These sessions are conducted for seven to ten days before the exhibition games are played. The crowds are generally smaller, which makes autograph acquisition more plentiful. Collectors must take the proper precautions — dress comfortably, wear good walking shoes, use sunblock, include hat, sunglasses and drink lots of fluids, otherwise they can become ill from dehydration or heatstroke.
- **Arrive early in the morning about 8 A.M.** Walk around the enormous complex and enter Holman Stadium to become acclimated to the player workout areas. Check out the players' indoor batting tunnel and parking lot, which is nearby. Locate the clubhouse

Retired players (including Steve Garvey, pictured) sign for children at Dodgers Fantasy Camp.

area, which is the beginning and ending point to garner many autographs. The morning practice session begins at 9 A.M. with all players stretching for about 30 minutes. The players break out into groups practicing for two-and-a-half hours. They return to the clubhouse around noon for lunch. Some of the players might sign for approximately ten minutes, while others promise to autograph items after lunch.

- **Walk over to each practice field where the players work on fundamental skills.** The players are grouped by their skill position — the pitchers work on one field, the infielders and outfielders on another field, the players work on running, bunting and sliding — so all of the players are placed at one of the six fields. A group of players head over to Holman Stadium, which is a five minute walk from the practice fields. Offer to hold the player's bag and equipment so he might be willing to autograph some items. Many of the players will sign inside the stadium after they arrive. The Dodgertown complex is wide open and the players walk past the fans whenever the go to different station areas to work on their skills. This facility has always been a baseball fan's dream for collecting autographs.

- **Approach the players at the completion of their skill practice.** At Dodgertown the players have to pass collectors to move from one field to another. They are encouraged to be fan-friendly, and most participate daily in signing memorabilia. The autograph seekers must always exhibit patience and be polite.

- **Initiate friendly conversation with the players.** Always know the correct facts when you make a statement. The players appreciate knowledgeable individuals, and might give away their bats, hats and batting glove with requests. They will autograph their items and pose for pictures with the fans.
- **The indoor batting tunnel, which is in the player parking lot area, is an easy place to obtain many signatures.** Players will pass by Campy's Bullpen (many of the facilities and streets are named after retired Dodgers) to use the batting tunnel. Most of the players provide autographs after completing their batting practice. This is an excellent area to interact with the players.
- **Arrive early at Dodgertown when the entire 40-player roster has reported.** Before the players have changed into their uniform, they will come outside the clubhouse area to meet the vendors, who provide them with fielding and batting gloves. Stand by the vendors' cars or trucks to greet the players. They have been receptive to autograph requests and taking photographs with the small crowd of fans.
- **The clubhouse area is a good meeting place when collectors arrive at Dodgertown.** Along the clubhouse side, walk a short distance to the pitching area adjacent to the tennis courts. You will find three or four pitchers practicing and throwing off the pitcher's mound. Sandy Koufax is usually in this area helping the pitchers. He doesn't wear a uniform and is often dressed in shorts. He may come along the roped fence when he is called by collectors who recognize him. He may sign for about five minutes and quickly walk away. He is not a very outgoing individual. Other coaches and camp instructors also congregate here.
- **Locate the outdoor batting cage adjacent to Holman Stadium.** Some of the players are practicing their bunting skills in this area. Collectors can approach this fenced-in cage while watching the players. At the completion of their practice session, the players will sign for the very few fans who found this area.
- **Head over to Holman Stadium where the Dodgers play their exhibition games.** A group of players will be on the field conducting batting practice, which usually lasts until lunchtime. Other players will join in during the morning practice session. There is no fee to enter the stadium and you can sit next to the Dodgers open dugout. The spring training instructors and players will lean over and pose for pictures with the fans. Most players will sign when they leave the stadium after batting practice.

Signing habits during the exhibition games — 10 to 15 games.

- **Plan to attend an exhibition game.** The Dodgers schedule a home exhibition game every Sunday at Holman Stadium. The game begins at 1:00 P.M., and the players work out before the game at one of the six practice fields from 10:00 A.M. until noon. Collectors can walk around the complex and obtain many autographs. Dodgertown is the easiest complex and most fan-friendly for collecting autographs.

• **Plan to attend Fan Appreciation Day.** Every Sunday afternoon the Dodgers play an exhibition game at Holman Stadium. When you make inquiries about spring training, you should call Dodgertown and request the exact Sunday date for Fan Appreciation Day. At this event, the fans are allowed on the field for a 30 minute autograph session with approximately 20 players participating. The players have always signed for the huge crowd of fans and this has been a most successful event. Fan Appreciation Day will probably continue when a new team arrives.

• **Frequent player substituting is common during the exhibition games.** When the players are replaced, they leave the field and head over to the clubhouse area. Some collectors leave with them. Some will sign at the clubhouse entrance, while others provide autographs after showering.

• **Purchase tickets by the dugout area on either side of the stadium.** Prior to the game you can reach over and hand items to the players to autograph. Most of the players are congenial and don't mind signing when they are sitting. At Holman Stadium, another good place for acquiring autographs is sitting by the bullpen bench on the third-base side of the stadium. You can easily hand items to the players. Some of the pitchers sitting on the bench might sign during the game. Most will sign prior to and at the end of the game.

• **Plan to stay after the completion of an exhibition game.** Some players will continue to workout after the game. They stay in the weight room or work on particular skills at one of the fields. If you stay until 5:00 P.M., some players will be easy to add to your collection. Some may even furnish you with their baseball equipment. Many times the equipment manager will provide cracked bats to the children standing outside the clubhouse area.

• **The player parking lot is usually vacant.** After showering, most of the players leave by the parking lot adjacent to the clubhouse. The players are approachable, and usually they may sign one item.

Before leaving Vero Beach, take State Road 60 east over the intracoastal bridge to A1A highway on the beach. Look for a local restaurant called Bobby's. It's a sports lounge with interesting Dodgers memorabilia displayed in the showcase window of the bar dining room. After the games, some of the players have dinner here. After spending an impressive day at Dodgertown, the baseball enthusiast will find reason to return again and again. It's a baseball haven that truly epitomizes what spring training is all about. As the Dodgers celebrate their 50th anniversary in California in 2008, the team is heading west again to another new spring training site in Arizona. For baseball fans and collectors, the memories are great, the history is rich and above all, this has been the greatest road trip.

The Washington Nationals spring training complex in Viera, Florida, is 40 miles north of Vero Beach. Travel north on Interstate 95 to Exit 195. Turn left onto Fiske Boulevard and follow it to the stadium. The surrounding fields with grazing cattle have been replaced with shopping centers, golf courses and restaurants, and new housing developments and office buildings are under construction. This area is a planned community with outdoor recreational facilities and like Port St. Lucie, Viera will blossom in about five years.

The team practice fields are about a half mile away from Space Coast Stadium, where the Nationals play their home games, and the players carpool over to the practice fields each day. Obtaining autographs and collecting baseballs at the Nationals spring training complex can be easily accomplished. If you stand and wait beyond the outfield fence when the Nationals are taking batting practice, many new baseballs travel over the fence and become a souvenir for the collectors. Some fans walk away with three baseballs from this outfield area. There is no need to purchase the official major league baseballs that are being sold here for $15 which will be used for col-

After completing their spring training workout, many players (including Ismael Valdes, pictured) sign after showering.

lecting autographs. The Nationals have many unknown new players and during week days there may be 50 to 75 fans at the spring training practice fields. There are no crowds and lines here. When the players complete their work they walk past the collectors and have been accommodating for all of the fans. The Nationals spring training site is great for the acquisition of signatures and collecting baseballs.

Spring training and collecting autographs have become a passion with baseball fans. It is the best time to approach the players and acquire their signatures on all of your memorabilia. The players are more relaxed, and most enjoy your interest. The ballparks are all small and cozy, which allows the collector to interact with the players. Hobbyists should use the suggestions that have been provided to help make collecting fun and enjoyable. On the next page is a directory listing of the Florida and Arizona spring training camps, complete with addresses and telephone numbers.

Spring Training Camp Directory

Team websites are listed in the Directory of Resources following.

Grapefruit League

Atlanta Braves
Walt Disney World
PO Box 470517
Celebration City, Florida 34747
(407) 839-3900

Baltimore Orioles
Fort Lauderdale Stadium
1301 NW 55th Street
Fort Lauderdale, Florida 33309
(954) 776-1921

Boston Red Sox
City of Palms Park
2201 Edison Avenue
Fort Myers, Florida 33901
Toll Free(617) 482-4SOX

Cincinnati Reds
1090 North Euclid Avenue
Sarasota, Florida 34237
(877) 647-7337

Cleveland Indians
Chain of Lakes Park
Winter Haven, Florida 33880
(866) 48-TRIBE

Detroit Tigers
Tigertown
2125 North Lake Avenue
Lakeland, Florida 33805
(863) 686-8075

Florida Marlins
Roger Dean Stadium
4751 Main Street
Jupiter, Florida 33458
(561) 775-1818

Houston Astros
Osceola County Stadium
631 Heritage Park Way
Kissimmee, Florida 34744
(407) 839-3900

Minnesota Twins
Lee County Sports Complex
14100 Six Mile Cypress Parkway
Fort Myers, Florida 33912
(800) 33-TWINS

New York Mets
Tradition Field
525 Northwest Peacock Blvd.
Port St. Lucie, Florida 34986
(772) 871-2115

New York Yankees
Steinbrenner Field
1 Steinbrenner Drive
Tampa, Florida 33614
(813) 879-2244

Philadelphia Phillies
Bright House Networks Field
601 N. Old Coachman Road
Clearwater, Florida 33765
(727) 467-4457

Pittsburgh Pirates
Pirate City
1701 27th Street East
Bradenton, Florida 34208
(941) 748-4610

St. Louis Cardinals
Cardinals Complex
4795 University Drive
Jupiter, Florida 33458
(561) 966-3309

Tampa Bay Rays
Progress Energy Park, home of
  Al Lang Field
180 2nd Avenue, SE
St. Petersburg, Florida 33701
(813) 282-RAYS

Toronto Blue Jays
Knology Park
373 Douglas Avenue
Dunedin, Florida 34698
(888) 525-5297

Washington Nationals
Space Coast Stadium
5800 Stadium Parkway
Viera, Florida 32940
(321) 633-9200

Cactus League

Arizona Diamondbacks
Tuscon Electric Park
2500 East Ajo Way
Tucson, Arizona 85713
(866) 672-1343

Chicago Cubs
PO Box 5770
Mesa, Arizona 85211
(800) 905-3315

Chicago White Sox
10710 W. Camelback Road

Phoenix, Arizona 85307
(623) 877-8585

Colorado Rockies
Hi Corbett Field
3400 East Camino Campestre
Tucson, Arizona 85716
(800) 388-7625

Kansas City Royals
Surprise Stadium
15946 N. Bullard Avenue
Surprise, Arizona 85374
(623) 222-2222

Los Angeles Angels of Anaheim
Tempe Diablo Stadium
2200 West Alameda Drive
Tempe, Arizona 85282
For Tickets: *www.angelsbaseball.com*

Los Angeles Dodgers
10710 W. Camelback Road
Phoenix, Arizona 85307
(623) 877-8585

Milwaukee Brewers
Maryvale Baseball Park
3600 North 51st Avenue
Phoenix, Arizona 85031
(800) 933-7890

Oakland Athletics
Phoenix Municipal Stadium
5999 East Van Buren
Phoenix, Arizona 85008
(602) 392-0217

San Diego Padres
Peoria Stadium
8131 West Paradise Lane
Peoria, Arizona 85382
For Tickets: www.padres.com

San Francisco Giants
Scottsdale Stadium
7408 East Osborn Road

Scottsdale, Arizona 85251
(877) 473-4849

Seattle Mariners
Peoria Sports Complex
15707 North 83rd Avenue
Peoria, Arizona 85382
(800) 677-1227

Texas Rangers
Surprise Recreation Campus
15754 North Bullard Avenue
Surprise, Arizona 85374
(623) 594-5600

Directory of Resources

General

The Baseball Autograph Collector's Handbook
R. J. "Jack" Smalling
2308 Van Buren Avenue
Ames, Iowa 50010
(515) 232-7599

Bud's Sports Cards & Collectibles
1300 E. Oakland Park Blvd.
Fort Lauderdale, FL 33334
(954) 561-0022
www.budssportscards.com

Cooperstown Bat Company
PO Box 415
Cooperstown, NY 13326
(888) 547-2415
www.cooperstownbat.com

Hollywood Collectibles
3311 Sheridan Street
Hollywood, FL 33021
Orders: (800) 844-7735
www.hollywoodcollectibles.com

Mounted Memories (Displays)
5000 NW 108th Avenue
Sunrise, Fl 33351
(800) 749-7529
www.mountedmemories.com

National Baseball Hall of Fame
PO Box 590
Cooperstown, NY 13326
(888) HALL OF FAME
www.baseballhalloffame.org

New Era Cap Company
160 Delaware Avenue
Buffalo, NY 14202
www.neweracap.com

Lin Terry (Display Cases)
185 6th Avenue
Patterson, NJ 07524
Orders: (800) LIN Terry
www.linterry.com

Authentication Services

PSA, Professional Sports Authenticator
P.O. Box 6180
Newport Beach, CA 92658
(800) 325-1121
www.info@psacard.com

Picture Framing

Design Crafters, Inc.
7848 Wiles Road
Coral Springs, FL 33067
(954) 340-8830

Baseballs and Equipment

Anaconda Sports
P.O. Box 660
Lake Katrine, NY 12449
(888) 914-6319
www.anacondasports.com

Baseball Photographs

Photo File
333Bedford Road
Mount Kisco, NY 10549
Orders: (800) 346-1678

Publication

Sports Collectors Digest
P.O. Box 420235
Palm Coast, FL 32142
Subscription Order: (800) 829-5561

Websites

For periodicals:
www.sportscollectorsdigest.com
www.krause.com/periodicals/

For shows:
www.krause.com/shows/

For books:
www.books.krause.com/

Also:
www.baseball-almanac.com
www.sportsline.com
www.springtrainingonline.com
www.sun-sentinel.com

Major League Baseball Directory

Baseball Commissioner's Office
777 East Wisconsin Avenue
Milwaukee, WI 53202
(414) 225-8900

American League
245 Park Avenue
New York, NY 10167
(212) 931-7800
www.mlb.com

Los Angeles Angels of Anaheim
2000 Gene Autry Way

Anaheim, CA 92806
(714) 940-2000
www.angelsbaseball.com

Baltimore Orioles
333 West Camden Street
Baltimore, MD 21201
(888) 848-BIRD
www.theorioles.com

Boston Red Sox
4 Yawkey Way
Boston, MA 02215
(617) 226-6000
www.redsox.com

Chicago White Sox
333 West 35th Street
Chicago, IL 60616
(312) 674-1000
www.chisox.com

Cleveland Indians
2401 Ontario Street
Cleveland, OH 44115
(216) 420-4200
www.indians.com

Detroit Tigers
2100 Woodward Avenue
Detroit, MI 48201
(313) 471-2000
www.detroittigers.com

Kansas City Royals
PO Box 419969
Kansas City, MO 64141
(816) 921-8000
www.royals.com

Minnesota Twins
34 Kirby Puckett Place
Minneapolis, MN 55415
(612) 375-1366
www.twinsbaseball.com

New York Yankees
161st Street and River Avenue
Bronx, NY 10451

(718) 293-4300
www.yankees.com

Oakland Athletics
McAfee Coliseum
Oakland, CA 94621
(510) 638-4900
www.oaklandathletics.com

Seattle Mariners
1250 First Avenue
Seattle, WA 98134
(206) 346-4000
www.seattlemariners.com

Tampa Bay Rays
One Tropicana Drive
St. Petersburg, FL 33705
(727) 825-3250
www.raysbaseball.com

Texas Rangers
1000 Ballpark Way
Arlington, TX 76011
(817) 273-5222
www.texasrangers.com

Toronto Blue Jays
One Blue Jays Way
Toronto, ONT M5V 1J1
(416) 341-1000
www.bluejays.ca

National League
245 Park Avenue
New York, NY 10167
(212) 931-7800

Arizona Diamondbacks
PO Box 2095
Phoenix, AZ 85001
(602) 462-6500
www.diamondbacks.com

Atlanta Braves
PO Box 4064
Atlanta, GA 30302

(404) 522-7630
www.atlantabraves.com

Chicago Cubs
1060 West Addison Street
Chicago, IL 60613
(773) 404-2827
www.cubs.com

Cincinnati Reds
100 Main Street
Cincinnati, OH 45202
(513) 765-7000
www. reds.com

Colorado Rockies
2001 Blake Street
Denver, CO 80205
(303) 292-0200
www.coloradorockies.com

Florida Marlins
2267 Dan Marino Blvd.
Miami Gardens, FL 33056
(305) 626-7400
www.flamarlins.com

Houston Astros
PO Box 288
Houston, TX 77001
(713) 259-8000
www.astros.com

Los Angeles Dodgers
1000 Elysian Park Avenue
Los Angeles, CA 90012
(323) 224-1500
www.dodgers.com

Milwaukee Brewers
One Brewers Way
Milwaukee, WI 53214
(414) 902-4400
www.brewers.com

New York Mets
123-01 Roosevelt Avenue
Flushing, NY 11368

(718) 507-6387
www.mets.com

Philadelphia Phillies
One Citizens Bank Way
Philadelphia, PA 19148
(215) 463-6000
www.phillies.com

Pittsburgh Pirates
115 Federal Street
Pittsburgh, PA 15212
(412) 323-5000
www.pirates.com

St. Louis Cardinals
700 Clark Street
St. Louis, MO 63102
(314) 345-9600
www.stlcardinals.com

San Diego Padres
PO Box 122000
San Diego, CA 92112
(619) 795-5000
www.padres.com

San Francisco Giants
24 Willie Mays Plaza
San Francisco, CA 94107
(415) 972-2000
www.sfgiants.com

Washington Nationals
1500 South Capitol Street SE
Washington, D.C. 20003
(202) 349-0400
www.nationals.com

Bibliography

Baker, Mark Allen. *Collector's Guide to Celebrity Autographs*. Iola, WI: Krause, 1996.
_____. *Sports Collectors Digest Baseball Autograph Handbook*, 2d ed. Iola, WI: Krause, 1991.
_____. *Sports Collectors Digest Team Baseballs*. Iola, WI: Krause, 1992.
The Baseball Encyclopedia. 10th ed. New York: Macmillan, 1996.
Cohen, Stanley. *Dodgers! The First 100 Years*. New York: Carol, 1990.
Larson, Mark K. *Sports Collectors Digest Complete Guide to Baseball Memorabilia*, 2d ed. Iola, WI: Krause, 1994.
Neft, David S., Michael L. Neft, and Richard M. Cohen. *The Sports Encyclopedia: Baseball 2005*, 25th ed. New York: St. Martin's Griffin, 2005.
Pahigian, Joshua R. *Spring Training Handbook*. Jefferson, NC: McFarland, 2005.
Sanders, George, Helen Sanders, and Ralph Roberts. *The Sanders Price Guide to Sports Autographs*. Sidney, OH: Scott, 1993.
Skipper, John C. *A Biographical Dictionary of the Baseball Hall of Fame*. Jefferson NC: McFarland, 2000.
Smalling, R.J. "Jack." The *Baseball Autograph Collector's Handbook, Number 14*. Ames, IA: R.J. Smalling, 2007.
Zachofsky, Dan. *Idols of the Spring*. Jefferson, NC: McFarland, 2001.

Index

Numbers in **_bold italics_** indicate pages with photographs.